Women and Mystical Experience
in the Middle Ages

Dedicated to the memory of
my mother
ROBERTA FRANCES BEER
(1909–1987)
and my brother
WILLIAM REED BEER
(1943–1991)

Women and Mystical Experience in the Middle Ages

Frances Beer

THE BOYDELL PRESS

First published 1992 by The Boydell Press, Woodbridge
Reprinted in hardback and paperback 1993, 1995

The Boydell Press is an imprint of Boydell & Brewer Ltd
PO Box 9, Woodbridge, Suffolk IP12 3DF, UK
and of Boydell & Brewer Inc.
PO Box 41026, Rochester, NY 14604–4126, USA

ISBN 0 85115 302 X hardback
ISBN 0 85115 343 7 paperback

British Library Cataloguing-in-Publication Data
Beer, Frances F.
  Women and Mystical Experience in the
  Middle Ages
  I. Title
  248.2092
  ISBN 0–85115–302–X
  ISBN 0–85115–343–7 pbk

Library of Congress Catalog Card Number: 92–15362

This publication is printed on acid-free paper

Printed in Great Britain by
St Edmundsbury Press Ltd, Bury St Edmunds, Suffolk

CONTENTS

ACKNOWLEDGEMENTS

I would like to express my gratitude to Atkinson College for granting the fellowship that allowed me time to do much of the reading and writing for this book; to Patricia Watson, Shelagh Wilkinson, Kevin Crossley-Holland and my father, Samuel Beer, for their thoughtful and encouraging comments in the course of its preparation; to Ann Hutchison for inspiration and advice; to Carol Davison for assistance with research; to Elizabeth Brady for helping me break the computer barrier; and to my family, David, Denis, Jessica, Kitty, for their support along the way.

Introduction

In Europe and North America alike, the past few years have seen a major effort to reclaim the vast range of female voices that have been lost through the centuries. Sometimes the loss has been the result of relatively benign neglect – a manuscript forgotten in an attic, or a novel allowed to go out of print, because they were not thought of as 'serious'. Other times a more active desire to efface the records left by powerful and independent women seems to have been at work – particularly if these figures were openly defiant of the patriarchal establishment. Of course many such records from the Middle Ages have been irretrievably lost to us; but some of them can be recovered, dusted off and polished up to reveal their original glory.

The testimonies of these women provide a perspective that can, if we are ready to listen, greatly augment our general understanding of the Middle Ages. In an attempt to 'comprehend' this earlier time we would not want to be without them any more than we would want to be without such voices as Augustine or Aquinas. The fact that the established canon of medieval literature has for so long been without female voices must indeed raise the question as to how full our comprehension can have been. What would the picture be if we could fill in all the blanks? Do women, even when writing about the same subjects as men, approach them differently? How might the philosophical enquiries of women modify the received 'orthodox' position on such questions as a rigorously hierarchical social chain descending through God and King to Husband; the 'handmaid' role of the Virgin Mary in relation to Father and Son; the notion of a tripartite God that includes no female component? If only to discover how imperfect has been our understanding of the European Middle Ages, we must listen to as many of these voices as we can.

But there are happier reasons for listening. These voices are exciting, creative, energetic – *new*. Hearing even a few of them, realizing that medieval women were not inevitably mute and subservient, is a little like finding out that the world is not flat after all and that there are wonderful unexplored continents on the other side. Further, in some extraordinary cases, we are allowed through the texts to enter into the personal lives of the authors, sharing in their most profound emotional and spiritual experiences. This is a marvellous gift, the recovery of these courageous, articulate foremothers, particularly when we are able to reconstruct from the texts a sense of what they, and their lives, were like. While it is impossible to calculate how many women's voices have been lost to us through the destruction of their works, a number have managed to survive the antifeminism of intervening generations, which would have preferred to leave them on the shelf. Perhaps more surprising is the fact that within their own lifetimes certain of these women managed to transcend the virulent misogyny that so dominated their cultures. How they were able to achieve this transcendence is one of the puzzles that may be answered by studying these texts. The negative conditioning faced by women was formidable, and must have required no less formidable inner resources to have been resisted.

Antifeminism in the Middle Ages came in many shapes and sizes, as it does today. The best known to us, perhaps, is the version descending from St Paul, who argued so effectively that because of their inferiority women could not preach and had to cover their heads in church; 'The head to which a wife is united is her husband', he says,

> just as the head to which every man is united is Christ . . . . A woman brings shame upon her head if she uncovers it to pray or prophesy . . . [But] a man has no need to veil his head; he is God's image, the pride of his creation . . . And women are to be silent in the churches; utterance is not permitted to them . . . : if they have any questions to raise, let them ask their husbands at home. (1 *Corinthians* XI, 3ff.; XIV, 34–5)

Of course Paul was in part passing on an older Judaic tradition, which held that uncleanness was part of the female condition. As Job notes: 'So frail man's life, woman-born, so full of trouble . . . Who can bring the clean from the unclean? Not one' (XIV, 1, 4). Parallel to this view was one articulated by the Greeks that presented women as defective males, lacking reason as they lacked that eminently reasonable male organ. 'We should look upon the female state', says Aristotle, 'as being as it were a deformity; though one', he kindly adds, 'which occurs in the ordinary course of nature'. Women were necessary vessels, contributing the base matter in the reproductive process; but it was men who provided the all-important form, the 'principle of the movement'.[1]

There are many more shades and subtleties to these complementary misogynist traditions, but to understand the legacy to which the Middle Ages were heir, one further ingredient needs to be considered: woman's

---

[1] See *Not in God's Image: Women in History from the Greeks to the Victorians*, Julia O'Faolain and Lauro Martines, eds. (New York, 1973) for these and many other antifeminist quotations; also Aristotle, *On the Generation of Animals*, trans. A. L. Peck (Cambridge, Mass., 1953).

perceived link with the powers of evil. 'There is a good principle which created order, light and man', observes Pythagoras, 'and an evil principle which created chaos, darkness and women'. 'Woman is the source of all evil', warns Socrates succinctly; 'her love is to be dreaded more than the hatred of men'. This notion was seized with relish by the early Church Fathers who saw women, beginning with Eve, as the 'devil's gateway'. Tertullian was unequivocal in placing responsibility for the Fall on women:

> You are the one who opened the door to the devil, you are the one who first deserted the divine law . . . All too easily you destroyed the image of God, man. Because of [you] . . . even the Son of God had to die.[2]

Consequently, observes St Clement, 'every woman should be overwhelmed with shame at the thought that she is a woman'.

Our notion of the 'double standard' seems in part to descend from this set of concepts. Women are inherently weak, defective; but beyond this, such potency as they do have – particularly if it is sexual – is emphatically negative, a source of active danger for men. It follows (one supposes) that if an illicit sexual connection between man and woman occurs, it is 'caused' by the corrupt, that is female, partner, who has led the male into temptation by appealing to his carnality. Clearly then, it is not his fault if he strays, and his wife ought not to object. For her part, the onus to prove her virtue is always upon her; obviously the only really good woman is one who is essentially asexual and keeps her physical attractions, such as they may be, a well-guarded secret. This logic has a familiar ring today, but was more emphatically articulated in the Middle Ages. One author, trying to warn his young female charges about the dangers of arousing lust in the opposite sex, provides the following illuminating analogy:

> it was commanded in the Old Law that a pit should always be covered; and if an animal fell into an uncovered pit, the man who had uncovered the pit had to pay the penalty. These are terrible words for the woman who shows herself to men's sight . . . *The pit is her fair face, and her white neck, and her light eye, and her hand* . . . *She is guilty* . . . and must pay for his soul on the Day of Judgment.[3]

Any sin which he commits, with or without her consent, is then her fault; while she is 'paying' for his soul at the End of the World, he will apparently be *en route*, scot-free, to the Pearly Gates. Since there is something inherently deficient in the state of being female, it is better to bow out as

---

[2] Tertullian, 'The Apparel of Women', trans. E.A. Quain, p. 188, in *The Fathers of the Church* (New York, 1959).

[3] *The Ancrene Riwle*, trans. M.B. Salu (London, 1955).

fully as possible – to be a virgin, and a religious, proving perhaps the safest combination, as it would involve the fullest rejection of conventional sexuality. In St Jerome's words, 'she who serves Christ will cease to be a woman and will be called a man'; only in this way can she offset the terrible liability of having been born female.

The effect of this antifeminist tradition on medieval society was profound. Such views were of course not limited to the Church Fathers – who remained enormously influential throughout the Middle Ages – but were perpetuated and disseminated by means of both sermons and popular literature, century after century, to form and control attitudes towards women at all social levels. Literary evidence of misogynist stereotypes abounds. 'Women do many things just because they are forbidden', remarks the German Gottfried von Strassburg in his thirteenth-century courtly romance, *Tristan*;

> God knows, these same thistles and thorns are inborn in them! . . . In the first thing she ever did . . . [Eve] proved true to her nature and did what was forbidden! . . . She wanted none but that one thing in which she devoured her honour! Thus they are all daughters of Eve who are formed in Eve's image after her.

Gottfried's indictment echoes the slightly earlier *Nun's Rule*, a severe didactic treatise from England, as it describes Eve's legacy:

> This apple, my dear sister, symbolizes all those things towards which desire and sinful delight turn. When you look upon a man you are in Eve's case; you are looking at the apple . . . [Eve] has many daughters who, following their mother, answer in the same way: 'But do you think . . . that I shall leap upon him because I look at him?' God knows, my dear sister, more surprising things have happened. Your mother, Eve, leapt after her eyes had leapt; from the eye to the apple, from the apple in paradise down to the earth, from earth to hell, where she remained, in prison, four thousand years and more, together with her husband, and she condemned all her children to leap after her, to endless death.

And both are corroborated by the comical and rather more bourgeois French 'Vices of Women', composed later in the same century:

> Who too much trusts in womankind
> Often leaves honor far behind;
> Who loves or prizes womankind
> Often ends up much maligned; . . .
> Ask: who first sinned – man or woman?
> Who got us exiled from the Garden? . . .
> Because of woman's weaker wit
> She fell into the snake's gambit . . .

4

Women were clearly dangerous not only to themselves, but to those around them; and it was the obligation of the husband to keep them in check, as this French statement, also from the thirteenth century, makes clear:[4]

> In a number of cases men may be excused for the injuries they inflict on their wives, nor should the law intervene. Provided he neither kills nor maims her, it is legal for a man to beat his wife when she wrongs him . . . It is the husband's office to be his wife's chastiser.

These popular texts usually offered an alternate view of the virtuous woman as well: one who was quiet, obedient, abstinent – and very rare. In describing this paradoxical creature, Gottfried recalls St Jerome:[5]

> When a woman grows in virtue despite her inherited instincts and gladly keeps her honour, reputation and person intact, she is only a women in name, but in spirit she is a man! . . . When a woman lays aside her woman's nature and assumes the heart of a man, it is as if the fir dripped with honey, . . . a nettle bore roses above ground!

Such a restrictive model must only have had the effect of making most women feel the hopelessness of ever surmounting their inherently base nature. More, one wonders how girls could possibly grow up in the face of such conditioning and emerge unscathed. And yet, sometimes, they did. Although the three women upon whom this study concentrates – Hildegard of Bingen, Mechthild of Magdeburg, and Julian of Norwich – are vastly different from each other temperamentally and intellectually, they share the fact not only of having survived, but of being among the grandest, most triumphant voices of the Middle Ages. Their stature was such that they managed to command considerable respect in the midst of their misogynist worlds: that their work is not more widely known today does not indicate that they were ignored in their own time, but rather results from the intervention of subsequent generations, evidently unsettled by these thrilling and courageous witnesses. It is telling to note the form this 'intervention' has taken. The works of Hildegard, Mechthild and Julian were not destroyed, as was the case with some more 'dangerous' women, but each was defused in a particular way: Hildegard has until the past few years been dismissed as an eccentric, while Mechthild

---

[4] These four quotations are, respectively, from Gottfried von Strassburg's *Tristan*, trans. A.T. Hatto (Harmondsworth, 1960), p. 277; Salu (*op. cit.*), 'The Custody of the Senses', p. 23; 'Le Blasme des Fames' in *Three Medieval Views of Women*, trans. and ed. Gloria K. Fiero, Wendy Pfeffer, Mathé Allain (New Haven, 1989), p. 121; 'Coutumes de Beauvaisis' in *Not in God's Image* (*op. cit.*), p.175.

[5] *Tristan* (*op. cit.*), p. 278.

has been seen as the victim of her own rampant libido (a curiosity, but essentially pathological in her relation to the divine); and Julian has been 'domesticated', rather like Jane Austen: she is 'our Julian', kind, gentle, lovable, a source of comfort, but not quite dependable theologically. The implication has been that if we want to be illuminated as to the heavy mysteries of Christianity, we must turn to the real, male experts.

All three of these women were mystics. Hildegard of Bingen was a twelfth-century Rhineland abbess, who wrote extensively and was known for her success as an administrator, preacher, scientist, musician and prophet as well as her authorship of three encyclopedic mystical commentaries. Mechthild of Magdeburg, a thirteenth-century nun from Saxony, wrote a composite visionary treatise entitled *The Flowing Light of the Godhead*. This outspoken text resulted in her being harassed by ecclesiastical authorities to the extent that she finally took refuge in Helfta, a Cistercian convent renowned as a centre of women's learning; there, though blind, she added the final chapter of her work (which, unquestionably, her persecutors would have liked to see consigned to oblivion). And Julian of Norwich, a fourteenth-century solitary, completed her *Revelations of Divine Love* in the privacy of her 'cell'; although she had formally withdrawn from the outside world, her reputation as a spiritual advisor was extensive, and she was often visited by troubled souls in search of spiritual reassurance.

Each of these women based her mystical account on an intensely personal series of spiritual experiences, which utterly altered her subsequent life, and which were evidently powerful enough to conteract the sense of inferiority – and the importance of women's silence – that contemporary society sought to impose. Although all express a degree of concern as to their own unworthiness, they are utterly confident about what they have experienced, and feel a surpassing commitment to record it; for them, the love of God far outweighs the prohibitions of man. These records give us the extraordinary opportunity to participate in these women's inner lives, to examine both the nature of their spiritual journeys and the ways in which they are expressed; and to ask whether the fact of their being female gives them a different 'window' onto the experience of the divine than their male counterparts.

It will have been noted that all of these women were committed to some form of religious life, which is to say that they had cut themselves off from the options of wife- and motherhood. Given the medieval view of women's accountability for the Fall in general, and of sexual corruption in particular, such a choice need hardly be seen as surprising. The best a wife could hope to be was submissive to her husband, and based on the evidence of their writings, these three women must all have been strong, independent thinkers. Although they are in no uncertainty as to their correct relation to their Creator, obedience to a husband would likely not have come easily to them; the acceptance of God's omnipotence was axiomatic, but the social custom of translating this image from the divine to the human – so that the husband was seen as standing for God within the marital unit – might well have presented difficulties.

The rejection of marriage need not, of course, mean the rejection of womanhood, and Hildegard, Mechthild and Julian all reveal themselves to have been, in their various ways, intensely female. Hildegard, inspired by the Germanic martial ideal, identifies on this level with her Creator, and sees herself as God's lieutenant. The history of the world is the history of the struggle between the forces of good and evil, and she recognizes her obligation to be militant; beyond this, as she reveals herself in her texts, she seems well suited temperamentally to be a soldier, not one to miss a good fight if there is one to be had. Evidently she does not see the dominant, active role as being the exclusive property of the male sex. Her work is populated by a range of mighty female figures – such as Sapientia/Wisdom; Synagogue/Mother of the Incarnation of the Word of God; or Ecclesia/The Church – who function to effect God's plan on earth. Although they are symbolic, these figures are not women in name alone, but are seen as explicitly female, endowed with breasts and wombs, performing particularly female functions such as cradling offspring or giving birth. One of Hildegard's most remarkable representations of the divine is as an enormous, star-filled, fiery cosmic egg – a grandly all-encompassing female image. Hildegard's own motherly impulses were lavished on the younger women in her convent, for whom she wrote hymns and a play, and whom she encouraged to adorn themselves, as a celebration of their beauty, on feast days. Hildegard herself seems to have identified with her more august female figures, such as Sapientia, but she saw her 'daughters' as brides of Christ and rejoiced in the fulfillment they would find in such a relationship.

Mechthild's predominant imagery is erotic. In her earliest visions she sees the divine through a child's eyes, but she soon moves on to represent divine union as consummation between two lovers, whereby the soul is transported in ecstasy to a secret and blissful place, and from which it is misery to return. In the absence of the lover, life itself is empty and seems to have no meaning; the soul can only wait, in longing, for the return of her beloved. Mechthild's regard for the maternal ideal is evident in her representation of the Virgin Mary, who is seen as a figure of limitless generosity, the mother of the perfect Child, who has also nurtured, with the milk of compassion, other wise men – prophets, apostles, subsequent devout Christians: in fact she is mother of us all. In Mechthild's celestial vision, Mary is situated on the left hand of God, the counterpart of Jesus on the right, her flowing milk the complement to his flowing blood.

Julian most dramatically reveals her femaleness in her understanding

7

of the motherhood of God, which seems to carry Mechthild's implication of Mary's divinity to its ultimate conclusion. Julian explains that the Trinity actually includes a female component; as well as being the Son, Jesus is our Mother, who feeds and nurtures us, and looks after us during our lifetime, as a mother does her young. Julian herself shows a surpassing tenderness to her fellow Christians, whose fears she longs to allay, and whose faith she strives to strengthen by her account of God's all-inclusive love. As she is reassured by the tenderness of 'Mother Jesus', Julian herself becomes infused with the maternal impulse, and turns to comfort the rest of us, affirming that Jesus wants us to imitate the child who naturally trusts its mother, and runs to her for help at the smallest threat. (Because of this quality of tenderness, tradition has affectionately dubbed her 'Mother Julian'.)

Are these sorts of 'female' observations the result of 'nature' or 'nurture', of biology or social conditioning? Impossible (as always) to say with finality. Obviously some sorts of cultural influence are in evidence. Hildegard's image of her 'daughters' as numbering among the brides of Christ cannot be separated from the medieval apocalyptic tradition, any more than Mechthild's erotic metaphor can be seen as distinct from the conventions of courtly love. On the other hand, the fact that Julian may have been brought up to equate womanliness and motherhood with gentleness, and may herself have had a particularly close bond with her own mother, cannot in itself have given rise to her understanding of Jesus as Mother, which was (and still is) in direct contradiction to the orthodox view of the Trinity. Nor can Hildegard's bold view of the procreatrix Ecclesia with her chalice, catching the blood as it flows from Christ's side and becoming the first Eucharistic agent, have been the reponse to any cultural conditioning beyond the mere fact of. Germanic partiality for strong women. In their personal humility, all three women tip their hats, so to speak, to contemporary misogyny; but they appear, finally, to repudiate its power. Though they dutifully acknowledge their 'unworthiness' as women, they proceed to go right ahead and repeat everything that has been shown to them, even – perhaps especially – when it is in flat contradiction to accepted doctrine.

Where this courageous independence came from raises another question. Was it because they were unusually strong-minded that they were able to resist the docility seen as appropriate to woman; or did the confidence to speak out result from their spiritual experiences? Probably a bit of each. Some special strength must have been required to enable them to receive and articulate such powerful, and potentially shattering, visionary experiences. But there seems to be evidence that they also became more assured in the wake of their revelations. However reluctant some modern readers may be to accept the validity of these revelations, there can be no question as to the absolute faith of Hildegard and Mechthild and Julian, their utter confidence in what they have been shown. A reading of any of their works indicates an intense, individual bond with their Creator which is all-absorbing, wholly fulfilling, the source of surpassing joy and wonder. In their experience of divine love, these women are lifted beyond mundane and petty prejudices: their relationship with their God gives them the perspective they need to recognize the irrelevance of such merely human forces as antifeminism.

This bond may also have recalled for Hildegard, Mechthild and Julian the evidence that had been before them all along, however obscured by the comments of the Church Fathers: the Gospels, which tell us that some of Christ's most trusted followers were women. It is Mary Magdalene, described as once having been 'a great sinner', who becomes the greatest of Christ's lovers. The figures of Mary and Martha, rather than two men, are chosen by Christ to illustrate the difference between the active and the contemplative lives. It is the Marys who wait by the cross as Christ dies, and then return to the sepulchre to anoint his body. And of course it is to Mary Magdalene that he first reveals his resurrected self, and upon whom he depends to carry the word to the disciples. The discrepancy between the feminist example of Christ, as presented in the Gospels, and the antifeminist view of the church, as spoken by the Fathers, perhaps became more obvious to them in the wake of their revelations.

The particular situations in which each woman lived may have further helped to develop their intellectual and emotional independence. Hildegard's 'official' religious life began the earliest of them all, at the age of seven, when she was placed in a Benedictine monastery by her parents. Here she had a strongly positive relationship with her tutor, the abbess Jutta, and was presented with educational opportunities quite extensive for a girl at that time. Although she would not have been free from the scathing voices of the Church Fathers, the fact that she was part of a close female 'family' within the larger male monastery may have provided some insulation; but when she later took over as abbess, she insisted on establishing her own, wholly female convent, apart from her Benedictine brothers. It was in this new home that Hildegard's creativity came into full play, and she began her work as writer and musician and artist and scientist in earnest.

Mechthild entered a religious community when she was twenty-three. Rather than joining a conventional convent for the daughters of the upper class, she instead committed herself to a group known as the Beguines, who included among their number women from a range of social backgrounds; they lived austerely, and communally, were dedicated to a life of helping the poor, and had very few rules and regulations constraining them. This combination seems to have suited Mechthild's independent and idealistic spirit – having rejected the distasteful privileges of class, she was able to enjoy the security of a woman's community without the discipline of the male hierarchy. In any event, it was about the time she joined the beguinage that she had her first ecstatic experience. And in her old age there is no question but that she was able to find the strength to finish her life's work by sheltering with the learned nuns at Helfta.

Unfortunately we know so little about Julian that we can only speculate as to how she lived her early years. She may have lived at home with her mother until her early thirties, as a child perhaps attending a school run by nuns; she may have joined a religious community at some point in her life. Eventually, she made the choice to become a solitary, and to live alone in a cell attached to the church of St Julian in Norwich; here she would have had the leisure to delve into a range of spiritual texts, and to pursue the meditations that resulted in a greatly expanded version of her *Revelations*. Of the three, Julian's character is the most serene and self-contained. The quiet life of privacy, away from the distractions of everyday life, seems to have allowed her the freedom to achieve her deepest happiness and to reach her full potential.

The conventual religious life, dominated as it was by confessors, priests, abbots and the ecclesiastical hierarchy, did not normally free women from male authority. The fact of Hildegard, Mechthild and Julian's liberation seems to be related to their mysticism, their transcendent perspective allowing them to see beyond the social structures – whether ecclesiastical or secular – that ordinarily ensured women's submission. And in escaping 'domestication', whether by the paternalist direction of priest or husband, they have managed to avoid being silenced as so many other women in the Middle Ages were; they are able to use the language of the dominant culture to its fullest potential, while bringing to bear their particular experience as women and visionaries.

The best way to come to a fuller understanding of what religious women's experience in the Middle Ages was like is, of course, to read what they have written; but some perspective can be gained, too, by looking at what men at the time wrote for them. Two sections of this study are devoted to such works, notably the *Nun's Rule*, written about 1200, and the fourteenth-century epistles of Richard Rolle. Although a harsh misogynist in his youth, the years seem to have tempered Rolle, and the letters that he addresses to his female disciple towards the end of his life show not only affection but a great measure of respect. The letters aim to give specific advice as to how to avoid the dangers that beset the soul on the path of spiritual growth, as well as precise information about the positive steps that must be taken to bring it to mystical joy. He does not cite the conventional male scholastic authorities to support his advice, but rather encourages his disciple to trust in her own powers of self-examination, and eventually to become her own spiritual advisor; he seems to view the 'female' soul as fully capable of taking reponsibility for itself, and of ultimately reaching the same mystical heights as he has achieved – presumably much of his 'good advice' is based on what he discovered as he pursued his own mystical journey. Rolle was a free thinker in many respects, and through him we see evidence that it was possible for a man reared in the thick of an antifeminist tradition to overcome the associated prejudices and learn to see his female kindred-spirit as no more, or less, disposed to sin than he was himself.

In the author of the *Nun's Rule*, we encounter a male spiritual advisor who, like Richard Rolle, was writing a guide of sorts for enclosed women. But here the resemblance ends; the *Rule*'s author was no doubt a rather more typical product of his environment. While he was clearly fond of his charges, he shows scant trust in their ability to make independent spiritual progress, having himself accepted the prevalent notion of women's inherently corruptible nature. To be sure, his goal is benevolent – he wants to rescue them from their dangerous selves – but the means he uses are coersive: he aims 'below the belt' – trying to engage them on their own base level, as he sees it – by exploiting a combination of fear and desire. They should renounce the flesh, he argues, because they will soon be food for worms, rotting in their graves; they should love Christ because he is the most attractive and ardent, the richest possible suitor. Insofar as the *Rule* does succeed in exciting the fear and love of its female readers, it ironically serves to ensure that their motivations remain self-centred and mundane; rather than counteracting his society's misogynist stereotypes, the author of this work in effect perpetuates them, helping to convince young women that they are not trustworthy, that they are by nature susceptible to vice, that they are, indeed, the daughters of Eve.

In Hildegard, Mechthild and Julian we see a range of powerful, articulate women who were acceptable in varying degrees within their own societies. Hildegard – who, though a nun, travelled and preached extensively, wrote indignant letters of reproof to figures at the height of the male establishment, and defied ecclesiastical authority despite the threat of excommunication – was enormously respected. Julian, in spite of her great personal modesty, was revered as a spiritual counsellor; she certainly achieved nothing approaching Hildegard's notoriety (nor would she have wanted to), but evidence of her East Anglian community's regard is attested by the existence of a number of wills in which she is named long after the time of her enclosure – such bequests ensuring that she would continue to be provided with all the necessities of life. Mechthild came the closest to running afoul of the ecclesiastical establishment, but managed to save both herself and her book by retreating to Helfta. What of the women who refused to be silent, yet crossed over the invisible line of acceptability? One such figure was

11

Bloemardinne of Brussels, a woman influential in her time who has since virtually been erased from historical record.

Bloemardinne was active during the first quarter of the fourteenth century, and perhaps died about 1335. She may have been a Beguine, having committed herself to a life of piety and charitable works; she may have come from an influential family and have founded a hospice for impoverished older women. The difficulty in reconstructing anything like an accurate portrait of her life or work is that the only accounts we have of her come from men, who for the most part – whether medieval or modern – believe her to have been a dangerous heretic. According to the Augustinian historian Pomerius, writing in 1420, Bloemardinne was a woman of 'perverse teaching'; she wrote extensively about the 'spirit of freedom', praising what she called 'seraphic love' but what Pomerius described as 'most abominable sensual love'. She seems to have had a flamboyant streak, as she was said to sit in a silver seat when teaching or writing, and was reportedly accompanied by two ranks of angels whenever she approached the altar. She must also have been compelling as a figure, since she had many followers, who credited her with being the founder of a 'new doctrine'; when she died her body was reputed to have healing powers, and was visited by numbers of the sick in hopes of being cured.

Bloemardinne was a contemporary of the Flemish mystic Jan van Ruysbroeck, who saw her teachings as heretical, and openly attacked her in a series of pamphlets. The evidence suggests that her rebuttal to his charges was published, and that a fierce debate ensued, with Ruysbroeck incurring the emnity of Bloemardinne's followers, who composed and circulated poems ridiculing him. But here the story suddenly ends. All the pamphlets pertaining to this debate have vanished. Even Ruysbroeck's admirers tend to agree that he had them destroyed, then proceeding to counter Bloemardinne's views in his susequent polemical works. His advocates depict him as a solitary hero with the courage and widsom to take on this pernicious woman – who, in contrast, is described as 'perverted through pride and luxury' – and eradicate all written trace of her heretical arguments. Pomerius, Bloemardinne's 'historian', was from the same Augustinian house as Ruysbroeck, who was its founder and first prior. The only actual witness we have to her writings is this same Pomerius, who admitted that they were so cleverly disguised by their 'aspect of truth and piety' that no one could perceive their heretical nature without special help from God. The subsequent and total disappearance of these works precludes an objective examination; so the question must arise: were they really heretical at all, or was he simply backing up his Augustinian colleague, Ruysbroeck, in corroborating his view of Bloemardinne's heresy? Certainly it is clear that Pomerius' scant description is insufficient evidence upon which to base the now-received assumption that because Bloemardinne advocated freedom of the spirit she also encouraged free love. Of course she may have been as her male critics describe her: proud, avaricious, lecherous, depraved; still it would have been interesting to know her, to be able to draw our own conclusions. On the other hand, perhaps she was an inspired teacher and mystic – threatening because of her power and independence – who was wilfully misread, and subsequently censored, by certain of her contemporaries. Unfortunately it seems that we will never know.[6]

There were other women, as diverse as the French 'heretic' Marguerite Porete and Joan of Arc, who were dealt with more harshly by the ecclesiastical establishment – both having been burned at the stake after imprisonment, interrogation and probably torture. But Bloemardinne stands as an example of how women's history can be distorted and/or suppressed by the successive efforts of antagonistic male chroniclers. Fortunately the writings of Hildegard, Mechthild and Julian have survived, and although the available information about their lives may be partial, we can come to know these extraordinary women through their work.

---

[6] Henricus Pomerius, *De origine monasterii Viridis Vallis*, in *Analecta bollandiana*, vol. IV (Brussels, 1885); A. Wautler D'Aygalliers, trans. F. Rothwell (Paris, 1923; London and New York, 1925), *Ruysbroeck the Admirable*, pp. 76–81; 'Bloemardinne', J. Van Mierlo, *Dictionnaire d'Histoire et de géographie ecclésiastiques* (Paris, 1937), cols. 207–12; *The Seven Steps of the Ladder of Spiritual Love*, Jan van Ruysbroeck, intro. Joseph Bolland, S.J., trans. F.S. Taylor (Westminster, 1944), pp. 10–12; *The Spiritual Espousals*, intro. and trans. E. Colledge (London, 1952).

Hildegard of Bingen

I

Hildegard of Bingen, born at Bemersheim in 1098, was a figure for whom superlatives seem inadequate. Peter Dronke, for example, author of the major biographical work on Hildegard, resorts to adjectives such as 'overpowering' and 'electrifying', while Matthew Fox, one of her most ardent contemporary admirers, places her among 'the greatest intellectuals of the West'; praising her as a 'woman of genius', instigator of the flowering of German mysticism, Rufus Jones had earlier written that she possessed the 'visionary power and moral passion of the Hebrew prophets'.[1] Her prodigious creative output includes a mystical trilogy for which justifiably she is now best known: *Scivias*, *The Book of Life's Merits*, and *The Book of Divine Works*. But she also composed medical/scientific treatises, poetry, music, a full-length morality play, and a magnificent series of illustrations intended to clarify and make more accessible her visions. In addition, she was an eminently successful administrator, conducted preaching tours up and down the Rhine, and carried on a voluminous correspondence with key religious and political figures of her day. Before turning to her visionary works, it is worth having a detailed look at her extraordinary life; this is made possible by the fact that we have a Latin *Vita*, substantially of her own composition, as well as many of the letters that she wrote in her capacity as administrator and spiritual advisor.[2]

By her own account, she started to have visions in her infancy; in their earliest manifestation, these took the form of a light of awesome brightness, and they continued on a regular basis throughout her early years. As she describes it, she was uncertain, even fearful of these experiences as a child. She neither knew what to make of them, nor what others would

---

[1] See Peter Dronke, *Women Writers of the Middle Ages* (Cambridge, 1984), pp. 144–201; Hildegard of Bingen, *Book of Divine Works with Letters and Songs*, ed, Matthew Fox, (Santa Fe, New Mexico, 1987), pp. ix–xix; Rufus Jones, *The Flowering of Mysticism* (1939, repr. New York, 1971), pp. 43–44.

[2] For the *Vita* and letters see *Hildegardis abbatissae Opera omnia* in *Patrologiae cursus completus, Ser. Latina* 197, 91–140, ed. J.-P. Migne (Paris, 1882).

think of her if they knew; so in predictable childlike fashion she tended to keep them to herself. As a child she was also frequently ill, and it seems likely that the two phenomena were linked. Leaving her feelings of anxiety and isolation aside, the very effort involved in keeping visions of such great intensity bottled up would almost inevitably result in headaches and other psychosomatic symptoms. Still, to turn it around, as some have, and argue that the illness caused the visions seems to reflect the limits of our imagination, not of hers.[3] She attributed these painful bouts of illness, which continued throughout her life, to 'aerial torments' which she described as drying up her veins and flesh – even the very marrow of her bones. They seem to have been particularly acute when she was facing some frustration or some undone work. In the Preface to *Scivias* she remarks that she refused to write down her visions until she 'became sick, pressed down by the scourge of God'; and a persistent bout of illness in her 70s ended with a vision of a most loving – 'amantissimus' – man who exorcized the tormenting demons, after which she was able to complete the *Book of Divine Works*.

When Hildegard was seven she was placed by her parents in a monastery named for its founder, the Celtic saint Disibodus, under the tutelage of a noblewoman, Jutta, the *magistra* who was later to become the abbess.[4] Perhaps they made this decision because she was the tenth child in the family, which, however aristocratic, may have been running out of dowries adequate to ensure a proper alliance. It seems possible that she would already have distinguished herself as an unusual child: high-strung, keenly intelligent, plagued by recurrent illness, uncannily able to foretell coming events. In any case her parents referred to her as their 'tithe' to God. She seems to have taken to monastic life naturally and with great success: when Jutta died some years later in 1136, Hildegard, by then 38, was the unanimous choice of the nuns to replace her as abbess. Other details reveal the extent of her personal devotion to her community: she and her sisters invented a secret language, to be used in front of strangers, for which she wrote the glossary; she composed a cycle of hymns – words and music – to be sung within the convent by the nuns; her play, *Ordo Virtutum*, was initially composed for their use.

The Disibodenberg was a Benedictine monastery in the Rhine valley, of

---

3 C. Singer (*From Magic to Science*, New York, 1958) and O. Sacks (*Migraine: Understanding a Common Disorder*, Berkeley, 1985) explore the connection between Hildegard's afflictions and migraine headaches.
4 For discussions of Hildegard's life see, in addition to Dronke (*op. cit.*), Lena Eckenstein, *Women Under Monasticism* (Cambridge, 1896), Dom Philibert Schmitz, *Histoire de l'Ordre de Saint-Benoît*, 'Les Moniales', tome VII (Maredsous, 1956), Kent Kraft's essay in *Medieval Women Writers*, ed. Katharina M. Wilson (Athens, Georgia, 1984), *Sister of Wisdom: St Hildegard's Theology of the Feminine*, Barbara Newman (Berkeley and Los Angeles, 1987), Fox's introduction in *Book of Divine Works* (*op. cit.*).

which only ruins now remain. As such it would have been a self- sufficient community, protected by high walls, within which would have been found gardens and orchards, bakehouse and granary, dormitory, dining hall, kitchen, pantry, guest houses – and, most important, church and cloister, the 'heart of the monastery'.[5] At the time of Hildegard's arrival in 1106 it was 400 years old, but the abbey's female unit – originally a hermitage – had only recently been added. Other young women, attracted by Jutta's reputation for holiness, placed themselves under her direction, and the number of nuns soon grew to eighteen. These tended to be from aristocratic families, usually bringing some money with them as a kind of dowry when they entered the convent. Limited as their education may have been in comparison with what was offered the men, it was much better than any alternatives outside the cloister; indeed, convents at this time were a haven for any woman who was at all intellectually inclined. Hildegard's education included some Latin, the Scriptures and service books, possibly some music – though in her *Vita* she claims to have composed her songs without having had any musical training. But she also was an avid reader and seemed to have had access to a range of texts: she was familiar enough with Boethuis' *Consolation of Philosophy* to quote from it freely; her mystical works show a pronounced Neoplatonic influence, though the source for this material is uncertain; her knowledge of the Scriptures was exhaustive, and their influence pervades her writing.

During the monastic revival of the eleventh and twelfth centuries, double houses – monasteries enclosing both men and women – were not unusual, though by the thirteenth century they had for the most part been phased out. Although the actual buildings housing the nuns and monks were separated by distance and interposing structures, the communities were jurisdictionally one unit, living under the same rule. There were many obvious advantages from the women's point of view; most of the major abbeys had communities for nuns, who were thus able to participate actively in the reform movement, satisfying their interest in both asceticism and study. But of course what happened, as long as men and women were enclosed together, was that the men were seen as superior; authority rested with the abbots, and the women tended to look to the monks for instruction and leadership. However, after she became abbess, Hildegard chose to move her community of nuns to a new location, at Rupertsberg. She was perhaps eccentric in her desire for independence,

---

5   Lowrie J. Daly, *Benedictine Monasticism, Its Formation and Development Through the 12th Century* (New York, 1965), p. 196. For further information on the Benedictine monastic tradition, see also Cuthbert Butler, *Benedictine Monachism*, 2nd ed. (London, 1924), Schmitz (*op. cit.*), *The Rule of St. Benedict*, trans. and intro. by Cardinal Gasquet (New York, 1966), *The Rule of St. Benedict*, ed. Timothy Fry, O.S.B. (Collegeville, Minnesota, 1980).

but her decision was evidently the right one, as her community grew and flourished after its secession.

The purpose of a monastic community's self-sufficiency was to avoid the distractions and entanglements, not to mention the corruption, of the outer world. Within the double houses rules of claustration differed, and were stricter for women than for men, the underlying assumption being that the women were more susceptible to temptation. In the strictest cases the rule was evidently so restrictive that women were only allowed to leave to be taken to the cemetery. But in both England and Germany claustration tended to be less firmly enforced; women could take part in pilgrimages, visit and be visited by their families. As an administrator Hildegard would have had even more freedom than usual. In other words, she had the advantages of the structure and security provided by her community without being immobilized; she travelled extensively in both Germany and France, visiting and preaching at numerous monastic communities along the way.[6]

The Benedictine schedule, which was minutely regulated, was based upon two central ideals: labour and communality. Personal property and privacy were supposedly non-existent (monastics were to 'claim no dominion even over their own bodies or wills'); meals, prayer, work all were all done together.[7]

Labour was to occupy a specific number of hours each day (St Benedict originally specified six); for the women in Hildegard's monastery this would have involved traditional work such as spinning and weaving: while the particular purpose of manual labour was to imitate the lives of the Apostles, it was also seen as an essential antidote to idleness, the great danger for any enclosed religious. Occasionally the nuns were occupied in copying manuscripts. Hildegard herself was employed in nursing when at the Disibodenberg, but later, at Rupertsberg, her group was noted for its work in manuscript illumination, of which Hildegard's own masterpieces are an outstanding example.[8]

Days for the Benedictines were organized around periods of communal prayer, which took place at three-hour intervals, even during the night. The *Rule* spelled out in meticulous detail which psalms should be sung at what hours, and on which days, and this order was strictly

---

6   Schmitz (*op. cit.*), tome VII, p. 235. See also Jane Tibbetts Schulenburg, 'Strict Active Enclosure and its Effects on the Female Monastic Experience', in *Distant Echoes*, ed. J. A. Nichols and L. T. Shank (Kalamazoo, Michigan, 1984).

7   See Gasquet (*op. cit*). This model was based on the ideal set down in the *Acts of the Apostles* (IV, 31ff.): 'And when they had prayed . . . they were all filled with the Holy Ghost . . . And the multitude of them that believed were of one heart and of one soul; . . . they had all things in common'.

8   According to Schmitz (*op. cit.*), tome VII, p. 271, 'la miniature' was widely practised in the German houses, 'notamment . . . à l'entourage de Hildegard'.

followed. Details ranging from the discipline of a disobedient member to the appropriate quantities of bread and wine to be consumed at dinner were also spelled out. Thus, clearly, the sense of order, stability, and dependable routine was an important part of the Benedictine life, probably a central reason for the survival of the monastic tradition during the chaotic period following the fall of the Roman Empire.[9] The commitment to study, considered an essential part of daily life, not only meant that the Benedictine houses were frequently responsible for rescuing classical knowledge that had been threatened with extinction during the preceding centuries, but also that the individual members of the community were provided with the opportunity for a rich intellectual life; there was 'great scope for local talent and learning'.[10]

It is not surprising that Hildegard would have been satisfied with this life; for someone who had been buffeted by spiritual and physical extremes since earliest childhood, the security and regularity of the Benedictine system would have been profoundly reassuring. The discipline too must have been welcome, providing the structure necessary to develop the confidence and personal strength upon which she would so frequently have to rely in her later career. And for someone as extraordinarily intelligent as Hildegard, who, as a woman, might otherwise have had no access to formal education, the scholarly opportunities would have been irresistible.

Hildegard seems to have been born in the right place at the right time, in a number of ways. A new spiritual emphasis within the Benedictine movement, originally inspired by St Anselm in the previous century, served to make her monastic environment particularly appropriate for her. To the letter of the *Rule*, which had tended to limit itself to questions of structure and discipline, Anselm brought a new dimension. He wrote of the ideal of spiritual development, of inner growth – of what could be described as a new kind of enclosure, within the mind, that would further insulate the soul from the confusions of the world and allow it to be closer to God. His emphasis was not in conflict with the old *Rule*, which had assumed that the personal relationship between God and the soul would progress naturally if the requisite humility and obedience were adhered to. But Anselm's contribution spoke much more explicitly of an intense, personal relationship with God, opening the way for an increased emphasis on individual meditation and, eventually, the visionary experience.[11] Dedicated as Hildegard was to the order and stability of the

---

[9] Praised both for its brevity and its broadness of vision, Benedict's *Rule* has been described as the 'most complete and masterful synthesis of monastic tradition' (Fry, *op. cit.*, p. 90).

[10] R.W. Southern, *The Making of the Middle Ages* (New Haven and London, 1961), p. 185.

[11] See Southern (*op. cit.*), p. 226 and ff.

Benedictine life, this added element must, as it gave validity to her visions, have made it even more appealing. The progress by which she came to confess to others her inner visions was gradual, but in the meantime her personal tranquility must have been greatly increased by this assurance.

St Anselm's innovations were foreshadowings of the twelfth-century renaissance, which is perhaps too often described in glowing generalities, but which nonetheless does seem to have been a period of remarkable spiritual and literary flowering, of renewed optimism, confidence in the individual, and emphasis on love. Generally this was a period of enormous expansion and influence for the reformed monasteries; the spirit of inquiry and intellectual growth was guided by renewed confidence in Christian faith and ideals, by a new respect for the intensity of the personal religious experience to be found in the monastic life. The church as a moral force gained enormous credibility.[12]

The tenth century had been a period of consolidation for medieval Germany: pagans to the east had been quelled or converted, to the west the kingdom of Burgundy annexed. The German emperor was considered to be the leader of the Western world, and he had absolute control over the church, its lands and officials. But in the next century, during Hildegard's lifetime, this control faltered. Religious leaders felt that lay control was inappropriate, that the superiority of church over state ought to be entrenched. Pope Gregory VII (1073–85) had greatly enhanced the papal image and actual power, and supporters of papal supremacy now urged increased power for all members of the church.[13]

In the middle of the twelfth century, however, the church's newly won credibility was jeopardized by a papal schism, and there was widespread ecclesiastical squabbling within Germany; here again Hildegard was very much in the right place. Deeply troubled by this pervasive instability, she spoke out fearlessly and her voice emerged as that of a serious and greatly respected social reformer. She believed that it was the responsibility of the church to act as 'regenerator to society', that the cure for social ills was 'more active faith, a higher standard of moral conduct'.[14] The king, Frederick Barbarossa (1152–1190), was a strong ruler, who endeavoured to keep the German church under his control; here he fell out with Hildegard, since they supported different candidates for the papacy. Acting as God's mouthpiece, she wrote him a letter expressing fierce

---

12 See, for example, Joseph R. Strayer, *Western Europe in the Middle Ages* (New York, 1955), pp. 91 ff., and Southern (*op. cit.*), *passim*.

13 See Josef Fleckenstein, trans. Bernard S. Smith, *Early Medieval Germany* (New York, 1978), pp. 190 ff.; cf. also J.B. Gillingham, *The Kingdom of Germany in the High Middle Ages (900–1200)* (London, 1971), and Alfred Haverkamp, trans. H. Braun and R. Mortimer, *Medieval Germany (1056–1273)* (London, 1990).

14 Eckenstein (*op. cit.*), pp. 256 ff.

condemnation of his stand, blaming him for perpetuating the schism, warning him in apocalyptic language of his error and of the punishment to come: 'Woe, woe upon the evildoing of the unjust who scorn me! Hear this, king, if you would live – else my sword will pierce through you!'

Frederick was not the only powerbroker to be challenged by Hildegard. She also admonished the archbishop of Mainz, predicting his imminent fall (her prophecy here, as was often the case, came true: Heinrich was soon deposed and exiled).[15] Certain as she was that she was speaking for God, she did not euphemize no matter how powerful the antagonist. It is perhaps surprising that as a woman she could criticize her antagonists so unreservedly without fear of reprisal (not that this would have deterred her); her evident immunity arose at least in part from the fact of her visionary writings having been given the papal seal of approval, by Eugenius III, at the synod of Trier in 1147 – he recognized her *Scivias* as being divinely inspired and encouraged her to continue recording her visions as they came to her.[16]

Hildegard was not one to let obstacles stand in the way of her iron will and passionate sense of purpose; so if circumstances did not favour her cause, she tried to ignore them. One of the most remarkable of her characteristics is what appears to be an effective imperviousness to the potent medieval tradition of antifeminism. The classical idea of woman as defective male was augmented by the Middle Ages' view of her as moral cripple: if Eve had not disobeyed, we would all still be in the Garden of Eden. Disobedience was Eve's worst sin, but only one of many. Her defective reason was passed along, with the result that all her daughters were also more prone to vice. Hildegard's French contemporary, Andreas the Chaplain, articulated a particularly comprehensive, and enthusiastic, view of female weakness:

according to the nature of [her] sex . . . every woman is by nature a miser, . . . she is also envious and a slanderer of other women, greedy, a slave to her belly, inconstant, fickle in her speech, disobedient and impatient of restraint, spotted with the sin of pride . . ., a liar, a drunkard, a babbler, no

15 Eckenstein, Dronke and others discuss this incident. Hildegard's reputation as a prophet led to her being nicknamed 'the Rhenish sybil', and lasted into the sixteenth century. She would regularly be cited, along with famous prophetic figures such as the Sybils, St Bridget, Joachim, and Gamaleon, when true authority was sought, or when a particular judgment (e.g. for or against a particular ruler) was desired (see Marjorie Reeves, *The Influence of Prophecy in the Later Middle Ages*, Oxford, 1969).
16 St Bernard, with whom Hildegard corresponded, had been similarly impressed, and himself asked that she pray for him and his community: 'Wherefore I entreat and humbly pray that you would make remembrance of me before God and of those who are joined with me in spiritual society. I trust that you are united to God in the Spirit'. (*Life and Works of St. Bernard*, ed. Dom John Mabillon, vol. 2, p. 915).

keeper of secrets, too much given to wantonness, prone to every evil, and never loving any man in her heart.[17]

Andreas was, of course, echoing ideas that had been promoted by the Church Fathers (whose works, incidentally, were read aloud at mealtimes in Benedictine houses). John Chrysostom's view – 'the woman taught once, and ruined all . . . The sex is weak and fickle . . .The whole female race transgressed' – echoes Tertullian's question: 'Do you not know that you are Eve? . . . God's sentence still hangs over all your sex and his punishment weighs down upon you . . .'. Women were 'at once repulsive and fatally attractive': lift the corner of the dress, observes Jerome, and you will find the tip of the tail. For men, perhaps the obvious solution was to avoid their corrupting presence entirely; for women, the only really safe virtue was chastity; such was their nature that if they actually tried to do anything, they could not help but sin.[18]

An exchange of letters between Hildegard and a Rhineland *magistra* shows how liberated Hildegard could be from this depressing idea of woman's baseness. She had been chided by a fellow administrator, Tenxwind of Andernach, for allowing her nuns to dress up on holidays: not only did they don white gowns and veils, but they adorned their heads with tiaras. In justifying her policy, Hildegard (who was not given to admitting that she was wrong) argued that as virgins, her sisters were untainted by the Fall; retaining 'the simplicity and beautiful integrity of paradise', they were permitted 'bridal splendour'.[19] (*Scivias* portrays a chorus of virgins similarly 'adorned with gold and gems. Some of these had their heads veiled in white, adorned with a gold circlet', signifying that 'they all shine before God more brightly than the sun does on earth; . . . and so are adorned beautifully with the highest wisdom'.)[20]

---

17 Andreas Capellanus, *The Art of Courtly Love*, trans. John Jay Parry (New York, 1969), p. 201.

18 See O'Faolain and Martines (*op. cit.*), pp. 129 ff. for the Chrysostom and Tertullian quotes. For a discussion of St Jerome and the ideal of chastity see Ann McMillan's introduction to her translation of the *Legend of Good Women* (Houston, Texas, 1987); also Eileen Power's 'The Position of Women' in *The Legacy of the Middle Ages* (ed. G.C. Crump and E.F. Jacob, Oxford, 1926, pp. 401 ff.), in which she discusses the growth of the parallel ideas of woman as temptress, and of chastity as the definition of female virtue and honour.

19 Dronke (*op. cit.*), p. 166. Hildegard was also criticized by Tenxwind for her exclusion of non-noble women from her convent. She defended her position with citations from the Old Testament and by upholding the traditional type of the 'noble saint'. Thus Tenxwind and Hildegard held opposing views of God: the former's 'pauper Christus' vs. Hildegard's '*rex potentissimus* . . . to whom one owes dread and honour' (see Haverkamp, *op. cit.*, p. 191).

20 Hildegard of Bingen, *Scivias*, II, 5, 7, p. 205; The Classics of Western Spirituality Series, trans. Mother Columba Hart and Jane Bishop, with an introduction by Barbara New-

Hildegard's imagery, if not her policy, is in this case comfortably traditional, as the use of the explicitly nuptial metaphor to describe the relationship between the virgin soul and Christ went back at least as far as the third century.[21] Hildegard is ultimately drawing upon the triumphant description of the New Jerusalem as found in the *Revelation* of St John the Divine (VII, 4 ff.; XIV, 1 ff.), by implication placing her sisters in the blessed, white-robed company which accompanies the Lamb in the heavenly city. And this is the same image that was to be so beautifully elaborated two centuries later by the fourteenth-century *Pearl*-poet at the culmination of his vision, when the bereaved dreamer sees his lost daughter amongst the heavenly company:

> This noble city of rich emprise
> Had suddenly a full array
> Of virgins all in the same guise
> As did my blessed one display,
> And all were crowned in the same way,
> Adorned in pearl and raiment white.
>
> (Þis noble cite of ryche enpresse
> Watȝ sodaynly ful wythouten sommoun
> Of such vergyneȝ in þe same gyse
> Þat watȝ my blysful anvnder croun
> & coronde wern alle of þe same fasoun
> Depaynt in perleȝ & wedeȝ qwyte . . .)[22]

Hildegard might be said to have taken liberties with the apocalyptic material in several ways: however imminent she may have thought it to

man (New York and Mahwah, 1990); cf. also *Scivias*, trans. Bruce Hozeski (Santa Fe, New Mexico, 1986). The complex role of virginity in the Christian tradition is well analyzed by John Bugge in *Virginitas: An Essay on the History of a Medieval Idea* (The Hague, 1975): humans were meant by nature to be asexual – this was their prelapsarian condition. Sexuality was the result of the Fall, before which life in Eden was comparable to that of angels; virginity could represent, and was an attempt to recreate, the angelic life on earth. Thus the souls of virgins, whether male or female, could be seen as belonging to a higher rank than others, however virtuous those others may have been. See also Newman (*op. cit.*), pp. 221–2.

[21] See Bugge (*op. cit.*), pp. 61 ff., who notes that as early as the fourth century the rite of consecration for Christian female virgins was similar to the nuptial ceremony.

[22] *The Pearl*, trans. Sara de Ford (Northbrook, Illinois, 1967), p. 93. It should be pointed out that the gender of St John's apocalyptic company is not specified, while that of the *Pearl*-poet seems undeniably feminine. As the figure of Christ came, in the course of the Middle Ages, to be seen in more explicitly human terms, the nuptial image of the Bride/soul's union with him-as-Bridegroom tended to be applied more narrowly to female virgins (see Bugge, *op. cit.*, p. 66).

be, the day of judgement had yet to arrive; her sisters were still very much alive and well; and the decision as to who will finally comprise the chosen company in the heavenly city was not hers to make. Yet it is difficult not to rejoice in Hildegard's courageous defiance of the gloomy, antifeminist tradition by which she was surrounded. Her view of her community of women was confident, proud, joyful: they were a splendid company, worthy to honour God on the special holy days with their beauty rather than their penitence; they were not so morally fragile that the donning of lovely garments as an expression of love for their Creator would tempt them to vanity.

In many other ways Hildegard projects a rare confidence in women's power; there is no sense that she equates strength in women with danger, nor does she see a powerful 'good' woman as a second-best man. Her visionary treatises are peopled – even sustained – by majestic female figures. Synagogue, for example, is 'mother of the incarnation of the Word of God', a tall woman who carries in her lap and arms the Old Testament prophets – 'in her heart stood Abraham and in her breast Moses'.[23] Ecclesia, wearing a gem-studded dress and sandals of onyx, gazes heavenward with a radiant face. The 'puella' Caritas, Hildegard's representation of heavenly love, with golden sandals and 'a cloak whiter than snow, brighter than the stars', embraces the sun and the moon.[24]

Hildegard's confidence in women's potential for positive power made her community, even at the Disibodenberg, a uniquely exciting place for religious women to be. As her reputation spread, she attracted more followers; the growing ranks, along with the longing for a fuller independence, seemed to point to expansion. Then in 1148 she received a heavenly command to undertake this move, and establish an independent convent at Rupertsberg, near Bingen.[25] The Benedictine enshrinement of obedience might have been a major obstacle at this point, for as the abbot was God's representative, utter obedience was owed him; and when Hildegard made this proposal to Kuno, her abbot, he rejected it categorically. The presence of Hildegard and her group at the Disibodenberg was desirable for a number of reasons (not the least of which were her fame and the nun's dowries), and, further, he felt that the proposed location was unpromising (evidently the site was arid and deserted). On learning that Kuno opposed her decision, Hildegard's response was hardly that of the docile handmaid: she assumed a rock-like rigidity from which she could not be moved, and lay 'tanquam saxea rupes' – like a

23 *Scivias* (Hart and Bishop), I, 5, p. 133.
24 See Dronke (*op. cit.*), pp. 170 ff.; he notes that Hildegard was 'the first of the women mystics to personify love as a beautiful woman'.
25 See Hildegard's *Vita* (*op. cit.*) PL 197.96b–97a. Cf. Kent Kraft, in Wilson (*op. cit.*), pp. 110–11, and Dronke (*op. cit.*), pp. 150 ff.

rock made of stone – until the stymied abbot finally surrendered and granted her permission.

However much divine aid Hildegard may have received in achieving this state of petrification – she describes herself as having been struck down as with an illness – it is to be assumed that her own fierce will was also a considerable asset. She was sure she would be following God's command in making the move, and this certainty overrode Kuno's temporal authority. She saw herself as comparable to Moses leading his people towards the promised land; when Kuno resisted her efforts, she did not hesitate to compare him and his followers to the wicked Amalekites, foes of the Israelites in the desert and 'from generation to generation' thereafter (*Exodus*, XVII, 8–16). The move to Rupertsberg, when it finally took place in 1150, was felicitous; the convent expanded to include some fifty women – it even had running water! – and was enriched by the decision of various wealthy families to bury their dead within its grounds. Its success was such that Hildegard susequently set up a second house across the river at Eibingen to which she regularly travelled by boat.

Generally we have no information as to Hildegard's private friendships, but she did have a 'favourite' nun, Richardis von Stade, who seems to have been a sort of personal secretary, and to whom she was particularly attached. However, through the influence of Richardis' brother, the archbishop Hartwig, her friend was offered a prestigious position as abbess at another convent. Hildegard, believing that Richardis' motivation for accepting promotion was based on ambition, tried every means to dissuade her. In her correspondence with Hartwig she was more than liberal with her insults, comparing him to the proud Nebuchadnezzar – punished by God for his presumption by being driven mad – and a 'simoniac', one of that despised species of sinners who traded in ecclesiastical offices, and who were consigned by Dante to the eighth circle of hell. She even appealed to Pope Eugenius in her attempt to block the appointment. But neither insult nor entreaty sufficed to keep her friend with her. Richardis departed; and although she eventually regretted her decision, she became ill before she was able to rejoin Hildegard, and died in 1152. This sad loss is an isolated instance of the failure of Hildegard's will, but she was able to accept it because of her belief that God needed Richardis more than she did; and she even wrote an eloquent letter of consolation to Hartwig.[26]

A final episode, more than 25 years later, shows Hildegard (by now an octogenarian) still in full possession of her great courage and independence. She had agreed to allow a nobleman to be buried in the

---

[26] See Dronke (*op. cit.*), pp. 150 ff. and Newman (*op. cit.*), pp. 222 ff.

convent cemetery, which was in itself hardly unusual; the catch was that he was generally thought to have died excommunicate. However, Hildegard knew that he had been given the last rites before his death, and had herself received a divine command to permit the burial. Her superiors ordered that the body be exhumed; Hildegard's response was to make the sign of the cross over the grave with her staff, and obscure the outline of the grave so that no one would be able to disturb it. As punishment for this defiance, the entire community was excommunicated. This was a terrible privation, as mass could not be performed nor communion taken; perhaps most painful of all for the sisters was the prohibition against singing. At length Hildegard appealed to a higher ecclesiastical authority, who arranged for the interdict to be lifted. The stalemate was thus resolved, but not because of Hildegard's capitulation; again, as God's agent, she evidently did not consider this to be an option – nothing 'would let her conscience be crushed by clerical legalism'.[27]

These characteristic anecdotes have to do with Hildegard's active life as an administrator, which was certainly of major importance to her. But far more vital was her inner spiritual existence, the sphere of her visionary life. As we know, she had been subject to intense spiritual experiences from earliest childhood; uncertain as to their significance, worried that others would think her abnormal or presumptuous, she kept them largely to herself. However, shortly after she was elected abbess, in 1140, 'when I was forty-two years and seven months old', a dramatic change occurred. As she reports in *Scivias*, 'a fiery light of exceeding brilliance came and permeated my whole brain, and inflamed my whole heart and my whole breast, not like a burning but like a warming flame, as the sun warms anything its rays touch'; a celestial voice instructed her to 'say and write what you see and hear . . . as you see and hear them on high in the heavenly places in the wonders of God.'[28] Hildegard says that, subsequently, she had the power to understand the meaning of 'the psaltery, . . . the evangelists and the volumes of the Old and New Testament'.

From this point on, although she continues to refer to herself as 'paupercula feminea forma' – a poor little figure of a woman – Hildegard's actions seem to indicate that her self-doubt has been dispelled to a

---

27 Dronke here compares Hildegard's resolution to that of Antigone, defying the unjust decree of Creon. He also quotes her directly on the question of whether she should bow to the ecclesiastical authorities: 'I saw in my soul that if we followed their command and exposed the corpse, such an expulsion would threaten our home with great danger, like a vast blackness – it would envelop like a dark cloud that looms before tempests and thunderstorms . . . [We did not want to] seem to injure Christ's sacraments . . . , yet, so as not to be wholly disobedient, we have till now ceased singing the songs of divine praise, in accordance with the interdict, and have abstained from partaking of the body of the Lord' (*op. cit.*), pp. 195 ff.

28 *Scivias* (Hart and Bishop), 'Declaration', pp. 59–61; also Eckenstein (*op. cit.*), p. 264.

significant degree. She now sees herself as the mouthpiece of God, and her role in the process of salvation – for as much of the world as she can manage to reach – is proportionately evident. Despite this new confidence, and an abiding desire to have things her own way, Hildegard's concern is never for herself: whether she is writing hymns, or books on medicine, or mystical treatises, her aim is always to share with those around her, to enhance their spiritual elevation; her generosity is prodigious.

Hildegard's transcendence of self-doubt may have been facilitated by the acquisition of a new model, the prophetic Old Testament figure of Sapientia: 'The wisdom that grants discernment is crying aloud . . . There she stands, on some high vantage-point by the public way . . . or at the city's approach . . . making proclamation. To every man, high and low, her voice calls: Here is better counsel for the simpleton; O foolish hearts, take warning! I have matters of high moment to unfold . . . A tongue that speaks truth, lips that scorn impiety; here all is sound doctrine' (*Proverbs* VIII, 1–8). Such an identification is what we would by now expect: Hildegard selects for emulation an impressive, active figure of authority – one who avers that 'the Lord made me his when first he went about his work, . . . before his creation began' (*Proverbs* VIII, 22) – as the most effective means, herself, of becoming God's adjutant and working his will. Another important biblical figure with whom she identifies – undeterred by sexual difference – is St John the Divine, who was similarly commanded to 'Write down thy vision of what now is, and what must befall thereafter' (*Revelation*, I, 19). As we shall see, Hildegard's use of apocalyptic imagery in her writings is pervasive; indeed, her kind of prophetic work has been said to be 'largely founded on the Apcalypse.'[29]

After hearing the command of the celestial voice, her obligation to write was imperative. As Hildegard was insistent that her words, as they came directly from God, not be altered at all, she was fortunate in finding a scribe, Volmar, who faithfully recorded every detail of her account, and who stayed with her throughout most of her life. In an illustration from the *Book of Divine Works*, Volmar can be seen in the act of transcription, as Hildegard receives her divine inspiration. Hildegard seems to be recording her revelation directly onto a set of wax tablets; from these Volmar may later have made his permanent copy. Any temptation to attribute a measure of Hildegard's eloquence to Volmar's intervention is dispelled by a letter that she composed after his death, which shows the sophistication of what must be her own prose style: 'she uses rhetoric, figures of speech, complex and fluent sentences with ease'.[30]

---

[29] Eckenstein (*op. cit.*), p. 260.
[30] Dronke (*op. cit.*), p. 195.

27

II

Since the substance of what Hildegard sought to communicate was based on her visions, we need to examine their nature before turning to her actual writings. Well along in her career, when she had become a figure of great renown, she acquired an admirer named Guibert, who wrote what amounted to a fan letter asking her to describe her visionary experiences. Although his first letter was not answered, he persisted, and fortunately she then replied at some length. From this response we learn in detail exactly what her revelations were like.[1] Her soul 'ascends . . . to the heights of the firmament, . . . and spreads itself out among various peoples, very distant from me, in far away regions'. She does not perceive these things with any of her senses, 'but rather in my soul, with my external eyes open'. In other words, her external faculties are not affected, and she goes right on seeing and hearing everything that is going on in the 'real' world even as the illumination proceeds. The light that she experiences, 'far brighter than a cloud that bears the sun on it', she calls 'the shadow of the living light', in which 'the scripture, the virtues, and certain works of men' are reflected, or mirrored, 'as the sun, the moon, and the stars appear on the waters'. The words that she hears 'are not like the words that resound from the mouth of a man, but shine out like flames, and like clouds moving in the pure air'. Not surprisingly, Hildegard reports that she is not able to 'comprehend the form of this light', any more than she would be able to stare directly at the sun. Finally she adds that she has – though rarely – been able to see, within the shadow, the Living Light itself, the 'lux vivens', and that when this happens all her sadness and anxiety disappear, she feels like a 'simple maiden rather than an old woman'; her exhaustion and pain are relieved, and her soul refreshed.

This account reveals a number of peculiarly Hildegardian features. Most obvious is perhaps the fact that her external faculties are not affected even in the midst of her mystical experiences, so that presumably she can go on with whatever she is doing and no one around her will be aware of her inner state. This is in striking contrast to the experiences of many mystics, for instance her contemporary Elisabeth of Schönau, who entirely lost the use of her senses during her ecstasies. Presumably this is why Hildegard was able to keep secret the fact of her visions for as long as she did; it is also what we might expect of someone who accomplished

---

1 See Kraft (in Wilson, *op. cit.*), p. 123 and Dronke (*op. cit.*), p. 168. The text of the letter (trans. Ronald Miller) is also reprinted in *Book of Divine Works* (*op. cit.*), pp. 347–51.

as much as she did – she must have always been doing at least two things at any one time.

Hints of what might be called her 'synthesistic' or 'holistic' view[2] appear in this passage when she compares the mirroring of divine truths to the reflection of created objects on water. The creation properly ordered, as represented by sun, moon and stars, is an accurate image of the Creator – that is, elements within the creation may be turned to bad effect, but are not themselves bad. Thus the natural, material process of reflection is an appropriate image for the spiritual process of revelation that Hildegard experiences.

Another characteristic feature is the immediate generalization of her vision: she is not interested in how glorious or exciting these revelations were for *her*, but points rather to the fact that her soul 'spreads itself out among various peoples . . . in far away regions': it follows that the truths she is granted are for the spiritual elucidation of as many souls as she can contrive to come in contact with – in keeping with her extensive correspondence and travels. The calm, technical precision of the description is typical of Hildegard's reportorial style within her accounts of the actual visions. She can describe something as astounding as the ascent of her soul into the heights of the firmament as if she were doing a newscast. This care is not despite the importance of her subject, but because of it. Her job is not to wax enthusiastic – for her God's truths need no promotion – but to be an utterly dependable witness/messenger. This fits with the almost parenthetic reference, in her letter to Guibert, to her vision of the Living Light – an experience which seems to coincide with the phenomenon of union so glowingly described in the accounts of other mystics: the supreme moment of bliss and triumph in the spiritual life. While it is clearly a source of great joy to Hildegard as well, it is simply not her focal point. So in this letter alone we are given the beginnings of a significant insight into Hildegard's particular relationship with her Creator; she sees herself as an adjutant, a lieutenant who can always be counted on, whose powerful, active will is redirected towards the service of her commander, whose courage is such that her own physical pain, by which she continues to be regularly afflicted, is entirely forgotten, perhaps even assuaged, as she carries out her mission.

After receiving the divine command to record what she saw in her visions, the first work that she undertook, in 1141, was *Scivias* (from the longer phrase 'Scito vias Domini', or 'Know the Ways of the Lord'); this was to be volume one of her mystical trilogy, and would be ten years in the writing. In it Hildegard, now abbess, sought with characteristic meticulousness to set down every detail of her visions; and in each of the

---

[2] Rufus Jones describes this quality as 'cosmic vitalism' (*op. cit.*), p. 45.

accounts, her presentation follows the same form. First, she is confronted by a bright light which radiates over a striking image, such as a mountain or an abyss; this image and the surrounding figures are then described in minute detail; finally, an extensive allegorical interpretation of the image, many times greater in length than the original description, is provided. The visual nature of Hildegard's revelation cannot be stressed strongly enough. Every one of her visions was literally that: visual; an elaborate, static, iconic tableau, which she first described, then allegorized. Finally she painted, or had paintings done, of these images, to complete the record and to serve in themselves as objects of further contemplation.[3]

The subject matter of *Scivias*, which has been described as a 'salvational encyclopedia',[4] is comprehensive – including the Creed, Scriptures, Incarnation and Trinity – and covering the history of creation from the Fall of Lucifer to the Day of Judgement. Its structure is tripartite: the first section is divided into six visions, the second into seven and the third into thirteen. What is immediately striking about this composition is its vastness, its boldness, the grandeur of its imagination. Part I, for instance, opens with a view of the enthroned Creator on a mountain top, bathed in a blinding glorious light; it includes along the way revelations to do with the Fall, the cosmic egg, the three stages of life, the grand figure of Synagogue; and it concludes with a vision of the angelic orders – 'armies of heavenly spirits' – ranged in concentric circles, all singing 'with marvellous voices all kinds of music about the wonders that God works in blessed souls, and by this God was magnificently glorified'. Hildegard's tone is unwavering, confident and courageous – this is no 'poor little woman' speaking.

There is a danger in discussing Hildegard's work of getting lost in the vastness and complexity, of struggling to give shape and order to a multitude of generalities but losing any sense of the specialness of what she has to offer. Some of the elements that she includes in her writing were common in the Middle Ages, for instance the Boethian/Neoplatonic view of the creation as image of the Creator, or the conviction that the Old Testament prefigured the New (and so the Old Testamant becomes a Christian document: Noah's flood looks forward to the sacrament of baptism, the sacrifice of Isaac prefigures the crucifixion); and some are intensely personal, perhaps most particularly her emphasis on

---

3 See Eckenstein (*op. cit.*), p. 265. The originals of Hildegard's paintings were lost during the Second World War, but fortunately copies had been made before this occurred. For reproductions of her illuminations see *Hildegardis Scivias*, eds. Adelgundis Führkötter and Angela Carlevaris, in *Corpus Christianorum: Continuatio Mediaeualis* XLIII and XLIIIa (Turnhout, 1978).

4 See Adelgundis Führkötter's Foreword to *Scivias* (Hozeski), p. xi. Führkötter cites Christel Meier's observation that the three-part structure of *Scivias* 'intimates the triune God'.

the importance of the feminine in the process of salvation. But the way these elements are linked and woven together and built upon provides the crucial blend that is Hildegard, and only by a minute and patient following, a turning over of ourselves to her as guide, can we expect to share the passionate, eccentric brilliance of her revelations. This discussion, then, will focus on Part I of *Scivias*, and examine its six visions, one at a time, in some detail.

The first *visio* includes five main images.[5] On an iron mountain sits a figure of great brightness, with 'a soft shadowlike wing of wonderful breadth and length'. At the foot of the mountain stand two figures, on the left an image 'full of eyes', on the right a child wearing a pale tunic and white shoes. 'Living sparks' descend from the figure on the mountain and surround these two images, and above them, in the mountain, are ten 'windows' through which pale pairs of heads can be seen. The fact that the mountain is iron, Hildegard explains, represents the stability and permanence of 'the eternal kingdom of God'; the brightness of the figure (so bright that 'it blinds your sight'), indicates that the celestial divinity is 'incomprehensible to human minds'; the softness of the wing reflects its 'sweet and gentle protection', the fusion of fairness with justice. Fear of the Lord is represented by the image full of eyes, which, gazing on the kingdom of God, 'counters all forgetfulness of God's justice'. The child, standing before this image, indicates that the poor in spirit follow after the fear of the Lord; they do not boast, or act for self-advancement, but choose to be simple and to walk in 'the serene footsteps of the Son of God'. The brightness that obscures the child's head – the 'glory that descends from the One enthroned' – reflects that our weak powers of contemplation are not sufficient 'to grasp His purpose'.

The powerful virtues that emanate from God are represented by the 'living sparks . . . darting fire in divine glory' that radiate from the seated image; they 'ardently embrace and captivate' those who fear the Lord and love the poor in spirit. The stars and the pairs of heads reveal that nothing, neither the positive nor the negative aspect of our actions, can be hidden from God; sincerity motivates those actions that are positive, while negative actions are marked by lukewarmness. Often our actions are characterized by both qualities because sometimes we are weak of heart, sometimes awake and vigilant.

Hildegard concludes the explication of this *visio* with a quotation from Solomon: 'The slothful hand has brought about poverty, but the hand of the industrious man prepares riches' (*Proverbs* X, 4). 'A person makes himself weak and poor', she says, interpreting the biblical text, 'when he will not work justice . . . But one who does strong works of salvation,

5   *Scivias* (Hart and Bishop), I, 1, pp. 67 ff.

31

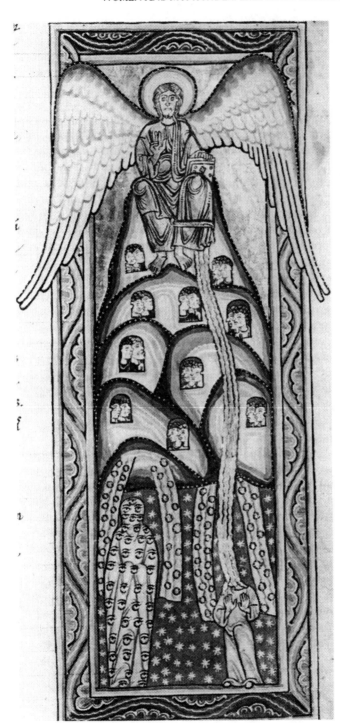

Visio One. In *Scivias'* first vision a wingéd figure of great brightness, from whom living sparks descend, sits atop an iron mountain. The image reveals that while absolute obedience to the Creator is required, security and serenity will be the reward. Wiesbaden 1,2; by permission of das Rheinische Bildarchiv.

running in the way of truth, obtains the upwelling fountain of glory'. The ideal of zealous activity expressed in *Proverbs* corresponds with the words of the figure on the mountain, who exhorts her – and through her, humanity in general – to cry out against corruption. Those who do not devote themselves to the preservation of justice are lukewarm and timid; we must extend ourselves 'into a fountain of abundance and overflow with mystical knowledge': this will be a knowledge that cannot be found through human understanding, but must be achieved through the process of revelation, by way of divine justice. God's bright serenity will 'shine strongly with glorious light among the shining ones'.

After the preliminary factual description of the first *visio*, Hildegard moves on to a more lengthy explication of the central images. Her method of interpretation derives from the traditional medieval system of interpretation, typological exegesis, according to which there can be several levels of meaning within a single text: literal, moral, allegorical and anagogical. The literal describes deeds, or tells the story; the allegorical teaches what we should believe, the moral how we should act, and the anagogical what we should strive towards. As the physical, literal world is a mirror of the spiritual one, it serves as a means whereby the secrets of the latter may be unlocked; and once the truth has been extracted, the literal level may be dispensed with – hence the notion of fruit and chaff, the former being the only really significant aspect of the text.[6] So Chaucer's Nun's Priest, at the end of his tale, reminds his audience of St Paul's advice: everything is written for our benefit, but we must labour to extract the truth, 'Taketh the fruyt, and lat the chaf be stille'.[7]

However, there is no 'chaff' in Hildegard's system: each aspect of her revelation, whether visual presentation, verbal description, or allegorical interpretation, constitutes a kind of 'fruit', a valid representation of divine truth.[8] Once explicated, the image itself continues to serve as a contemplative focal point and an ongoing source of inspiration and understanding; it stands as an alternate expression of the *visio*'s spritual message.

---

[6] 'Litera gesta docet,/ Quid credas allegoria,/ Moralis quid agas,/ Quo tendas anagogia'. See, for example, *Exégèse Médiévale*, H. de Lubac (Paris, 1964). The fourfold notion of interpretation was advocated by figures such as Augustine and Bede. There was also a threefold theory advanced by others, for example Jerome. In *The Middle English Mystics* (London, 1981), Wolfgang Riehle examines in detail the metaphorical language used by medieval mystics.

[7] *The Canterbury Tales*, Geoffrey Chaucer, 'The Nun's Priest's Tale' VII, 3443 (*The Riverside Chaucer*, ed. L. Benson, Boston, 1987).

[8] Dronke (*op. cit.*), p. 146 compares Hildegard's revelations with the third level of visions described by her contemporary, Richard of St Victor, in his commentary on the *Apocalypse*: those which are perceived with the help of the Holy Spirit by the 'eyes of the heart', whereby the human spirit is led through the 'likeness of visible things or figures and signs . . . to knowledge of invisible ones' (*PL* 196, 686).

What then of the content of Hildegard's first *visio*? How is this revelation, and her understanding of it, characteristic? The arresting focal point
of the *visio* is the figure seated on the mountain. Hildegard's God is
emphatically central and powerful, and adjures humanity, through
Hildegard, in tones that are resolutely awesome, but not necessarily
dreadful. Scorn is reserved for those who are susceptible to corruption,
while the active, alert followers are not threatened; indeed, the admonition specifies that the reward of God's serenity will become available to
those who participate in the process of revelation. As the agent of the
divine, the receiver and transmitter of this information, Hildegard is very
much in the background, even off-stage, again like the dependable repor-
ter. She does not say how excited or how pleased she is to be so selected
by God, but is fulfilled simply by carrying out her mission.

The *visio* makes clear a number of times that absolute obedience to God
is required, that fear is an essential part of the soul's relation to God; love
is not mentioned, nor indeed is any explicitly Christological influence in
evidence. Two kinds of fear seem to emerge from within the vision: the
fear of being excluded or rejected by God if we are lukewarm and timid is
a negative force; but the fear felt by the faithful follower for the good
commander is positive, equatable with reverential respect. And the commander does not obtain obedience through fear, as much as through
being trustworthy – those who obey and carry out their part of the duties
will always be protected. Fear and courage are not exclusive, but coexistent, complementary.

Thus, despite the initially daunting impression of the figure on the
mountain, the image is not a threatening one, nor is the prospect of
punishment used as motivation. The iron of the mountain reflects security, permanence, the stability of the reign of God. The huge wing with
its implication of gentle enfolding represents both 'sweet and gentle protection' and 'true equity'.[9] The sparkling rays that envelop the two figures
at the foot of the mountain reinforce the sense of caring and protection;
they represent the divine virtues which 'ardently embrace' those who fear
and serve the Lord. And the rewards that are promised the faithful are
described in life-giving terms of water and light: the 'fountain of abundance', the 'glorious light' of serenity. Hildegard sees her Creator as an
inseparable mix of justice and mercy, intolerant of weakness but ready to
forgive. As the pairs of pale heads indicate, both our good and our bad
deeds are known to God; but further, no one is expected to be all good all
the time, and this is not a cause for fear; everyone experiences lapses in
alertness and zeal. And as the next vision makes even more explicit, the

---

[9]   Alert to the dangers of complacency, which can so easily lead to the despised lukewarmness, Hildegard is always clear that divine mercy is evenly tempered with justice.

system is designed to allow for, and pardon, our failings, as long as they are followed by repentance and reform.

Other features that later show themselves to be of importance are introduced in this first vision. The fact that the stability of the mountain and the brightness of the stars are seen as apt images for divine attributes suggests the correlation between Creator and creation that is so central to Hildegard's view. Her insistence that human understanding, in itself too weak to grasp divine truth, must rely on revelation and the assistance of the Holy Spirit, looks forward to her view of the importance of the prophetic role in the process of salvation and her belief in the supremacy of faith over reason.[10] The emphasis on the vice of corruption implies a political concern which overlaps with Hildegard's ongoing involvement in secular affairs, her conviction that the church should play an active role in social reform. Hers is not an ideal of wholesale withdrawal from a corrupt and confusing world: we have an obligation to tend and reform the disordered creation. In fact it is tempting to speculate that Hildegard would have seen an exclusively antiworldly ideal as perilously close to lukewarmness. Her agenda is as large as the history of creation: judgement day may be at hand, but until then the battle against the forces of evil will rage and must be tirelessly waged on all possible fronts.

III

Scivias' first illumination reveals an image of the Creator as almighty commander, the feudal lord, with Hildegard in the position of loyal follower, or retainer. Without danger, however, and without a serious opponent, a lord and vassal are rather at loose ends. Fortunately, Hildegard loves a good fight, and a hard-won victory; for although she has not a shadow of doubt as to the omnipotence of her Creator, and therefore the inevitability of God's ultimate victory, her world view is emphatically not one in which evil is perceived simply as the absence of good. Lucifer and Antichrist are envious, ruthless, vengeful. They are utterly committed to

---

[10] Hildegard nonetheless shares Boethius' regard for the faculty of reason. As he explains, it is in being reasonable that man is like God; the abandonment of reason means the loss of the divine image, the distortion of the soul – and thence the descent into a condition of sinfulness, for the soul can no longer correctly govern itself or its body. Kent Kraft (in Wilson, *op. cit.,* p. 115) points out that Hildegard's view of the universe becomes more orderly as she progresses towards the *Book of Divine Works,* increasingly 'restructured by the imposition of *ratio,* of measuring reason'.

Visio Two. Although presided over by a multitude of bright stars, this vision reveals the danger presented by the forces of evil. A small, vulnerable figure hangs precariously over the mouth of a dark lake, from which emerge foul smoke and a sinister serpentine form. Wiesbaden 1,4; by permission of das Rheinische Bildarchiv.

God's overthrow, and the battle they wage continues without interruption throughout the entire history of the world. The guard of the vigilant must never be relaxed. We must take full measure of the foe and continually maintain the battle.

It is not surprising, then, that the second vision in *Scivias* introduces the element of evil.[1] Again the *visio* includes five central images, and again the strong voice speaks to Hildegard, though this time it is heard intermittently throughout the discussion rather than in one long address. First, a bright multitude of 'living lamps' is revealed, then a wide, deep lake; the lake has a mouth like the opening of a well, which emits a dark, stinking smoke. A serpentine form with a 'deceitful' appearance stretches forth from the smoke; from its mouth emerges a white cloud that contains many stars, which in turn produces through itself the figure of a man. This vulnerable naked man is suspended by a slight thread from the cloud, and is dangling directly over the ominous mouth of the dark lake; in the lower right corner are two trees, one bearing what might well be the fruit of knowledge; in the four corners of the illumination's frame are depicted the four elements: the lighter air and fire at the top, at the bottom the heavier water and earth. As an apparent result of the lake/snake/cloud/man sequence, the elements of the world, which previously existed in harmony, are 'turned to the greatest agitation and [display] horrible terrors'.

Hildegard begins her interpretation with the same painstaking care and precision as she brought to the first illumination; the commentary for the more difficult second illumination is five times the length as that for *Vision One*. The brilliant star-like multitude represents the angels before the Fall, those who did not themselves strive for glory, but were content to contemplate the glory, or brightness, of God. Those angels that fell into darkness with Lucifer, however, 'embraced the torpor of ignorance'. Their dullness represents the absolute loss of their mirroring ability, of their divine likeness – their perpetual exile from God; we recall, in contrast, the perfect mirroring ability of 'the shadow of the living light' described in Hildegard's letter to Guibert. This loss, more than any physical torment, constitutes the definition of hell: damnation's worst pain is the pain of separation from God. As Chaucer's Parson explains, 'he that is in helle shal have defaute of the sighte of God', hell's deathly darkness will prevent him from seeing the face of God, 'right as dooth a derk clowde bitwixe us and the sonne'. Conversely, the joy of heaven is to be forever in the presence of God. So in Dante's *Paradise* the most blessed souls comprise the white mystic rose, and, arranged in semicircles, they sit in eternal contemplation of the 'First Love', the 'Light which is true in Itself'.

---

[1] *Scivias* (Hart and Bishop), I, 2, 73 ff.

God describes to Hildegard the creation of hell, 'outside the world's framework, . . . neither sun nor moon shed any radiance there . . . In the light we behold God's work . . . and in the darkness God's absence'.[2]

In *Scivias*, the uncorrupted angels who remained in heaven understood 'that God continues immoveable', the failure of Lucifer's rebellion confirming God's unalterable omnipotence. But the once splendid Lucifer, failing to recognize his limitations, and having set himself in competition with God, was cast with his rebel angels into the 'fiery blackness', where, deprived of the brightness of God, their own was also blackened. Hildegard's commentary points out that for God not to have exiled the rebel angels would have been unjust, and specifies that the nature of Lucifer's wrong was the wish to divide up the wholeness of the divinity: there cannot be two Gods in one heaven.

For Hildegard, wholeness, the integrated harmony of the universe, is of central importance, and this second *visio* reveals not only the particular nature of Lucifer's crime, but the way in which it initiated the ongoing process of evil, bringing about imbalance on earth, the disruption of its natural wholeness: the black mouth of the lake – the lower world – opens ominously; it emits a deceptive smoke which obscures the truth; the envious serpentine figure – the devil – menaces the vulnerable naked man, tempts him with the false promise of pleasure; the four elements, angered at man's disobedience, are now unbalanced, displaying fear and restlessness; the creatures of the world set themselves in opposition to a degraded humanity, and woman sets herself in opposition to man instead of helping him. The process of salvation will involve not only the defeat of the old enemy, Lucifer, but the restoration of this lost harmony, so that the creation will once again perfectly reflect its Creator.

Hildegard's ability to recapitulate the whole history of creation in a single image is apparent in this *visio*. Most obviously, the connection between the two Falls – of Lucifer, and of Adam and Eve – is shown. The black lake was created originally for the rebel angels, but of course is not only for them: their torment foreshadows the ongoing process of punishment for those who, in imitation of Lucifer, will subsequently choose to disobey God, and join his treacherous company in the outer darkness. Some, Hildegard explains, will be banished forever; others, if they repent before their death, will eventually be released.

The teachings of her commentary are bolstered by quotations from the Old Testament, *Job* (XXI:17–18) and *Ezekiel* (XVIII:30). Job describes the response of the angry God to the disloyal: they will be extinguished, as an oil lamp; they will be as chaff and ash before a mighty wind. Ezekiel

2 *The Canterbury Tales*, Geoffrey Chaucer, 'The Parson's Tale', X, 183, 184 (*op. cit.*); *The Divine Comedy*, Dante Alighieri (trans. H.R. House, New York, 1954), *Paradise*, Canto XXXII–XXXIII; *Book of Divine Works* (*op. cit.*), pp. 87, 88.

urges man to be busy with repentance, in order to avoid the ruin that follows from sin. The use of these Old Testament voices, while evoking a powerful reminder of the vengeful aspect of God's nature, also emphasizes that the process of salvation is one which is taking place throughout the whole expanse of history, thus encompassing the scope of both testaments.

So the commentary on *Vision Two* evolves towards an explicit revelation of the role played by the incarnation in the process of salvation. God's anger is essentially modified by forgiveness: the 'most gentle Father sent his Only-Begotten to die for the people, to deliver humanity from the power of the Devil'; 'the Son saved [humanity from the Devil] by His blood and brought him gloriously to the glory of Heaven'. The array of divine virtues is augmented at the time of the incarnation by the two chief Christian virtues, humility and charity, which will be necessary to effect the final defeat of Lucifer: 'Humility caused the Son of God to be born of the Virgin . . . The Son of God lay in a manger, because His Mother was a poor maiden . . . And charity took the Only-Begotten of God, who was in the bosom of the Father in Heaven, and placed Him in the womb of a mother on earth'. The nature of the exchange involved in the crucifixion is made explicit: 'When the innocent lamb was suspended on the cross . . . the lost sheep was brought back to the pastures of life'.[3]

In the course of Hildegard's commentary we have been reassured that despite Adam and Eve's departure, paradise has never ceased to exist; its perfection was immediately reestablished after their expulsion, its wholeness maintained: 'a luminous splendor surrounded that region' and it was fortified 'with His glory, so that from then on it would be touched by no encroachment': this reassurance recalls God's covenant with Noah in *Genesis* (IX, 11) – 'Never more will the living creation be destroyed by the waters of a flood' – where a rainbow signals the restoration of harmony. Then, with the ringing conclusion of her commentary, Hildegard banishes any residual fear created by the threatening image of the yawning black lake: certainly the danger persists, but there is a solution, and it is more powerful. Armed with humilty and charity, she assures her readers, you 'shall not fear the Devil's snares but shall have everlasting life'.

Hildegard's account of the Fall in this *visio* must take into consideration the reason that the devil chose to tempt Eve rather than Adam: he knew that 'the susceptibility of the woman would be more easily conquered than the strength of a man', and that Adam loved Eve so passionately he would do whatever she told him. In addition, the devil was particularly envious of Eve, since she would give birth to the race that is destined to replace the fallen angels in heaven. Eve was responsible for the Fall, 'since she, more than any other creature could lead Adam to

---

[3] *Scivias* (Hart and Bishop), I, 2, 30–33, pp. 87–90.

disobedience'; seeing the rebellion of Adam and Eve, 'the Creation, which had been created for the service of humanity, turned against humans [and] . . . now opposed itself to them': thus earth's correct hierarchy was distorted, each fall leading to the next like so many dominoes.[4]

What of Hildegard's view of Eve? Does it undermine her presentation of female figures who are both powerful and virtuous? On the surface, Hildegard seems to be in agreement with the conventional medieval view of soulful Adam as innocent victim, and corruptible Eve as cause of the Fall. Yet this dualistic approach is in fundamental conflict with Hildegard's view of the ordered creation as image of its Creator; whatever is made by God must by definition be good, and to despise any aspect of the creation (even if it *is* female) is in effect to despise its Maker. Furthermore, to see aspects of the creation as inherently corrupt is to give too much power to the forces of evil, and suggests that the ultimate triumph of good may actually be in question. For at the heart of dualism 'lies a horror at the beastly fascination of the flesh . . . Flesh and spirit were of different stuff . . . The soul was to be purged by hurting the body . . . The flesh should be tried to the utmost so that the spirit could escape this mortality and live'.[5]

Such a view cannot be reconciled with the ideal of the ordered creation as the perfect image of the Creator, of the universe in which each thing has a correct place to which (if out of it) it naturally longs to go, and in doing so honours and worships its Creator. Historically, this hierarchical view has been abused in the process of justifying social and economic inequalities, but it has not been responsible for – and is at variance with – the crippling revulsion from the flesh that has been dualism's legacy. Hildegard's love for the creation does not allow for the rejection of any of its parts. Certainly the desires of the body can tempt the soul away from its correct direction; but the soul also can

> take possession of the whole body in which it exists, in order to achieve its own work by means of that body . . . That body has been formed by God . . . The soul urges the body to be vigilant and revives it to do its proper work . . . ; from this time forward the body renews its powers, . . . will turn again totally to God's service.[6]

Rather than seeking oppositions, or antitheses, Hildegard looks for correspondences, parallels, resolution. In one of her medical works, *Physica*, she speaks of the correspondences between the elements, the creatures and the plants, and of their correct relation to humanity: as a means of

---

4 *Ibid.*, I, 2, 26; 33; 27.
5 See *Ancrene Wisse*, ed. Geoffrey Shepherd (London and Edinburgh, 1959), pp. xli, xliv.
6 *Book of Divine Works (op. cit.)*, I, 4,19, pp. 95, 96.

restoring or maintaining health. In her *Book of Life's Merits* she presents a catalogue of the vices and virtues, in corresponding pairs, explaining that illness is the result of vice, that health can be regained through the virtues; in other words the flesh is not inherently evil, and can, as flesh, be restored to goodness/health. In the *Book of Divine Works* Hildegard presents a 'system of metaphorical correspondences between the elemental layers of the universe and various parts of the body'; she aims to establish correspondences between the geography of the earth and the soul, the weather and the humours, between the literal and the allegorical, the physical and the spiritual, the human and the divine – 'all with the view of glorifying God and his works':[7]

> as the word of God has penetrated everything in creation, the soul penetrates the whole body . . . The soul is the green lifeforce of the flesh, . . . the body grows and progresses through the soul, just as the earth becomes fruitful through moisture.[8]

The soul, through reason, perceives the correct course of action, but it is integrally bound with the body; like the elements, and the rest of created things, they must stand in correct relation to one another. And as the soul and body need one another, so do man and woman:

> God gave the first man a helper in the form of woman, who was man's mirror image . . . Man and woman are in this way so involved with each other that one of them is the work of the other . . . Neither of them could . . . live without the other . . . Man is . . . an indication of the Godhead while woman is an indication of the humanity of God's Son.[9]

And when woman was first created, she was pure, an embodiment of Adam's love; their paradisal love was 'free of carnality'.[10] Woman's correct relation to man, as helper and partner, is clear – technically 'inferior', perhaps, she is nonetheless worthy to represent Christ's humanity. Thus Hildegard rejects the medieval cliché of woman as either lustful temptress or pristine angel. Instead she indicates a progression in which Eve, the old mother, prefigures Mary, the new one. Mother of humanity, she is also strangely linked with Christ: as Adam, 'who was not injured' by the birth of Eve, 'joyfully beheld that [first] woman', so Mary, 'who was also full of joy, enclosed her Son within the womb';

---

[7] See Eckenstein (*op. cit.*) and Kraft (in Wilson, *op. cit.*, p. 120n), where he also claims the *Book of Divine Works* to be 'one of the most fully articulated statements of the relationship between the macrocosm and the microcosm found in twelfth-century thought'.
[8] *Book of Divine Works* (*op. cit.*, I, 4, 21), pp. 96, 97.
[9] *Ibid.* (I, 4, 100), pp. 122, 123.
[10] See Dronke (*op. cit.*), pp. 170 ff.

Eve [like the Son of God] was not created from a man's seed but from the flesh of a man . . . God created her by the same power through which God sent the Son to the Virgin. Neither Eve, the virgin and mother, nor Mary the mother and Virgin, has found any woman like herself. In this way God put on a human form.[11]

Hildegard's refusal to accept the polarization of man and woman, and of 'good' and 'bad' women, ties in with her recognition that none of us on this earth can be either absolutely virtuous or utterly vicious; the tendency towards sinfulness is an essential quality of our humanity, and so is the capacity for repentance. It also reflects a rejection of the simplistic notion that the flesh is automatically more 'susceptible' to sin; sins of the spirit are equally pernicious, starting with the pride of Lucifer, and including the despicable 'lukewarmness', which seems to be a kind of sloth.[12] So, at the conclusion to her commentary on *Vision Two*, she is able to use the body-soul bond to describe the interdependence of the essential Christian virtues of humility and charity: they 'are like a soul and a body . . . Humility is like the soul and charity like the body, and they cannot be separated from eachother but work together . . . And as the various members of the body are subject . . . to the soul and the body, so also the other virtues cooperate . . . with humility and charity'.[13] Both are necessary.

Hildegard's ability to reconcile these conventional antitheses liberates her scope, permitting her the inclusion of such magnificent female figures

---

[11] *Book of Divine Works* (*op. cit.*), III, 7,13, p. 199. For a fuller examination of this question, and more generally of Hildegard's treatment of women in her works, see Barbara Newman's excellent study, *Sister of Wisdom* (*op. cit.*). It is intriguing to note that Jung describes four stages to the development of the *anima*, the first of which is symbolized by Eve, the third by the Virgin Mary, and the fourth by Sapientia, with whom we have already seen Hildegard identify (*Man and his Symbols*, ed. Carl G. Jung, New York, 1964, p. 195).

[12] Chaucer's Parson lists a number of similar spiritual errors under the heading of *Accidia*, e.g. 'wanhope, that is despeir of the mercy of God', 'sompnolence, that is sloggy slombrynge', 'necligence', who, when he does something, cares not 'wheither he do it weel or baddely' (*The Canterbury Tales, op. cit.*, X, 692 ff.)

[13] *Scivias* (Hart and Bishop), p. 90. It should be noted that Dronke (*op. cit.*), pp. 171 ff. argues that Hildegard's thought on these subjects is marked by unresolved conflict: on the one hand, God is omnipotent, has created everything, and humanity is part of the harmonious whole; on the other, Lucifer's terrible power raises the question of whether the flesh belongs to him. According to Dronke, Hildegard's *Causae et curae* best reflects her ambivalence, but he also remarks that she moves towards a reconciliation of this conflict through her music, which 'is earthly but not earthbound'. Newman too refers to Hildegard's oscillation 'between a joyful affirmation of the world and the body, and a melancholy horror of the flesh' (*op. cit.*), p. 21. As we have seen, Hildegard does not deny that the body can lead the soul astray (as Eve did to Adam); but it can also cooperate in perfect harmony with the soul: thus our physical beings are not intrinsically corrupt.

as Synagogue in *Scivias* I, and of powerful female imagery, such as the cosmic egg, which appears in the third *visio*. And conversely, within the second vision, Hildegard has been able to make her depiction of the process by which the unwary are trapped all the more terrifying by her combined use of male and female sexual imagery, the serpent and the well: as both elements can cooperate in the process of salvation, so in their evil manifestation can they work together to hasten damnation.

IV

Hildegard's third *visio*, of the cosmic egg, is astonishing even in the context of her other revelations.[1] At the start of her description she emphasizes that what she sees, 'a vast instrument, rounded and shadowed', is specifically egg-shaped, narrower at the top, fuller in the middle, and narrow again at the bottom. It consists of a series of concentric ovals, the outermost of which is a ring of bright flame, blown by a great wind. The next layer is darker, and contains a 'dark fire' so horrible that Hildegard can not bear to look at it; this dark layer is shaken by violence: it is full of thunder, storms, and sharp stones, and a turbulent wind rages inside it. There is an integral link between the two layers, as the outer, bright fire is described as having 'felt within itself the turbulence of the thunder'.

After the dark layer a region of pure ether is found, within which are many clear starlike spheres; inside the oval of ether is a circular region of moisture, described as 'watery air with a white zone beneath it, which diffused itself here and there and imparted moisture' – either 'sudden rain with great noise' or 'a pleasant and softly falling rain'. Both these regions, of air and of water, have their own winds creating their own particular turbulence.

Towards the top of the region of pure air, suspended from a sequence of torches, is a globe of reddish fire that illuminates the whole inside of the egg, and causes the clear spheres to shine with its light; it sometimes 'raised itself up' and 'sometimes sank downward'. At the egg's centre, in the midst of these concentric ovals, sits a large, sandy globe, kept in position by the surrounding elements – though sometimes the buffeting of the winds is strong enough to cause it to move a little. And within the

---

[1] *Scivias* (Hart and Bishop), I, 3, pp. 93 ff. Peter Dronke (*Fabula: Explorations into the Uses of Myth in Medieval Platonism*, Leiden and Cologne, 1974, p. 96) points out that the image of the cosmic egg comes from antiquity, but that Hildegard's is 'the most richly individual transformation of the fable of the world-egg'.

Visio Three. Hildegard's cosmic egg includes a number of concentric ovals. Outermost is a ring of bright flame, followed by a layer of dark, violent fire. A star-filled region of pure ether surrounds a circle of moisture. At the centre sits a globe, within which is a great mountain. As a whole, the egg represents both the majesty and the mystery of the Creator. Wiesbaden 1,14; by permission of das Rheinische Bildarchiv.

dry globe a great mountain is seen, dark towards the north, and light towards the east. The light does not reach the darkness, nor can the darkness reach the light. Again the voice speaks to Hildegard, and her commentary begins.

Hildegard's commentary reminds us at the outset that this *visio* has been created for the understanding and honour of the divine name, that it is a manifestation of things invisible and eternal: the egg itself in its wholeness represents the majesty and mystery of the all-powerful God, the hope of the faithful.

Each of the elements within the egg is then examined in turn, and the correspondences with divine verities are explained. The outer ring of bright fire signifies that God both burns and purifies, whether through the fire of vengeance or of consolation; the red globe indicates that the Son's glory is such that it illuminates all creatures; the three torches keep the fire from falling onto the globe even as the Son of God aided humanity through the revelation of heavenly truth. The rising of the globe parallels the raising up of humanity through the will of God, specifically by means of the incarnation; the downwards motion of the globe signifies the hardship and suffering experienced by the Only-Begotten while on earth.

The bright ring's wind indicates that from God, who 'fills the whole world with his power, truth rushes forth and spreads with words of justice', while the turbulence of the darker layer indicates the rage of the devil. The dark fire represents the murder that 'the ancient betrayer's most evil and most vile snares vomit forth' – specifically Cain's murder of Abel. The thunder, storms and sharp stones indicate that this murder is full of greed, drunkenness and hard-heartedness, while the shaking of the outer fire represents 'an increased disposition to vengeance on the part of right judgment'. That the bright fire 'felt within itself' the violence of the darker layer confirms that evil will be overcome and crushed by divine power.

As the commentary continues, the correspondences become almost predictable: the pure ether is the sereneness of faith, the clear spheres are the splendid works of piety; the red globe, as it stands for the glory of Christ, also represents the unconquered church. The winds from the ether indicate the unity of faith, and those from the moist air the cleansing power of baptism. The mountain within the sandy globe, separating the light from the darkness, assures us that no matter how much the devil tries he cannot reach the light – the joy of redemption cannot be contaminated by the misery of damnation.

What becomes evident is that, despite our initial reaction of astonishment at the image of an enormous flaming, rattling, windy, star-filled, glowing egg, this is really a most comforting and reassuring revelation. In its perfection it is indeed the ideal object to represent God, 'incomprehensible in His majesty and inestimable in His mysteries'. All the elements, all the contradictions, the chaos and harmony, the disruption and resolution of creation are represented; the correspondences between nature and man, macrocosm and microcosm, are revealed. As the violence of the dark fire and the atrocity of Cain's crime are linked, so the illuminating power of our pious acts is seen to correspond to the shining of the spheres. As long as creation continues, of course, the dark fire will burn and its violent winds will blow. But at the centre of it all is the mountain, ever stable, ever assuring the separation of good and evil, and the eventual defeat of the devil.

The egg, the smallest unit of creation, emerges in its perfect unity as the optimal figure for the oneness of the universe, the object of contemplation best suited to express the perfection of God's order and the process of salvation. The vision is ultimately reassuring because it reveals how evil can exist and, at the same time as it is part of the creation, be counterbalanced and controlled by the forces of good.

Following the cosmic egg in *Scivias* are two visions that also make dramatic use of female images.[2] In the fourth *visio* a small human figure is seen within a woman's womb; a brightness descends and fills its mind, after which the figure – a soul – is born, and undertakes a journey of great hardship. In the course of this journey, 'returning by God's grace from the path of error to Zion', the soul mourns its separation from its mother: 'O mother, O mother Zion, . . . Oh, how long, how long have I been deprived of your maternal sweetness, in which with many delights you gently brought me up!' After much remorse it is consoled and strengthened as the memory of the mother is restored: 'A most sweet fragrance touched my nostrils, like a gentle breath exhaled by my mother . . . I delighted in [my] tears as if I saw my mother'. An arduous trial, in which the soul is threatened by a swarm of scorpions, serpents and adders, is overcome with the help of the mother's exhortation: 'O daughter, run! For the Most Powerful Giver . . . has given you wings to fly with. Therefore fly swiftly over all these obstacles!' And I, comforted with great consolation, took wing and passed swiftly over all those poisonous and deadly things'.

The fifth *visio* focuses on Synagogue, an enormous female figure 'like the tower of a city' who has 'on her head a circlet like the dawn', and is described as the Mother of the Incarnation of the Son of God. 'In her heart stood Abraham, and in her breast Moses, and in her womb the rest of the prophets'. Being Synagogue, she also represents the errors of the Jews before the coming of Christ, and thus, though her upper half is light, is dark from the waist down. So she, too, is a figure of wholeness, representing specifically the way in which the Old foreshadows the New and is subsumed into the Christian process of salvation:

2   *Ibid.*, I, 4 and I, 5, pp. 109–29, 133–36.

The dawn recedes, and the sun's brightness remains. How is this? The Old Testament receded and the truth of the Gospel remains . . . Circumcision has not passed away, because it has been transformed into baptism . . . Hence the old precepts have not passed away but are transformed into better ones; and in the last times the Synagogue will transform itself faithfully into the Church.

V

But the egg is a good object for our further contemplation because, as well as providing the ideal symbol for the creation as it was revealed to Hildegard, it also serves as a kind of model for her own personal relationships. At the centre of the egg is of course the yolk, the source of life, and this stands for Hildegard's relationship to her Creator, the essential spiritual bond of her existence. The shell, the tough, protective exterior, is representative of her political/administrative side, which regularly and fearlessly challenged the male power structure, criticizing political and social corruption, protecting her own community and ensuring its ability to fulfill the divine command to grow and become independent. In this 'hard' external role Hildegard is clearly seen to be acting as God's lieutenant, as a wielder of the sword of justice, threatening dire consequences if the commander's orders are not followed.

What then of the egg's softer white? It can be seen as comparable to that aspect of herself that was bound up with the women of her convent, the arena in which her whole emotional life took place. This was her family: they were sisters, and she, as abbess, was their mother. The specifically maternal female images in Hildegard's visions thus take on a greater significance, since these are figures with whom she would have identified: the lost-and-then-found-again rescuing mother Zion; Synagogue cradling a whole testament's worth of prophets in her bosom. And the figure of Ecclesia, who appears in Part II of *Scivias*, provides an even more striking example, worthy of fuller consideration.[1]

As she first appears, Ecclesia is 'a woman as large as a great city', before an altar which she embraces. Her womb is described as being like a net, 'with a huge multitude of people running in and out'; she is splendidly arrayed, and 'on her breast shone a red glow like the dawn'. She has no feet or legs, 'but stands balanced on her womb . . . for she is always pregnant and procreating children'. Her motherly motto, which she

---

[1]   *Ibid.*, II, 3–6, pp. 169–85, 189–97, 201–34, 237–89.

Visio Five. Synagogue, as tall as a tower, is Mother of the Incarnation of the Son of God, and carries the prophets in her lap. She represents the foreshadowing of the New Testament by the Old. Wiesbaden 1,35; by permission of das Rheinische Bildarchiv.

waves on a banner above her head, says 'I must conceive and give birth!' And this is how she does it: black infants are drawn in through the holes in her womb, and breathed forth from her mouth. They are cleansed in the process (their black skins are removed, and replaced by white garments) and she remains pure throughout the birthing process: 'in this that mother suffers no hurt, for she will remain forever in the wholeness of virginity . . . That Bride will remain untouched, so that no schism can corrupt her'. (This fascination with the paradox of coexistent virginity and motherhood is echoed by Chaucer's Prioress and Second Nun in their invocations to the Virgin: 'O mooder Mayde! o mayde Mooder free!/ O bussh unbrent, brennynge in Moyses sighte . . .'; 'Thou Mayde and Mooder, doghter of thy Sone,/ . . . Baar of thy body – and dweltest mayden pure – / The Creatour of every creature'.)[2]

Although some of Ecclesia's children later turn heretic and attack her, she looks with kindness on them all, ready to forgive even the most wayward of 'these children of mine' if they want to return to her. Later, Ecclesia appears in an even larger manifestation, so tall that the top of her crown is cut off by the frame of the accompanying illustration (here recalling Boethius' Lady Philosophy whose head reaches into the clouds). She is bathed in bands of light – 'white as snow' from head to throat, red from throat to breasts, purple and blue from breasts to navel. In the red zone, at her breast, she enfolds a cluster of bright, bejewelled figures of purity, who surround a beautiful maiden with black hair, clad in a red tunic.

Finally she appears standing by the cross, in the attitude of the three Marys, with blood flowing over her, catching Christ's blood in a chalice as it pours from his side. Baptized by the blood, Ecclesia becomes the Eucharistic agent, bearing the sacramental blood to the altar, mediating between God and man in the nurturing act of communion.

Repeatedly the images of Ecclesia the Church are heavily maternal; she is the procreatrix, the nurturer, the protector, the tender enfolder. She gives birth to all the infants, is ready to forgive the disobedient ones, cradles the pure ones in her bosom – especially Mary, the beautiful dark-haired maiden, the flower who, when it blossoms, will bear, 'a most renowned posterity'.

For the sisters, her daughters, Hildegard produced some special compositions: a musical morality play, the *Ordo virtutum*, which could be performed by them within the convent,[3] and a cycle of hymns, the

---

2 *The Canterbury Tales (op. cit.)*, VII, 467–8, VIII, 36, 48–9.
3 The *Ordo virtutum* is the final revelation in *Scivias* (III, 13); unlike the others it is auditory as well as visual. A *psychomachia* in which the virutes contend (successfully, of course) with the devil for possession of the soul, Hildegard's play precedes by some two hundred years the main body of medeival drama (see 'Hildegard of Bingen's *Ordo*

Large as a city, Ecclesia stands balanced on her net-like womb, as she is always both pregnant and giving birth. Her children are breathed forth from her mouth, so that despite her many offspring, she always retains her virginity. From *Scivias* II,3. Wiesbaden 1,51; by permission of das Rheinische Bildarchiv.

Ecclesia, here so tall that her crown extends beyond the frame of the illumination, is bathed in bands of light – white, red, purple and blue. The bejewelled figures at her breast surround the beautiful Mary, clad in a red tunic. From *Scivias* II, 5. Wiesbaden 1, 66; by permission of das Rheinische Bildarchiv.

Symphony of the Harmony of Heavenly Revelations, which includes seventy-seven brilliantly innovative songs. The hymns, 'in melody and design, range and melismatic technique, . . . [go] beyond the limits of ordinary Gregorian chant', abandoning the 'strict metrical conventions of similar twelfth-century compositions for what we would call free verse'.[4] In these songs the theme of chaste fecundity reappears, for example in 'O viridissima virga', in which the Virgin's *viriditas*, or greenness, is celebrated. Mary is the 'most fertile branch', which 'brought forth blossoms'. Her fecundity spreads out from the central act of giving birth to the Saviour – the 'pulcher flos' – to include the whole phenomenon of seasonal rebirth: 'all the herbs . . . / which were dry / . . . spring forth in fullest green/ . . . the whole Earth rejoices'. On account of Mary the earth brings forth its harvest, the birds build their nests, and nourishment is provided for a grateful mankind. Her role here appears to merge with that of the goddess Natura, whom we later see as 'the vicaire of the almyghty Lord' in Chaucer's 'Parliament of Fowls'. The Chaucerian figure of Nature acts as the agent of Providence in restoring order to the raucous avian company, and oversees the pairing of the birds – 'To every foul Nature yaf his make/ By evene acord'. Necks intertwined, they then proceed to express their gratitude in a vernal hymn:

> 'Now welcome, somer, with thy sonne softe,
> That hast this wintres wedres overshake,
> And driven away the longe nyghtes blake'![5]

Both figures are the agents of regeneration, sponsors of fecundity, while themselves remaining chaste; and so is Hildegard's Ecclesia.

Perhaps even more common in the Middle Ages than the exalted and paradoxical goddess-of-chaste-fecundity figure was the image of the soul as bride, longing to be united with her Lord, the bridegroom. We have seen that Hildegard presents the Virgin Mary in this role as well – the flower who is both betrothed to, and will bear, the Saviour. Yet Hildegard does not herself adopt the nuptial image to describe the bond between her soul and God; it would hardly be compatible with her view of herself as faithful warrior.

---

virtutum: The Earliest Discovered Liturgical Morality Play', Bruce Hozeski, *American Benedictine Review* 26 (1975), 251–29).

4 Kraft, in Wilson (*op. cit.*), pp. 116–17. See Peter Dronke, *Poetic Individuality in the Middle Ages*, chapter V, for an assessment of Hildegard's songs and play; Barbara Newman has published a critical edition, *Symphonia armonie celesium revelationum* (Ithaca, N.Y., 1988). Twelve of the songs (trans. Jerry Dybdal and Matthew Fox) are included in the *Book of Divine Works* (*op. cit.*), pp. 366–93, and several recordings of Hildegard's compositions are now available.

5 'The Parliament of Fowls' (*op. cit.*), ll. 379, 667–8, 680–82.

In the attitude of the three Marys, Ecclesia
stands by the cross and catches Christ's
blood in a chalice. Then, as the Eucharistic
agent, she places the blood on the altar.
Above her are four signs – of the nativity,
the passion, the burial and the resurrection
of Christ. From *Scivias* II, 6. Wiesbaden 1, 86;
by permission of das Rheinische Bildarchiv.

Further, the nature of her bond with the other nuns operates to render the nuptial image inappropriate: Hildegard sees herself as the nurturing mother, not the ecstatic lover. So on those occasions that she does use sexual imagery to explain her relation to God, she emphasizes that it is procreative, rather than erotic, in nature. Ecclesia is the bride who, 'subjected to her bridegroom, . . . receives from Him a gift of fertility and a pact of love for procreating children'. This bond makes her not only mother, but also leader: she 'educates them as to their inheritance, . . . and sends those souls to Heaven'.[6] The analogy here is between semen and blood, conception and communion; Ecclesia's 'intercourse' takes place not as the consummation of individual erotic passion, but for the practical, altruistic purpose of procreation of children whom she will then tend and, again as her Creator's assistant, bring to salvation.

Similarly, in her hymn to the courageous virgin martyr, St Ursula[7] (linked with Ecclesia and thus Hildegard herself), Ursula is described as falling 'in love with the Son of God', rejecting earthly men. Her desire, she says, is to join him in a 'heavenly marriage feast', but what follows is hardly a consummation scene. Rather, all those who mocked her for her choice are possessed by the devil, who proceeds to destroy 'all that was noblest [in those bodies]'; in other words, the result is not love but war, specifically 'the apocalyptic war between Christ and Satan, in a symmetrical array' that matches angel against scoffer, 'the body of Christ against the devil's body'.[8]

Here we see that the ideal of virginity did not have to be construed as mere passive avoidance of lechery. Nor should we conclude that Hildegard's advocacy of the virgin state in any way suggests agreement with the misogynist position articulated by the likes of Jerome, whose view of virginity was coloured by his mistrust of women – he advocated chastity for men because women were so dangerous, and for women as the best way of keeping them out of trouble. The earliest Christian notion of celibacy, in fact, was an active, political ideal – not so much against sex as for freedom – and the martyrs were political rebels. Chastity was seen as a virtue equally valuable for men and women; as it was equated with prelapsarian innocence, it could indicate a kind of spiritual incorruptibility, and thus came to constitute a cornerstone of monasticism.[9]

These are views which we can easily imagine Hildegard sharing. In her

6 *Scivias* (Hart and Bishop), II, 6, 1 (p. 238).
7 St Ursula was famed for rejecting marriage in favour of chastity, and for being martyred, along with her many thousand virgin followers, by the Huns at Cologne. See Newman (*op. cit.*), p. 226 for a translation of this poem.
8 Newman (*op. cit.*), p. 227.
9 Cf. Elaine Pagels, *Adam, Eve and the Serpent* (New York, 1988); also Bugge (*op. cit.*), pp. 30 ff.

case we are particularly reminded of the apocalyptic context, in which spiritual armour is of distinct relevance: the end of the world was imminent, the struggle between good and evil a global as much as an individual one. Ursula's virginity represents not only her commitment to God, but also her fierce independence in the face of massive, corrupt social pressure – and it is this combination that ensures her power in the epic battle.

Hildegard does not, however, entirely reject the erotic image; rather, she saves it for her daughters. Her 'Symphony of Virgins', composed for her nuns, recognizes the power of erotic love – 'Hard it is to resist/ what tastes of the apple' – and offers, as a solution, the embrace of Christ as the best of all possible lovers: 'raise us up, O Savior Christ! . . . O fairest form, O sweetest fragrance/ of the delights we long for:/ Always we sigh for you with tears, in exile'.[10] And we are reminded of Hildegard's decision to allow her daughters, in imitation of the apocalyptic brides of the Lamb, to wear bejewelled tiaras and white dresses on their holy days. Their role as lovers of Christ she supported unequivocally, but this was not for her, the militant warrior-mother, the vassal faithful unto death.

[10] Newman (*op. cit.*), p. 224.

From Warrior to Lover

There has never been anyone, male or female, before or since, quite like Hildegard. Her passion, militancy, courage, devotion, and prodigious creativity are an inimitable combination. Still, her individual relation to her Creator can be seen as emerging from a particular cultural tradition; in its character it is generally feudal, but there is a more specific link with her ancient Germanic past. In his study of the Germanic peoples, *Germania*, written in AD 98, the Roman historian Tacitus recorded the phenomenon of the *comitatus*, a small band, whose function was chiefly military, characterized by an immensely powerful bond between lord and retainer. An examination of this model may provide us with a richer understanding of Hildegard's blend of characteristics.

The primary virtues of the *comitatus* were, on the part of the retainers, loyalty, self-sacrifice, utter obedience to the tribal chieftain. For his part, the lord owed protection and reward, often in the form of booty, to his retainers. As loyalty and trustworthiness are at a particular premium on the battlefield, so a foundation of unshakeable mutual trust was basic to this life-long bond. A desire for fame and glory was intense on both sides of the relationship, though it was never meant to interfere with the primary reciprocal obligations of lord and thane.[1]

Two important things happened to the *comitatus* tradition as it crossed over from history into literature: it travelled, and it was Christianized. The material of the Teutonic heroic age was preserved and passed on orally by the Germanic tribes; when they moved, it moved with them. So, along with the Angles, Saxons, and Jutes it arrived in Britain – the very word *thane*, for example, comes from Old Saxon *thegan* (=man) and Old High German *degan* (=warrior, hero) – and became fully assimilated into

---

[1] See *De Origine et Situ Germanorum*, ed. J.G.C. Anderson (Oxford, 1938). Cf. also Stanley B. Greenfield, *A Critical History of Old English Literature* (New York, 1965), pp. 80 ff and Rosemary Woolf, 'The Ideal of Men Dying with their Lord', in *Art and Doctrine: Essays on Medieval Literature*, ed. Heather O'Donoghue (London, 1986). Woolf points out that Tacitus' recording of the *comitatus* ideal may have been partly based on romantic longing, as he wanted to contrast the noble German savages with the decadent Romans; certainly by the time it appears in Old English poetry it is a 'poetic fiction and not a historical reality' (p. 181).

the indigenous literary tradition. The *comitatus* ideal, and the associated theme of loyalty *vs.* disloyalty, was celebrated in many subsequent medieval epics, such as *La Chanson de Roland* and *El Cid*. But it seems to have taken a particularly strong hold on the Anglo-Saxon imagination. The bleak desolation of the Wanderer, separated by death from his beloved 'gold-friend' and kinsmen; the despair of Beowulf's retainers as they wait, heart-sick, by the mere, dreading their leader's death; the courageous loyalty of Byrthnoth's followers who refuse to leave their dead lord's side though they face certain death at the hands of the Danes – these are a few of the best-known Old English literary treatments.

In both its Germanic homeland and in the Anglo-Saxon England to which it immigrated, the *comitatus* model was modified by the introduction and integration of Christian material as their respective populations were converted. The Old Saxon *Heliand*, for example, composed in the ninth century, was 'designed to make the Christian religion more easily acceptable to the [newly and reluctantly converted] Saxons'. It transplants the story of Christ's life from the New Testament to an epic Germanic setting: Christ is the ruler, 'the generous protector', and the disciples are his 'retinue', 'the loyalest men on earth'.[2] Thus contemporary iconographic representations of Christ show him as vigorous and vital, even when on the cross. However villainous, Herod, too, is a commander who is the 'ring-giver' to his followers. In what is perhaps the best example of this heroic amplification, the author of the *Heliand* expands a single verse (*John* XVIII, 10), where Peter draws his sword and cuts off Malchus' ear, to twelve resoundingly epic lines in which 'the courageous warrior in his anger went and stood staunchly in front of his King and Lord . . . his spirit did not waver . . .; he struck out at the enemy leader with the power of his hands . . . His ear was hewn off: . . . the blood spurted forth . . .'.

Perhaps the best Anglo-Saxon example of the synthesis of heroic and Christian theme, diction and imagery is the Old English poem, 'Dream of the Rood'.[3] Christ, 'the Lord of mankind', 'the young Hero', appears as a warrior who steps boldly up to the cross and eagerly participates in the crucifixion: 'firm and unflinching' Christ 'stripped Himself; . . . mounted on the high cross, brave in the sight of many, when he was minded to redeem mankind'. The cross (which narrates the middle portion of the poem) becomes the faithful retainer, who must, ironically, serve his lord

---

[2] See J. Knight Bostock, *A Handbook on Old High German Literature*, 2nd ed. rev. K.C. King and D.R. McLintock (Oxford, 1976), pp. 169 ff. The Teutonic/ heroic influence is evident throughout much of Old English poetry; *Genesis B*, for example, even seems to be a translation of a Saxon original; but the exchange became reciprocal, with the ninth-century *Heliand* showing signs of Northumbrian influence.

[3] The 'Dream of the Rood', found in the Vercelli Book, is translated in R.K. Gordon, *Anglo-Saxon Poetry* (Cambridge, 1954).

Like the 'Dream of the Rood', the Aaby Crucifix (c.1050–1100) shows Christ as a victorious hero even while on the cross. His head is upright, his body unbroken, his crown and garments those of a king. National Museum, Copenhagen.

by himself becoming the instrument of death: 'I trembled when the Hero clasped me; yet I durst not bow to the earth, . . . I must needs stand firm'; he is, however, able to share in his Lord's pain – 'They pierced me with dark nails; the wounds are still plain to view in me' – and as a participant in the crucifixion, he becomes the 'cross of victory', and helps to bring about the resurrection. With the retelling of the story of the crucifixion to the dreamer, the cross is fully consoled by becoming an agent of revelation: 'I bid thee, my loved man, declare this vision unto men; reveal in words that it is the glorious tree on which Almighty God suffered for the many sins of mankind . . .'. Significantly, the poem concludes with a reference to the harrowing of hell and the victorious return of the hero Christ, 'triumphant . . . mighty and successful', leading the souls he has released 'into God's kingdom'. And the dreamer's final vision of heaven, inspired by the cross's narrative, is as a heavenly feast where the faithful retainers are gathered together and reunited with their lord everlastingly.

In Hildegard's case, there is no evidence that she was specifically familiar with the Old Saxon *Heliand*; nonetheless she has evidently been influenced by this tradition, an amalgam of Teutonic and Christian material, which was so strong a part of her culture. From all we have been able to learn through her various writings, she consistently sees herself as a retainer who owes unwavering loyalty and obedience to her Lord, and who, in return, is assured of his trust and protection. Like Wiglaf, who remains with the dying Beowulf after all his other comrades have fled, Hildegard is the truest of the true, seeking no glory or reward for herself, finding fulfillment through faithful service and the glory of her Lord. Is it odd for her on the one hand to be so aware of her role as matriarch within her female community, and yet to be able to identify so eagerly with what seems to be a resolutely male model? Is there evidence that other women of her time might also have aspired to such a synthesis?

As a matter of fact, there are three extant Old English poems – *Juliana*, *Judith* and *Elene*[4] – which suggest that within the Germanic tradition such a combination was not anomalous. All three poems are religious epics that have female fighting saints as their central heroic characters; all three women are committed to an ideal of chastity, but far from being a passive virtue, it is a source of martial prowess, to be used in defeating the forces of evil.[5]

---

4 Cynewulf is the author of the ninth-century *Juliana* and *Elene* (found respectively in the Exeter and the Vercelli Books); the tenth-century *Judith* is found in the *Beowulf* manuscript.

5 See Jane Chance's comprehensive study, *Woman as Hero in Old English Literature* (Syracuse, New York, 1986), ch. 3. Chance argues that the three women represent three different grades of *castitas* – Juliana the virgin, Judith the chaste wife, and Elene the abstinent mother – and that the struggles of each are representative of the struggle between good and evil.

Juliana is a beautiful Christian maiden, living in Roman times, whose pagan father offers her in marriage to a powerful official, also pagan, named Eleusius.[6] She has made a personal vow of chastity, and most particularly she does not want to have anything to do with a pagan. She defiantly tells her suitor that before she can think of marrying him he must first convert to Christianity; otherwise, 'thou shalt never in thy fierce hatred prepare pain so sore . . . as to turn me from these words'. Juliana's father, who is enraged that she would presume to disobey him, turns her over to Eleusius; he is at first moved by her beauty, but when she refuses his offer he swiftly drops his suitor's stance, and orders that she be stretched naked on a rack and scourged, while he laughs at her torment. Still she continues to defy him: 'Accursed foul foe', she retorts, 'I fear not thy judgments, nor the harm of thy torments!'

Eleusius then has her hung by the hair from a tree for six hours, and cast into prison. It is here that Juliana encounters her real challenge.[7] The paltry efforts of her father and suitor have been easily dealt with, but in prison she is tempted by a devil (who later admits to being Belial), disguised as an angel, who counsels her to give in – in fact, he says, 'God . . . bade thee be commanded to avert those [further torments] from thee'. Juliana, with her keen individual sense of justice and truth, does not believe him, nor does she seem to be remotely tempted by the prospect of avoiding subsequent torture. She prays directly to God, who immediately reveals to her that her apparently angelic companion is a fraud, and asks that she seize him and extract a full confession.

Juliana literally wrestles the devil to the cell floor, where she holds him powerless throughout a lengthy dialogue. She wrings the truth from him in successive stages, during which he admits to having been responsible for much evil in general (specifically the deeds committed by such major wrong-doers as Cain and Judas Iscariot), and explains that the fiends are punished by their leader, 'the king of the hell-dwellers', if they fail in their assignments. We are reminded throughout the confession that Juliana physically holds the devil down by the power of her own hands, which he refers to as 'fetters'. Eventually he arrives at a grudging respect for his opponent, 'bold in combat beyond the whole race of women', admitting that he suffers affliction when he recounts his evil deeds and that she is guiltless and wholly wise; he even begs her 'by the grace of heaven's

---

6   *Juliana*, in Gordon (*op. cit.*), pp. 165–177.
7   Rosemary Woolf points out that as a result of Cynewulf's alterations to the source, the scene between Juliana and the devil has become 'the dramatic core of the work' (*Juliana*, ed. Rosemary Woolf, Methuen Old English Library , New York, 1966, p. 15). Further, as Jocelyn Price notes, Cynewulf has extended paganism beyond a specific historical time, so that it represents 'an area dominated by the devil within God's eternal framework'. ('The Liflade of Seinte Iuliene and Hagiographic Convention', *Medievalia et Humanistica* (New Series, 14), 1986, pp. 37–58.)

King' to have mercy on him. In other words he is as close to contrition as a fiend can possibly be. She is, he says, the most courageous spirit he has ever encountered, and the only one (including the patriarchs and prophets) entirely able to withstand his diabolical assaults: none 'durst lay hands upon me as boldly as thou in thy holiness now'; 'thou hast constrained me by painful blows . . . I have found no woman in the world early or late like unto thee'.

When Juliana is finally called back from prison to face her last ordeal, she is merciful enough to set the devil free, rather than dragging him along to face further humiliation. She welcomes her martyrdom joyfully, and sails through a number of final torments, including being stretched on a wheel set with swords and boiled in molten lead: 'Still the saint stood, with beauty unblemished; neither hem nor garment, neither hair nor skin, neither body nor limbs, was marked . . .'; finally she dies by decapitation – or rather, 'her soul . . . was borne away from the body to its lasting joy' – but not before great numbers of pagans, inspired by her courageous example and by her stirring words, have been converted to Christianity. In conclusion, Cynewulf, the poem's author, explicitly evokes the *comitatus* image: the evil Eleusius and his comrades are drowned at sea; the soldiers are 'thanes' who, now in 'that dark abode . . . that low den', cannot look to 'the chieftain for treasures to be bestowed', or hope 'that in the wine hall on the beer bench they should receive rings . . .'.

But for Juliana it is 'far otherwise'; her body is brought into the city by a ' mighty throng, . . . a great host', who are singing out in praise of their heroic leader. Here, as elsewhere in the poem, the comparison between Juliana and Christ becomes inescapable – when she is hung on the tree for six hours, Christ's crucifixion is recalled; when she resists the devil's temptation in prison, we are reminded of Christ's temptation; when she overcomes the devil, the harrowing of hell comes to mind; and here, her triumphant re-entry into the city reiterates Christ's entry into Jerusalem on Palm Sunday. In Juliana, the idea of a female figure who identified with, and stood for, a male deity, evidently presented no problem what-soever for either Anglo-Saxon poet or audience.

The story of Judith comes from the apocryphal Old Testament book named for its Hebrew heroine.[8] In this poem, more than in *Juliana*, Germanic heroic diction is conspicuously employed, initially to charac-terize the villain Holofernes and his men: he, their 'gold-friend', 'bade all the eldest thanes come; the shield-bearing warriors attended'; they were the 'daring shield-warriors, doomed to death'. Judith, a widow, is initially described in terms of nobility, wisdom, and radiance, but she turns out to

---

8 *Judith*, in Gordon (*op. cit.*), pp. 320–26.

be a very powerful and courageous warrior indeed. A particular instance of her bravery is her bold infiltration of the Assyrian camp with the goal of slaying their leader. As recounted in the Apocrypha, she has taken off her widow's sackcloth and adorned herself so as to be at her most alluring; 'she anointed herself with the finest myrrh, parted and tied her hair . . . took bracelet and anklet, ear-ring and finger-ring' (*Judith* X, 2 ff.); posing as a traitor, she presents herself at her enemies' camp. She claims to seek asylum with them because her people, the Hebrews, are destined to defeat; further, she promises to provide Holofernes with information that will ensure his victory, and counts on his wanting to be left alone with her because of her great beauty. Significantly, however interested she may be in her own chastity, she is prepared to risk it for the possibility of helping her beleaguered people.

The start of the Old English poem has unfortunately been lost, so the action begins in mid-scene, with the depraved Holofernes, 'the fiendish wanton', organizing an orgy for himself and his followers. Their feast, in which Holofernes 'drenched his officers all day in wine, till they lay swooning', is a grotesque perversion of the *comitatus* ideal – such as that evoked at the conclusion of the 'Dream of the Rood' – of a devoted band gathered peacefully round their dear lord in the mead hall: as a chieftain who ought to be responsible for the protection of his retainers, Holofernes' behaviour is particularly reprehensible, and is directly linked to their eventual destruction. At the conclusion of the feast the lecherous chieftain, captivated by her charms, does indeed have Judith brought to his tent; but thanks to his besotted condition there is a significant discrepancy (as Macbeth's porter might say) between his desire and his performance, and he falls into a drunken stupor. Thus Judith evades his sexual advances – but escape is not what she has in mind. She wants vengeance, and she prays eloquently – sword in hand – for victory: 'give me, O Lord of heaven, victory and true faith, that with this sword I may cut down this dealer of sudden death'. Filled with courage, she 'struck the hostile foe with gleaming sword'. Although two blows are needed to complete the decapitation, Judith shows no sign of revulsion: the 'woman of valour', who has 'won illustrious fame in fight', stows the bloody head in a bag and hastens back through the Assyrian ranks to her own city, where she presents her people with her gory trophy, and uses it to spur them on to a victorious assault on their enemies.

She is their inspiration, their leader, the positive counterpart to the degenerate figure of Holofernes, the failed lord. 'Then the band of bold men', Judith's army, is 'quickly made ready', and the unsuspecting, hungover Assyrians are attacked. The victory is glorious, resulting in huge quantities of booty; for a month the 'warlike earls' continue to bring back to their leader the spoils of war – helmets, swords, corslets, 'treasures more splendid than any man among the sages can tell', and perhaps most gratifying to Judith, Holofernes' sword and helmet. She thanks God for the victory, but the poet gives the immediate credit to Judith: 'The warriors won all that by courage, bold in battle under the banners by the wise counsel of Judith, the valorous virgin'. Interestingly, this final battle does not occur in the earlier version of the story, in which the victory of Judith and her people is secured simply by the flight of the Assyrians. Evidently, the Anglo-Saxon poet has tinkered with his biblical source in order to emphasize the martial aspect of the conflict, and particularly of Judith's role. She has not just outwitted the Assyrians; she has inspired and led her followers into a long, bloody and glorious battle, in which the foe is decimated.

For a model of chastity, Judith is distinctly on the assertive side, and it is probably no coincidence that she has been chosen to play this particular role at this time and place. In the *Acta Sanctorum* there are long lists of maidens who were martyred rather than sacrifice their chastity: yet *Judith*'s poet chose to go back to the Old Testament, and find a heroine who was not a saint, was not even a Christian, was not technically a virgin, and was certainly not martyred; Holofernes never so much as lays a hand on her, and throughout the narrative Judith is firmly in control, physically and intellectually, as well as spiritually. Evidently the poet wanted – and must have assumed the audience did – an active heroine who could be seen as a retainer of the Lord, and who could in turn lead her own *comitatus* to victorious salvation; to find such a figure was important enough to justify the rejection of an enormous body of conventional, officially sanctioned material about female martyrs.

Looking back to Juliana, we recall that Cynewulf, too, selected a heroine who, though martyred, had the physical power to wrestle a demon into submission with her bare hands, and extract from him a full confession. But if we look at Cynewulf's other religious heroine, Elene, we find an even clearer instance of the Anglo-Saxon predilection for mighty women.[9] The poem's initial focus is not on Elene, but her son, the emperor Constantine, who is at war with the barbarians, and facing near-certain defeat. As the result of a vision, Constantine has an image of the cross made, which he carries into battle; in the midst of the fray, as the

---

[9] *Elene*, in Gordon (*op. cit.*), pp. 211–34. The fact that neither Judith nor Elene are actually virgins may relate to a generally more flexible attitude towards female chastity amonst the Anglo Saxons than that stipulated by the Church Fathers. In his late seventh-century 'De Virginitate', which was dedicated to the abbess Hildelith of Barking, Aldhelm diverges from Sts Paul, Jerome and Ambrose, in identifying three grades of virginity, the second grade, *castitas*, being allotted to those who 'having been assigned to marital contracts', have 'scorned the commerce of matrimony for the sake of the heavenly kingdom'; the monastery at Barking itself included a number of members who had dissolved their marriages in order to assume a religious life (see *Aldhelm: The Prose Works*, ed. Michael Lapidge and Michael Herren (Ipswich, 1979), pp. 73 ff.).

enemy are scattered, he bids the image of the cross be raised. 'It was plain that the King almighty . . . had granted to Constantine . . . triumph under the heavens, by his rood-tree'. The victory is seen to be directly responsible for his conversion to Christianity, and convinces him of the importance of finding the true cross in the Holy Land. To this point Constantine's roles as warrior and Christian hero are comfortably conflated: he is 'the ring-giver, war-chief of armies', 'the protector of armies . . . exulting in booty, . . . with his band of followers'; similarly the battle is described in conventional heroic terms: 'fierce foemen . . . sent forth flights of arrows, spears above the yellow shields, adders of war . . . Steadfast in mind they marched on'. Overlooking the scene are the traditional raven, eagle and wolf, ready to move in on the dead and claim their own gruesome form of booty when the battle is over.

But since Constantine has other commitments he must find a delegate to search for the cross, and the person he chooses is his mother. Here an interesting transference takes place, for as she assumes the mantle of power she also takes on all of her son's martial prowess, and though a middle-aged matron (Constantine would have been 38 at the time of the poem's action) she turns out to be remarkably successful in her quest. Her army is now the 'band of earls', their ships are 'sea horses, . . . wave horses' loaded with armour and weapons; as they sail the waves crash over the sides of the ships, 'the sea resounded . . . Blithe were the warriors . . .; the queen rejoiced in the journey'. Once in Jerusalem, the 'emperor's kinswoman [sat] in majesty on her throne, the stately warlike queen decked with gold'. The details of Elene's quest are too complex to recount; but, through her courage and iron-willed determination, she succeeds in finding not only the true cross but also the nails used in the crucifixion: 'Tears fell on the nails of twisted wire. The queen's desire was gloriously fulfilled . . . She thanked . . . the Lord of victories'. As well as being a successful military commander, Elene also shows herself to be a remarkable administrator: she converts large numbers of Jews, personally undertaking their instruction; she builds a church for the cross, which she orders to be overlaid with gold and gems; and she establishes a bishopric in Jerusalem, which soon becomes famous far and wide.

All of these three women then, though chaste, are not valued chiefly for their chastity; rather, their chastity is valuable because it gives them added strength, and represents the power of their will.[10] They are strong,

---

[10] The Anglo-Saxon tradition included a view of spiritual life-as-warfare which saw the condition of chastity as conferring power on women rather than assuring their submission. Bugge (*op. cit.*), p. 41, discusses the Christian idea of the *militia Christi*, which considered angels to be sexless and their invincibility linked to this sexlessness; in the case of earthly virgins, 'abstention would safeguard [the soul's] deiform integrity', and thus be a crucial aid in the struggle against evil.

responsible, worthy: able to serve their Lord with fierce, unquestioning loyalty, and also able to lead their own followers to salvation, whether military or spiritual. Juliana is linked most directly with Christ himself; Judith is the lieutenant, Elene the emperor's proxy. Each is a different variation on the theme, but in all cases there is no hesitation, on the part of poet, or, presumably, audience, about assigning strong women to traditional male power roles. The Germanic tradition is anomalous in this respect; both Church Fathers and later medieval churchmen, sharing a deep mistrust of women as an entire species, preferred to consign them to more passive and less powerful positions.[11] Happily, Hildegard was born into this tradition, and was able to glory in it. She would surely have revelled in any of these activities – wrestling with Belial, decapitating Holofernes, sailing to Jerusalem at the head of an army.

This was the end of an era, however. The vigorous, active model of female valour was soon to be overshadowed by the emergence of a new force that first made its appearance in twelfth-century Provence; from there, courtly love – *l'amour courtois* – was to spread rapidly throughout Europe in the course of the next hundred years. This was a 'system' of love, with Arabic and Ovidian roots, that was based on an inversion of the feudal model, with the aloof lady in the position of lord, holding all the power, and the lover-as-vassal perpetually at her feet, seeking favour. This love could be of varying degrees of spirituality, depending on who was doing the loving. Some 'vassals' were clearly hopeful of physical reward, sooner rather than later; others, most notably Dante and the poets of the *dolce stil nouvo*, saw their ladies as divine intermediaries, angelic messengers who would help them transcend their manly desires – and as a means to salvation, they accepted their daily suffering joyfully. As the courtly love system adapted and exploited the feudal model, so it did with Christianity; frequently we see the lady as the actual object of worship, even her accessories being treated as relics (Chrétien de Troyes' Lancelot reverently carries around with him a comb of Guinevere's that contains strands of her hair), the idolatrous lover's duty to his mistress overriding that to either lord or Lord.

Whether or not the extramarital shenanigans advocated by the courtly love system were ever much of a social reality is a matter of ongoing debate, but that it was a powerfully influential literary convention is unquestionable: some of the most moving love stories of Western culture, from *Romeo and Juliet* to *Wuthering Heights*, descend directly from this

---

[11] Nikki Stiller observes that the 'tribal egalitarianism of the Anglo Saxons seems to have allowed for much more scope and strength in the female character', a phenomenon that led to the emergence of the great abbesses in pre-Conquest England (*Eve's Orphans: Mothers and Daughters in Medieval English Literature*, Westport, Conn. and London, 1980, p. 21).

tradition. Within its own time, it fed and was fed by the growing Cult of the Virgin, with which it coincided chronologically, and this reciprocal influence perhaps helps to explain the peculiar phenomenon of something like a religion of women in the midst of what was generally a profoundly misogynistic era. Mariolatry helped to strengthen the idealization of women basic to the courtly system, and the imagery used to describe the revered mistress was turned around and applied to Mary, the bright lady, queen of heaven.

On the negative side, however, the courtly system finally tended to reinforce what might be called a dualistic view of women: if they were not all good, they were all bad, either on the pedestal or in the gutter.[12] The sensuality implicit in the literary convention gave renewed currency to the notion of the fundamentally corruptible nature of Eve's daughters – some very nasty poems indeed were written about ladies who refused to accept their lover's advances or, worse, chose someone else instead. And the system thus emphasized the polarization between men and women as well; in the wake of courtly love it is difficult to imagine a young woman taking pride in her martial prowess as the Lord's retainer, or being able to identify with a powerful leader.[13]

What might be called the 'orthodox' version of the courtly love system – witty, worldly and very polished; adulterous, secretive and distinctly erotic – was nurtured in the courts of several powerful French rulers – Eleanor of Aquitaine and her daughters Marie de Champagne and Alix de Blois. When Eleanor came to England as the wife of Henry II in 1152, she brought her retinue along, and with them came the whole body of courtly conventions.[14] Sexy, naughty, deliciously decadent, *l'amours courtois* as introduced by the Anglo-Norman aristocrats must have proved intriguing and sometimes irresistible to the austere Anglo Saxons. In the case of those who were supposedly committed to the renunciation of religious life, it would have been a particularly difficult temptation to deal with: Chaucer's Prioress, Madame Eglentyne,[15] is actually characterized in terms of her courtly affectations. Her aspirations to French, her elegant manners and emulation of the courtly style, her pleasure in her

---

12 For an interesting presentation of both the pro- and anti-female views see *Three Medieval Views of Women (op. cit.)*, which includes editions of three Old French *dits* describing alternately how vicious and how virtuous women are.

13 Joan of Arc is an obvious exception, but perhaps the virulence of the establishment's response proves the point.

14 In London Eleanor's influence was considerable. As J.J. Parry points out, 'Thomas of Britain wrote his *Tristram and Ysolt* under her inspiration, . . . Wace dedicated to her his *Brut,* and it is generally believed that she is the noble lady to whom Benoît Sainte-More dedicated his romance of Troy' (see the Introduction to *The Art of Courtly Love, op. cit.,* p. 13).

15 *The Canterbury Tales (op. cit.),* I, 118–162.

own prettiness, her brooch bearing the ambiguous motto, 'Amor vincit omnia', are all utterly inappropriate for a woman of her position – but also apparently common enough to raise no eyebrows amongst the other pilgrims. Indeed she seems quite to excite the ardent admiration of the General Prologue's narrator.

Throughout Europe the new eroticism seems to have played a part in modifying both male attitudes towards religious women, and these women's own view of themselves. In England, a fascinating body of texts composed towards the end of the twelfth century provides us with a close look at the transition, both linguistic and cultural, that was under way in the broad wake of the Conquest. These compositions include a guide for nuns called the *Ancrene Riwle*, or *Nun's Rule*, and a cluster known as the Katherine Group. They are written in a similar literary West Midlands dialect, indicating that there was something of a cultural centre at the time in or around Hertfordshire; and that Old English had been suffi-ciently modified by the influence of Anglo Norman in the century after the Conquest to produce a new language – Middle English – of which these texts are commonly considered to be the first literary examples.[16]

Among the texts of the Katherine Group are found the stories of three female saints – Katherine (for whom the Group is named), Margaret, and, again, Juliana; a treatise warning women against the woes of marriage, *Holy Maidenhood*; and an emotional address to the crucified Christ, *The Wooing of Our Lord*.[17] These works, and the *Nun's Rule*, share with the Anglo-Saxon saints' lives a reverence for the condition of chastity, but they have a markedly different slant. The emphasis is more strictly on the state of literal virginity, with the explicit agenda that the religious women to whom the works are addressed should save themselves for the better lover: that is, Christ. The emphasis on martial prowess fades for both partners in this relationship; the women are presented rather as courtly ladies, passively accepting the ardent advances of their aristocratic suitor, and his worth as a warrior is in specific relation to his ability to protect his vulnerable mistress. The 'ladies' in the *Nun's Rule*, for example, are fragile creatures, susceptible both to their emotions and their senses, barely

---

[16] See R.W. Chambers, 'On the Continuity of English Prose from Alfred to More and his School' (Oxford, 1933); also J.R.R. Tolkien's 'Ancrene Wisse and Hali Meiðhad', *E&S* 14 (1929), 104–26, and S.T.R.O d'Ardenne's introduction to *The Liflade ant te Passiun of Seinte Iuliene* for a fuller discussion of the Katherine Group/ *Ancrene Riwle* dialect.

[17] The texts of the Katherine Group have been published by the Early English Text Society; see *EETS* 18, 29, 34, 80, 193, 223, 225, 229, 241, 248, 284, 402. See also *Ancrene Riwle*, trans. M.B. Salu (*op. cit.*), and *Medieval English Prose for Women: The Katherine Group and Ancrene Wisse*, ed. Bella Millett and Jocelyn Wogan-Browne (London, 1990). Various of the introductions discuss the sources for these saints' lives; Price (*op. cit.*) offers a thorough analysis of the *Liflade of Seinte Iuliene*.

trustworthy, certainly not the sort you would choose to send off to Jerusalem in search of the true cross.

Side by side with the exploitation of this courtly metaphor comes its misogynist corollary: while the *Rule*'s nuns are urged to favour Christ-as-wooer, they are reminded that their bodies are foul, mere bags of excrement, their lovely hands fit only to dig the dirt of the graves in which they will rot. This view of the flesh as repulsive can be traced, as we might expect, to the Church Fathers, believing as they did that sexuality itself, even within marriage, was hopelessly tainted by concupisence; virginity was a way of imitating the angels while we were yet obliged to endure life on this wretchedly carnal earth.[18] The psychological process ensuing from this radical mistrust of the body seems to have been one in which the female object of desire – when that very desire was seen as loathsome – came to be blamed for the desire itself; and thus herself to be considered as essentially corrupt. It is not surprising that the state of utter continence would assume far greater importance when the fear of sex was so intense.

A movement away from the 'heroic' view of women seems actually to be taking place *within* the Katherine Group itself. The stories of Juliana and Margaret still present the heroines as physically powerful and courageous; both challenge the conventional male power structure in rejecting undesirable marriages, both engage in literal combat with a demon and are victorious; however, the heroic diction and imagery found in the Old English saints' lives have here become less pronounced.

Juliana's effect on Eleusius is more explicitly erotic in the Katherine Group's version, and the torments he inflicts seem the more pathological as they are imposed on a 'desired' body. Yet though he uses ardent language in his addresses, his view of her is only faintly courtly; he sees her as an object that ought correctly to be subject to his will. In rejecting Eleusius, Juliana tells her father that she is 'wedded to another . . . He is Ihesu, son of God . . . I love him and believe in him as my Lord'. But while she does employ the nuptial image to describe her relationship to her 'husband', her virginity seems finally to be defined as a spiritual condition which provides strength in the struggle against evil; it is not primarily related to her role as 'betrothed'. Eleusius has her stretched, stripped and beaten until she is bloody, but her prayer is hardly that of a helpless maiden in distress. Rather, she asks God to help her as he helped Abraham and Daniel, and is forthwith instructed to 'seize the false angel and bind him fast'; using her own chains (which she apparently is strong enough to burst), she binds the devil's hands so tightly that 'each nail ached and grew black with blood'. She then throws him down and beats him with the remaining chains.

---

[18] See Bugge (*op. cit.*); also Bella Millett in her introduction to *Hali Meiðhad* (EETS 284, London, 1982).

To this point her struggle with the fiend parallels that of the Old English Juliana. However, when she is again taken before Eleusius, she drags the devil with her, rather than letting him go as does her Anglo-Saxon counterpart. He is mocked by the crowds, who throw stones and bones at him; and finally he is cast by Juliana into a pit of filth. She shows none of the compassion here that she does in Cynewulf's version. Though her martial prowess is similar, the identification between her and Christ is diminished; yet a blessed woman, Sophia, later wraps Juliana's body in precious clothes, in an action that seems to recall the Marys tending Christ's body after the crucifixion.[19]

St Margaret's story shows an increased use of the erotic, courtly metaphor to describe the relationship between Christ and the virgin martyr. We are told that she has chosen Christ as her 'love and her lover'; beyond this, she asks that Christ protect her maidenhead – which she describes as a 'dear gemstone' she has entrusted to him – and that he not allow the impure to defile it. The introduction of what might be called a rape image – with the 'impure' cast in the role of rapists – brings the sexual nature of her bond with Christ sharply into focus. And by the use of this image Margaret also casts herself in the role of victim, an identification that is subsequently intensified by her reference to herself as a 'lamb among wolves' and a 'bird caught in a snare', both the lamb and the bird being powerless, at the mercy of their hunters, in need of rescue.

When Margaret is brought before Olibrius – Eleusius' counterpart – he too uses amorous language, and she defies him because, as she says, she already has a lover, one 'who I will give up for no one', from whom she will not be separated even by death: he is better than any earthly love; 'all bow down to him because he is so mighty . . . he is the loveliest to look upon and the sweetest to smell'. As she elaborates this material, her identity as betrothed becomes more pronounced. And significantly, when she describes the way in which she identifies with her Lord, it is not through fighting but through suffering: 'as our Lord died for us I am not afraid to die for him'. What all this adds up to is that her view of herself, and the way in which she would have been viewed by her audience, is markedly more 'feminine' than in Juliana's case.

In prison (where, like Juliana, she is thrown for rejecting her suitor's unwelcome advances) Margaret is first swallowed by the fiend who has taken the form of a dragon. The method of her escape once more results in a modification of the martial image; although she does free herself, she does so not through personal strength, but because the cross with which she is armed causes his body to burst open. The dragon is soon followed by a 'black fiend', whom she successfully wrestles into submission, but

---

[19] References in the discussion of Juliana's life are drawn from the *EETS* 248 edition (translations are mine).

only after he has been enfeebled by her prayers. Certainly a degree of physical power is indicated thereafter, when Margaret lifts the fiend up by the hair, casts him to the earth, and holds him there by placing her foot on his neck; and again, when he asks her to loosen her foot a little so that he can more easily deliver the confession which she is forcibly extracting from him. Having confessed, and hoping for some Christ-like mercy, he begs her not to cast him back into hell. But, like the Katherine Group's Juliana, Margaret is obdurate; the earth opens and, roaring, he falls backwards into the pit.

In the course of Margaret's story the echoes of Anglo-Saxon heroism seem to grow fainter as they yield to the erotic courtly influence, an impression that is strengthened by the concluding passage in which, after her decapitation, and as she is borne aloft by angels, Margaret receives this ardent message from her Lord:[20]

> 'Come now to your bridegroom, bride, for I await you. Come dear one, to your life, for I longingly await your arrival, the brightest bower awaits you. Dear one, hurry to me; come now to my kingdom.'

Seinte Katerine shows even more entrenched signs of the new influence, perhaps because it may have been composed as much as twenty years after the lives of Juliana and Margaret.[21] The author has chosen as his subject a martyr traditionally noted for intellectual rather than physical skills – in particular contrast to the Old English poets' choice of figures such as Judith and Elene, to whom martial prowess could be convincingly attributed. Katherine, an orphan, eighteen, living in Alexandria, is distinguished by the passive trait of *not* having learned 'foolish songs' – that is love songs or tales of love – but has rather kept her eyes and her heart on holy scripture: an excellent student, she has long been able to outwit her masters. Hearing a disturbing noise coming from the temple of the heathens as they praise their gods, she enters and challenges the 'keiser' Maxentius on his faith. An effort at mutual conversion ensues, during which Katherine predictably trounces all of Maxentius' scholars, having been promised by God that he will always provide both 'tongue and tale' with which 'to cast down your enemies': words will be her

---

20 References in the discussion of Margaret's life are from the *EETS* 193 edition (translations are mine).
21 See *Seinte Katerine*, ed. S.R.T.O. d'Ardenne and E.J. Dobson, *EETS SS* 7 (Oxford, 1981), Introduction, which places the composition of the 'Liflades' of Juliana and Margaret in the last decade of the twelfth century, and that of Katherine between 1200 and 1210. Quotations in the discussion of Katherine's life are taken from this edition (the translations are mine).

weapons. The emperor then tries bribery, which, as we would expect, Katherine disdains; and she replies in the following manner:[22]

'Whatever you do will not succeed in turning me away from the love of my lover ... I have wedded him to my maidenhood with the ring of true belief and I have truly taken him to me. We are so fastened and bound together, the knot that binds us two is so knotted, that neither mere strength nor living man may loose it ...'

'He is my love, he it is that gladdens me – my true bliss above me, my joy ... I want nothing else, my sweet life, so sweetly he tastes and smells to me that everything he sends to me seems pleasant and soft.'

Here Christ is fully the lover; Katherine, no longer the warrior, can be wholly the bride. Their relationship is a personal, private one in which her desire is completely fulfilled; she herself articulates much more fully than her Katherine Group comrades the extent to which she has surrendered to the erotic role. While her virginity may still provide her with spiritual strength, the focus has clearly shifted; as bride, her role is amorous rather than martial, and she will be faithful because she has bound herself to, is wedded to another. And her heroism is appropriately decorous: she converts many, but wrestles with no one. The notion of virginity has here been so thoroughly 'feminized' as to allow for the passivity considered appropriate to the compliant bride within a conventional heterosexual relationship.[23]

Holy Maidenhood continues in a similar vein, with the argument that virginity is the best state because Christ is the best husband. 'The king of all kings desires you as his lover'; 'Blessed is his spouse whose maidenhead is unspotted when he makes love to her' (literally, *on hire streoneth*, from the OE (*ge*)*streonon* = to beget), 'and when she gives birth to his children, she will have no hardship or pain'. In contrast to human experience, these children can never die, 'and shall always play before her in heaven'. Along the way this text also makes some energetic and very colourful arguments as to why human marriage ought best be eschewed. Husbands and wives are forever at odds, the housewife's life alternating between crisis and drudgery (burning food, screaming babies, spilt milk); sexually, men are brutes, and intercourse is ugly, painful and hopelessly corrupted by concupiscence: it is

[22] Bugge points to the Katherine Group's 'warm-blooded fascination . . . for sensuous aspects of Christ's person'; of the story of St Katherine he remarks that the experience she has of Christ is described as a 'hazy, dreamlike softness which gladdens her and casts a delicious sweetness over all that befalls her' (*op. cit.*), p. 99.

[23] Cf. Bugge (*op. cit.*), p. 106.

that coarse burning of the flesh, the burning itch of bodily lust that comes before the disgusting act, that beastly intercourse, that shameless union which is full of filth, that stinking and wanton deed.

The hidden persuader here – the device by which the 'holy maidens' are convinced to save themselves for Christ – is not only how attractive he is, but how ghastly the alternative (they are incidentally advised that to engage in human coition is to sell one's maidenhead too cheaply, though the sexual act is the price one must pay to keep a male provider). The virgin state here recommends itself not because it represents inner virtue or yields spiritual rigour, but because it offers relief from the active evil of human misery.[24]

Yet while *Holy Maidenhood* endorses the idea that the virgin life is as close as we can get to the angels on this earth (and the implied corollary that intercourse is little better than fornication), it also exploits the sexuality of the nuptial image. Christ is seen in graphically physical, male terms; he is ardent, generous, and far more attractive than any earthly counterpart could be: marriage with him is simply quantitatively much the better deal.

Chastity is of central importance in the life of any monastic, but it is treated in a peculiar way by the male authors of these texts, written for the training of young religious women. The reason becomes increasingly clear in the course of the *Nun's Rule*. Although there is ample evidence that the *Rule*'s author was fond of the women for whom he was writing – affectionately addressing them as 'my dear sisters', urging them to exercise moderation in their penitential acts, such as fasts and vigils[25] – it is also clear that he fully accepts the concept of woman as morally defective, as without sufficient reason to look after herself, as responsible for the first Fall and that of many a man since. He explains that, if a man should succumb to lust as a result of their beauty, they are 'guilty . . . and must answer for his soul on the Day of Judgement'; it is their duty to keep themselves hidden. In fact, since he is aware of their special weakness as women, he has all the greater obligation to watch out for their safety. As susceptible females, he is aware of the particular dangers presented to them by the heady influence of courtly love; but rather than avoiding it, he exploits it – and the nuns' sexuality – towards the eventual end of winning them for Christ. The *Rule* is divided into eight sections, which culminate in Parts VI and VII, 'On Penance' and 'On Love', but through-

---

24 Cf. Millett's introduction to *Hali Meiðhad* (*op. cit.*), pp. xxxii ff.

25 Other extremes of the penitential tradition, from which the author of the *Rule* sought to protect his charges, include such well-known phenomena as the wearing of hair shirts and flagellation, as well more obscure practices such as 'sleeping in water, on nettles, on nutshells, with a corpse in a grave, or in a cold church'. See *Medieval Handbooks of Penance* (ed. John T. McNeill and Helena M. Gamer, New York, 1938).

out, the author bases his approach on a skillful alternation between desire and guilt, fear and love.

He opens by invoking the erotic image of the union of soul and God: after the 'kiss of peace in the Mass . . . with burning love embrace your Beloved who has come down from heaven to your heart's bower, and hold Him fast until He has granted you all that you ask'; 'I am not a bold lover', says Christ, 'I will embrace my love only in a retired place'; 'thou shouldst in the bower of thy heart ask me for kisses like my beloved who says to me, . . . Let my lover kiss me with the kiss of his mouth, sweetest of mouths'; 'This kiss, dear sisters, is a sweetness and a delight of heart . . . immeasurably sweet'.[26] On the other hand, recalling the dualism of the Church Fathers, the *Rule's* author insistently reminds the sisters of their foul corruption, linked of course to their repulsive flesh: 'any . . . kind of touch between a man and an anchoress is . . . so loathsome . . . I would rather see . . . you, my dear sisters, to me the dearest of women, hanging on a gibbet'; 'The soul on earth is set . . . in prison, shut in a torture-chamber' (how far a cry from Hildegard!), the flesh 'like a worm . . . gnaws and destroys itself, . . . becomes putrid'; 'what fruit does your flesh bear at all its apertures? In the middle of your face . . . have you not as it were two privy holes? Have you not come from foul slime? Are you not a vessel of filth? Are you not destined to be food for worms?'

The *Rule's* portrayal of the contest between Judith and Holofernes, in contrast with the Old English poem, is merely figurative, representing the struggle between body and spirit: an anchoress 'must slay, as Judith did, the evil Holofernes, and tame her flesh well'. The nun's guilt at her own baseness is exacerbated by pathetic references to Christ's suffering on the cross – endured for her sake – at the same time as the evocation of his beautiful, naked, wounded body functions as another sort of erotic stimulus. She is reminded of her connection with Eve, 'our first mother', whose great sin 'has since spread over the whole world': but she is offered escape from this terrible cumulative burden of self-hatred through obedience, and through the choice of Christ as lover.

In the sixth section, 'On Penance', the young women are shown the link between the suffering of penance and the process by which they may be numbered amongst God's elect; 'all [your] joy lies in being crucified in pain and dishonour with Jesus on His cross'. The causes for penance on their part have been fully detailed. They are shown the necessity of suffering because of their unworthiness, reminded of the persistent susceptibility of the 'undisciplined' flesh: 'Who ever was chaste in the midst of pleasures and ease and bodily comfort? Whoever fed a fire within her and did not burn?' They are reminded of St Agatha, whose tortures

---

[26] All quotes from the *Ancrene Riwle* are from Salu (*op. cit.*).

included the amputation of her breasts, and who refused the healing salve offered by a divine messenger: 'I have never used any medicine of the flesh for my body'. The physical difficulty of their lives is only for their own good: 'young trees are encircled about with thorns for fear animals will feed on them when they are tender . . . [Your] hardships are thorns, and it is necessary for you to be encircled with them'.

The seventh section of the *Rule*, 'On Love', begins with an elaborate parable that makes clear to the sisters the degree of their obligation to their heavenly suitor.[27] A lady, defenceless, destitute, once was completely surrounded by her enemies; a powerful king sent sustenance, gifts, his whole army; but she was unmoved. He went himself, showed her the 'beauty of his face', spoke words of tenderness and delight; but still she disdained him. At last, he offered her his life in the battle against her foes, so that, at least, she would love him in death. He was 'himself outrageously tortured and finally slain . . . Would not this lady be of an evil nature had she not loved him thereafter beyond everything else?'

The stimulus of obligation is then sweetened and enhanced by its honeyed corollary. This king is, after all, immeasurably more desirable than any earthly lover. 'Am I not fairer than any other', he says, pleading for her love; 'Am I not the richest of Kings? Am I not of the noblest kindred? Am I not the wisest . . . the most gracious . . . the most generous . . . gentle and more tender than any other?' To beauty and ardour are added the rather more wordly incentives of class and wealth. Finally, extravagant rewards of rank and power are promised her: 'I will . . . make you the queen of the kingdom of heaven. You yourself shall be seven times brighter than the sun . . . all that you want shall be done in heaven, and on earth, too'; and – in case this does not suffice – 'yes,' he adds, 'even in hell'. The author seems intentionally to fan the nuns' desire: 'stretch out your love to Jesus Christ', he urges them, 'You have won him! Touch him with as much love as you sometimes feel for a man. He is yours to do with all that you will'. However, if they are so foolish as to reject these offers, they are abruptly reminded that they will be plunged, body and soul, into the fires of hell, 'to be whores to the devil in shame and sorrow, world without end!' And so ends the manipulation of the 'dear sisters'. An enormous emotional armory – the longing for love and security, sexual passion, social ambition, greed, desire for power, self-hatred, fear, guilt – has been deployed to win these young women for

27 Rosemary Woolf points out that the allegory of Christ as the lover-knight became common with the passage of the military ideal equating redemption with defeat of the devil: 'From the 12th century onwards there developed a perfect parallelism between the theological stress upon Christ's display of love on the Cross and the conception of chivalric conduct in the Arthurian romances, wherein a knight by brave endurance and heroic encounters would save a lady whom he loved' ('The Theme of Christ the Lover-Knight', in *Art and Doctrine* (*op. cit.*), p. 99 ff).

Christ, and this very earthly approach is directly attributable to the author's view of their venal susceptibility, their spiritual and intellectual insufficiency. It is difficult to imagine that his manipulative approach can have done other than reinforce his charges' belief in their baseness and inadequacy, leaving them less able than ever to manage their own spiritual affairs.

At the end of the Katherine Group's progression comes the *Wooing of Our Lord*, a passionate prose treatise written in the first person as a direct address to Christ. As with the other pieces in this group, the author is unknown, but in this case it seems likely that she may have been a woman. The *Wooing* takes up where the *Rule* left off, with an elaboration of its closing argument: Christ should be loved because he possesses all of the qualities most desirable in a lover. He is the most beautiful, the richest, the most generous, the wisest and most courageous, the strongest, gentlest, and the most noble. Christ's role of rescuer of the frail soul is emphasized; he has saved her from her three foes – the world, the flesh and the devil – who 'grinned for gladness . . . as mad wolves that rejoice over their prey . . . But thou wilt have me for thy beloved and thy spouse, so that thou didst not permit them fully to rejoice over me; . . . where the danger was greatest of all, there was succour nearest'.[28] But the approach differs from the *Rule*'s in that the woman does not have to be convinced to choose Christ; she fully recognizes his desirability, and addresses him as his committed lover. Her sensitivity to the degree of sacrifice made for her in particular seems to distance her from the aloof and ungrateful lady of the *Rule*'s section 'On Love', though perhaps the *Wooing* represents the lady's point of view at a later stage of development. She seems to have modified her interest in literal wealth – 'Ah! why should I be rich and thou, my beloved, so poor?' 'Therefore . . . will I be poor for thee . . . so that I may be rich with thee in thy eternal bliss'. Overall, Christ is being loved much more for what he is and has done than for what he has to offer. The *Wooing* is, in fact, an astonishingly beautiful love poem in prose, richly sensual, but spiritually earnest, its language rhythmic, hypnotic, throbbing with emotion. At regular intervals the lover repeats her passionate refrain, 'A iesu mi swete iesu leue þat te luue of þe beo al mi likinge' ('grant that the love of thee be all my delight'), and throughout makes fertile use of the language of love: 'Iesu swete iesu', she begins, 'mi druþ. mi derling. mi dritin. mi healend. mi huniter. mi haliwei. Swetter is munegunge of þe þen mildeu o muðe' ('my love, my darling, my Lord, my Saviour, my honeydrop, my balm! Sweeter is the remembrance of thee than honey in the mouth').

---

[28] R. Morris provides an *en face* translation of the *Wohunge of Ure Lauerd* in his *EETS OS* 29 edition; but see also W. Meredith Thompson's more recent edition *EETS* 241 (London, 1958).

As in the *Wooing of Our Lord*, this thirteenth-century portrayal of the crucified Christ shows him as a suffering, human victim, his bowed head crowned with thorns, his hands torn by the nails. The pathos of the scene is enhanced by the grief of his two mourners. Evesham Psalter, the Crucifixion, British Library Additional MS 44874, fol. 6; by permission of the British Library.

Her moving use of language, however, is not confined to expressions of tenderness for her beloved. A powerful element in the *Wooing* is the intense pathos surrounding the image of the crucified Christ, the aching compassion expressed by a woman for the agony of her lover: 'A hwat schal i nu don? Nu min herte mai to breke. min ehne flowen al o water. A nu is mi lefmon demd for to deien' ('Ah! what shall I do now? Now my heart may break, my eyes flow all with water. Ah! now is my beloved doomed to die'). Thus the events leading up to the crucifixion, and the details of Christ's ordeal on the cross, are described at great length: 'A lo he beres his rode up on his bare schuldres . . . A nu raise þai up þe rode . . . A nu nacnes mon mi lef. A. nu driuen ha him up wið swepes and wið schurges. A hu liue i for reowþe þat seo mi lefmon up o rode. and swa to drahen hise limes þat i mai in his bodi euch ban tellen' ('Ah, lo! he bears his rood upon his bare shoulders . . . Ah! now they raise up the rood . . . Ah! now they strip my beloved. Ah! now they drive him up with whips and with scourges. Ah! how can I live for grief, seeing my beloved upon the cross, and his limbs so drawn asunder that I may tell each bone in his body'). As in the *Rule*, the element of obligation is there – Christ has gone through all this for her – but this woman freely accepts her obligation, and finds union with her beloved through identification with his suffering, through compassion. Unlike the sisters in the *Rule*, she achieves her humility without the negative goad of fear and fleshly revulsion. We might say that the level of the *Wooing*'s experience does not compare with that of the great mystics, that no grand spiritual truths are revealed. Yet as a literary counterpart of the iconographic portrayal of Christ as suffering, human victim – rather than conquering hero – that was to emerge in the course of the thirteenth century, the *Wooing* is of major historical and cultural value; and in the earnest purity of its ardour, as a heart-rending expression of the bond between lover and beloved, it holds its own along side its larger contemplative relatives. Its composition coincides chronologically with the birth of our next subject, Mechthild of Magdeburg; and as it foreshadows her pervasive reliance on love language and her ardent bond with her Creator, the *Wooing* provides an appropriate introduction both to the woman and her work.

Mechthild of Magdeburg

I

Mechthild of Magdeburg (1210–1297) was born to an aristocratic family in Saxony, to the north-east of Hildegard's Rhineland. Aside from the scant biographical information that she provides, we know very little about her 'outer', or everyday existence; but her masterpiece, *The Flowing Light of the Godhead*, provides us with a rich view of her spiritual life. She spent much of her adult life working on this treatise, commencing the actual writing when she was forty, and completing the final book by dictation in old age when she was blind and infirm. Her method of composition was to write as the inspiration struck her, sometimes in prose, sometimes in poetry, on loose sheets – which were collected and preserved by her lifelong friend, the Dominican Heinrich of Halle. Whether Mechthild and Heinrich conferred as to how the pages and books were to be assembled, or whether the order in which they have been passed down was Heinrich's own, is not known. This uncertainty makes it difficult to examine Mechthild's work for clear evidence of spiritual change or progress; the books seem to be organized according to subject rather than chronology. However, close as Heinrich and Mechthild were, it seems possible that the existing order reflects in some degree her own preference.[1] Certainly she did not write the work so that others could study *her*; she saw herself simply as an instrument of God's will, and was baffled as to why he had chosen her.

A striking feature of Mechthild's writing is that she composed in her native tongue, Low German, rather than Latin.[2] The literary use of the

---

[1] See Eckenstein (*op. cit.*), p. 332; Mechthild of Magdeburg, *The Flowing Light of the Godhead*, trans. Lucy Menzies (London, 1953), p. xxii; and *Flowing Light of the Divinity*, trans. Christine Mesch Galvani (New York and London, 1991).

[2] Mechthild's friend, Heinrich of Halle, translated her work into Latin (rescuing it, as he put it, from the 'barbara lingua' of German). Fortunately – since Mechthild's original is now lost to us – a translation into High German was also undertaken by Heinrich of Nördlingen in 1344–5; this, along with the Latin version, forms the basis of subsequent editions. See *Offenbarungen der Schwester Mechthild von Magdeburg, oder das fliessende*

vernacular was beginning to spread during this period, for example among the Provençal poets; Dante was soon to write his *Divine Comedy* in Italian, and Chaucer would begin composing his earliest poem, the *Book of the Duchess*, in Middle English in the 1360s (in contrast to his more conservative contemporary, Gower – whose first composition was in Latin, his second in the court language, French, and only the final work, *Confessio Amantis*, in Middle English). But generally in the thirteenth century it was felt that any work that was to be taken seriously ought to be in Latin. What Mechthild's choice meant, aside from helping to give an early boost to Low German's respectability, was that her work was accessible to a more varied audience. Substantial parts of her book were in circulation during her lifetime, which meant not only that she had many enthusiastic admirers, but also numerous and powerful critics. When she was in her early sixties, in fact, she was forced by the persecution of these adversaries – corrupt members of the clergy who were incensed at her fearless and outspoken criticism – to take refuge in an established Cistercian convent, Helfta, where her writings were known and admired. Here she was warmly welcomed by the abbess Gertrude, and here she remained in comfort and security until her death at eighty seven.[3]

But for some forty years before moving to Helfta, Mechthild had lived in Magdeburg as a Beguine. The Beguines were an idealistic association of religious women, living communally – they were most common in Flanders, but also settled in Germany and northern France. The twelfth-century movement 'was a spontaneous, local outgrowth of the urge to apostolic life'; the first beguinages, sometimes supported by wealthy patrons, were intended to provide lodging for women who would otherwise be homeless – perhaps rather like our modern hostels, with a certain variety of background occurring amongst the members. After entering the community, the women were expected to support themselves as best they could, perhaps by nursing the sick, or by manual labour; basically they lived on charity. Mystical works played a central role in the religious life of these communities, which also found powerful inspiration in the ascetic model of the mendicant orders; on occasion a beguinage would be 'adopted' by neighbouring Dominicans, who felt a close ideological bond with the Beguines. As theirs was an unofficial association, there were no

Licht der Gottheit, ed. G. Morel (Ratisbonne, 1869, repr. 1963, 1967; Heinrich of Halle's Latin translation (Poitiers and Paris, 1877); and the most recent edition of Mechthild's work, by Hans Neumann (Munich, 1990).

3   See Eckenstein (*op. cit.*), pp. 329 ff.; Lucy Menzies, *Mirrors of the Holy: Ten Studies in Sanctity* (London, 1928), pp. 27 ff.; and Menzies' 1953 introduction to *The Flowing Light* (*op. cit.*) for information about Mechthild's life. Mechthild herself provides us with an autobiographical chapter in *The Flowing Light* (4,2). Specialists disagree amongst themselves as to the various dates in Mechthild's life, some placing her death as early as 1282.

vows required in undertaking this life, but it was one that – particularly in Mechthild's case – was marked by a strong commitment to social good, a mixing of the active and contemplative ideals. As the thirteenth century progressed, the Beguines were viewed with increasing suspicion by the established church; the subsequent charges of heresy against them, though ill-founded, resulted in more active persecution in the next century.[4]

Before entering the beguinage, and having at twenty-three made the decision to undertake a religious life, Mechthild had applied to a traditional convent; admission to this house depended on being presented by one's parents, along with a 'dowry'. But Mechthild refused to follow this route, instead applying on her own, without money. She was rejected. Possibly she was not surprised by this turn of events. Her choice of the beguinage indicates, in any case, her strength of principle: her unequivocal preference for the imitation of Christ, here through poverty, and her rejection of the social ease and material comfort to which she had been born.

About this time, she had what might be referred to as her first ecstatic experience, described in *The Flowing Light of the Godhead*. Mechthild speaks of her soul being taken out of her body, which remained behind, and transported to a region set 'between heaven and earth', where for a time it communed with God, forgetting its earthly connections.

> And I saw with the eyes of my soul in heavenly bliss, the beautiful humanity of our lord Jesus Christ and I knew Him by His shining countenance. I saw the Holy Trinity, the Eternity of the Father, the work of the Son and the sweetness of the Holy Spirit.

This experience, she explains, 'comes from the heavenly flood out of the spring of the flowing Trinity'. It takes 'all strength from the body', which remains 'as it were in a sweet sleep'; the soul is 'laid bare . . ., sees itself as one of the blessed and receives in itself divine glory'. God then takes the soul further, 'to a secret place . . ., where [He] alone will play with it . . . Thus God and the soul soar further to a blissful place of which I neither can nor will say much'.[5] It would be an understatement to say that her life was never to be the same after this experience. At its inevitable

---

[4] Giving an idea of the scope of the movement during Mechthild's lifetime, Haverkamp notes that 'around the middle of the 13th century about two thousand Beguines and Beghards are said to have lived in Cologne and its surroundings', the great majority of them being women (*op. cit.*), p. 318. For more information see Rufus Jones (*op. cit.*), p. 58 ff.; Malcolm Lambert, *Medieval Heresy: Popular Movements from Bogomil to Huss* (New York, 1976), p. 174 ff.; Ernest W. McDonnell, *The Beguines and Beghards in Medieval Culture* (New Brunswick, N.J., 1954).

[5] *The Flowing Light* (Menzies, *op. cit.*), 1,2; 4,2. Hereafter references to Mechthild's work will be included in the text.

conclusion, her soul was filled with contempt for the body with which it was forcibly reunited, and waited in a state of longing for a recurrence. Happily, these were frequent, and her work is filled with many and varied descriptions of these joyous spiritual encounters.

Earlier, at twelve, she entered what might be described as the first stage of her spiritual life; she describes it as a greeting from the Holy Spirit: this 'loving greeting came every day and caused me both love and sorrow; the sweetness and glory increased daily'. Thereafter she says that it was impossible for her to commit any serious sin, though she continues to refer to herself as an unworthy sinner, and makes clear that she never presumed to ask for the special revelations that were granted her. This early stage was marked by what she calls a desire to be 'despised', but it is important to be clear as to what she means here; Mechthild is not weighed down by anything that we would recognize as self-hatred. She wants to be rid of her body, not because she particularly loathes the flesh, but because she longs to be free to join God in the 'secret place'. She wants to be scorned on earth, particularly by her corrupt adversaries, so that she can be more like Christ, as he was also scorned on the way to Calvary – but clearly this kind of 'scorn' only proves the value of the object towards which it is directed. She herself points out that the persecution of God's children is intended as a way to allow them to be like his Son (1,25). So perhaps it would be more accurate to say that this stage was marked by a passionate desire to imitate Christ, and indeed this longing remained central throughout her life.

Certainly the struggle for liberation from the body was long and arduous; according to Mechthild's account it was a twenty-year fight, which left her exhausted and worn: 'Sighing, weeping, confession, fasting, watching/ Recollection, discipline prayer – / These I must constantly practise' (4,2). But towards the end she confesses to a grudging affection for the body, which she describes as a faithful servant, and admits to having used rather harshly in her youthful enthusiasm. In Mechthild's final poem the body addresses the soul, asking that when she reaches Jesus in 'the blissful heights' she will 'Thank him there . . . for me/ And pray that poor and unworthy as I am/ In his mercy He may be mine'. 'Ah! beloved prison', replies the soul to the body, 'I thank thee for all/ In which thou hast followed me./ . . . Therefore we will lament no more,/ But will be filled with gladness/ For all that God has done to us both' (7,65).

Yet despite her earlier struggles with the flesh, Mechthild's work reflects an acceptance of the physical: her vision of heaven after judgement day stresses explicitly the reunion of bodies with their souls; married couples, too, will be reunited, and will 'look lovingly at each other yet with restraint' (3,1); and the Bride and Bridegroom will be placed so 'that love may come to love, body to soul'. Mechthild's rejection of dualism's loathing for the body is perhaps more evident in her depiction of prelapsarian innocence in the Garden of Eden: Adam and Eve were created 'nobly after the pattern of the Everlasting Son', and, further, 'if they had not eaten the forbidden fruit they would have been able to 'conceive their children in holy love as the sun plays upon the waters and leaves them untroubled' (3,9).[6]

Although we have access to so few recorded facts of Mechthild's life, certain external factors were of great influence and can help us to understand her more fully. During Mechthild's early life the mendicant orders of St Dominic and St Francis were at a glorious high point – in fact their founders were still alive – and her brother Baldwin himself became a Dominican. It is difficult to exaggerate the impact that the purity and fervour of the 'new friars' had on Europe as their followers moved north from Italy. Their unequivocal commitment to poverty, in contrast to the pomp of the established church, offered new hope for the whole institution, sadly eroded by clerical decadence. Their commitment to a life of teaching and preaching, themselves going barefoot to the people, renouncing all earthly goods and supporting themselves by begging alone, stood in stark contrast to the idleness and indifference of the clergy at large, as their profound compassion for the suffering of every one, no matter how poor or lowly, was a welcome contrast to the elitism of the ecclesiastical establishment, with its undisguised preference for the wealthy and well-born.[7]

Mechthild shared the mendicant ideals of renunciation and humilty, and the optimism inspired by the coming of the friars. God, described in one of her visions as being unable to salvage wayward humanity with the existing forces, sends two new children, the Dominicans and Franciscans, to assist him; 'when the people recognize this holy life', she says, 'they will be so edified [they] will wash the hardened feet of the brethren with fervour . . . as Mary Magdalene did to our Lord' (4,27). Fortunately Mechthild did not live to see the depths of greed and lechery to which these orders had already fallen by the time the *Canterbury Tales* and *Piers Plowman*, with their bitter exposés of the friars, were composed.

Mechthild also shared the mendicants' reforming zeal, evident in the scathing passages in which she attacks clerical corruption. Holy Church's crown, she writes (here recalling her prophetic predecessor, Hildegard),

is dimmed in the filth of evil desires; . . . thy purity is burned up in the

---

6   Mechthild's concept of sex before the Fall recalls Augustine's argument that since there was no lust in Paradise, intercourse would have been accomplished as an act of will, without 'agitation of libidinous longing' (Bugge, *op. cit.*, p. 27).

7   The first settlements of Franciscans and Dominicans in Germany took place around 1220–1, and soon expanded into Mechthild's neighbourhood of Saxony and Thuringia. The Dominicans, concentrating on the major urban centres, were more influential in the north (see Haverkamp, *op. cit.*, pp. 32–1).

consuming fire of greed; thy humility is sunk in the swamp of thy flesh . . .! Alas! for the fallen crown of the priesthood! . . . [God's] vengeance will come upon thee . . . For thus saith the Lord: '. . . My sheep from Jerusalem have become wolves and murderers: for before my eyes they slay the white lambs'. (6,21)

Elsewhere, she dares to take specific aim at the canon of Magdeburg, on whose behalf she prayed to God for advice; she quotes God's reply in detail:

'He should clothe himself more modestly than he now does; moreover, he shall wear a hair shirt next his skin to guard against the softness he has accepted in the flesh . . . He shall sleep on a straw pallet . . . He shall also keep two rods beside his bed to discipline himself when he awakes . . . He shall hold himself always in fear like a mouse that sits in a trap and awaits its death . . . When he eats he shall eat sparingly; when he sleeps he shall be chaste and alone with Me'. (6,2)

The canon can hardly have been pleased, either by the ascetic model proposed for him, or by the clear implication that his current life was one of self-indulgence and luxury. Not surprisingly, the burning of Mechthild's uncomfortably honest book was sought; her subsequent self-doubt led her to ask God for advice. 'The Truth may no man burn', was the unequivocal reply to her prayer; 'Those who would take this book out of My hand/ Must be stronger than I!' And God then gently turns to reassure Mechthild as to the question of her 'unworthiness'; it is this very humility that has led him to choose her:

'Daughter! Many a wise man loses his precious gold
Carelessly on the great highway . . .
But someone must find it!
I have long acted thus:
Wherever I gave special grace
I sought for the lowest and smallest and most hidden.
The highest mountains may not receive
The revelations of My Grace,
For the flood of My Holy Spirit
Flows by nature down into the valleys.' (2,26)

83

II

Concrete evidence of Mechthild's humility has been seen in her decision to enter a beguinage, rejecting material comfort and social privilege, living in imitation of Christ as a means of carrying this out: her integrity required that she live as she believed. But we also know that she sought this life because of an active belief in social good, and it is characteristic of her integrity that her 'favourite' saints – beyond Dominic ('whom I love above all saints')[1] and Francis – reveal in their lives these same values. Mechthild's favourites can be divided into two groups, the 'new' and the 'old', the new group – all of whom died within her lifetime – including Elizabeth of Hungary, Jutta of Sangerhausen, and Peter the Martyr.[2]

Of aristocratic birth, Elizabeth was happily married for six years to Ludwig IV of Thuringia until his death *en route* to a crusade. Defenseless, she was turned out of the castle by an unscrupulous brother-in-law; after providing for her three young children, she proceeded to join the Franciscans and dedicate the rest of her life to working with the poor and sick – like Mechthild, renouncing all claim to material or social advantage. In 1228 she founded a hospital under the patronage of St Francis ouside Marburg; her grave became a centre of pilgrimage after her death in 1231, and the foundation stone for St Elisabethkirke was laid directly after her canonization four years later.[3]

Jutta, who was actually a friend of Mechthild's, followed a pattern similar to that of Elizabeth: she, too, was happily married, bore several children, and was widowed when her husband died on a crusade; she, too, renounced her property, arranged for her children to be cared for in religious houses, and dedicated herself to the care of lepers until her death in 1260. Peter the Martyr, attempting to maintain the Dominican ideal of conversion by persuasion rather than force, was nonetheless murdered in 1252 by the heretical Cathars he was trying to save. The new friars' idealistic model of self-renunciation and dedication to the aid of the needy is common to all three of these saints.

---

[1] See *The Flowing Light*, 4,20, 'Of Six Virtues of St. Dominic', which describes his generosity towards his brethren, and concludes, quoting God, 'when Dominic laughed he laughed with real sweetness of the Holy Spirit and when he wept he wept with such fidelity that he thought first of his brethren and set them before My eyes.' Mechthild's later, more forgiving attitude towards her body may have been the result of Franciscan influence; 'it is only in the spirituality of Francis of Assisi', points out José de Vinck, 'that "Brother Body" begins to receive his humble due', *Revelations of Women Mystics: From Middle Ages to Modern Times* (New York, 1985), p. 12.

[2] See *The Flowing Light*, 5,34, pp. 159n, 160n; also Donald Attwater, *The Penguin Dictionary of Saints* (Harmondsworth, 1965), pp. 113, 209.

[3] Haverkamp (*op. cit.*), p. 319.

Mechthild's favourite 'old' saints include John the Baptist, John the Evangelist and St Peter (patron saint of the Dominicans); their records as devoted followers and imitators of Christ hardly need repeating. But she encounters these three saints in a marvellous vision, 'Of a poor maid and of the Mass of John the Baptist' – subtitled 'An allegory of justification by faith' – which is recorded in her second book. This dream-like vision, as it is seen from the point of view of a wide-eyed girl, seems likely to have occurred when Mechthild was still quite young – though evidently after her first transcendental experience, since 'God took from her her earthly senses and brought her wondrously into a great church' (2,4). Arriving in the empty church, the poor maid at first fears that she has missed Mass, but is reassured when four youths arrive and strew the aisles with flowers – violets, roses, lilies; the youths are followed by two scholars bearing candles, which they place on the altar. Then comes a tall man, who

> was very thin, yet not old. His garments were so ragged that his limbs showed through. He carried a white lamb on his breast and had two hanging lamps in his hands. He went to the altar and set the Lamb thereon and bowed himself lovingly before it. That was John the Baptist who should sing the Mass.
>
> Next came a youth in fine garments who carried an eagle before his breast: he was St. John the Evangelist. Then came an ordinary man, St. Peter; and then a tall youth brought the vestments for the Mass wherein the three robed themselves.

The church soon fills with a grand heavenly company, richly attired in handsome robes of white or rose, wearing crowns. Weak and poorly dressed, the little maid feels out of place; when she notes the exalted company in the choir, 'robed in gleaming gold/ . . . surrounded by a cloud of rapture/ Brighter than the sun' – and including the Virgin Mary, St Catherine and St Cecilia[4] – her doubts grow: 'she looked down at herself and wondered, whether in her pitiful garments she dared to stay'. Suddenly she sees that she is wearing a 'reddish-brown cloak . . . fashioned of love [that] signified her longing for God and all holy things . . . and had embroidered on it these words: *Gladly would I die of love!*'

This is the turning point of the vision: the girl's doubt turns to confidence; 'she saw herself as a noble maiden, wearing in her hair a wreath of gleaming gold' with the words –

---

[4] This is the same St Katherine we encountered in the Katherine Group. St Cecilia, whose story is recounted in Chaucer's 'Second Nun's Tale', was similarly courageous, enduring terrible persecution for the sake of her faith, and converting throngs of pagans by her example before finally dying by decapitation.

His eyes in my eyes,
His heart in my heart,
His soul in my soul
Embraced and unwearied.
(And her face seemed the face of an angel).

While before she has seemed invisible, she now is warmly welcomed by the company in the choir, who 'looked at her with smiling delight'; best of all, 'our Lady beckoned to her/ That she should stand in front of St Catherine'; and throughout the rest of the dream the Mother gently tends and encourages the uncertain child. At this point Mechthild's indentification with the girl becomes explicit. 'Ah!, wretched being that I am', she laments, 'For I am not [now] so blessed as I saw myself there'; and, after being beckoned by Mary, 'I went and stood by our Lady'.

The Mass itself commences. The maid expresses a fervent wish to take communion, and Mary replies 'Yes! dear Child! Make your confession!' Incredibly, as if the girl's wildest hopes had not already been fulfilled, the Mother calls over John the Evangelist himself to hear it – which he gladly does, gently responding to her questions. In reply to the child's whispered wish to make an offering, Mary herself gives her a special gold coin: 'It is thine own will. Offer it in all things to my Lord and Son'. The offering – which 'thou wilt never take . . . back' – enables her to receive communion from John the Baptist, and the vision approaches its climax.

As he took the white wafer in his hands, the Lamb which was on the Altar stood up and was changed into the wafer and the wafer into the Lamb, so that I saw the wafer no more but instead a bleeding Lamb which hung on a red cross. He looked on us with such sweet eyes that never can I forget it.

The miracle of transubstantiation has taken place before her very eyes. Having seen this much she cannot but want the rest, her own actual union with the Lamb. For the last time she seeks Mary's intercession: 'Ah! dear Mother! pray thy Lord and Son that He give Himself to me!' and she sees 'a gleam of light from out the mouth of our Lady strike the Altar and touch the Lamb with the request'. Christ gladly accedes to his mother's wish, and the maid approaches the altar 'with great love and widely opened soul'.

John the Baptist took the white Lamb with the red wounds and laid it on the mouth of the maid. Thus the pure Lamb laid itself on its own image in the stall of her body and sucked her heart with its tender lips. The more it sucked the more she gave herself to it.

This passage reveals a great deal about Mechthild's emotional and spiritual realm. Through the vision of a Mass conducted by heaven's noblest saints, reaching down to an insignificant, helpless child, we begin to make contact with the rich variety of her inner reality. What is at first most striking about this vision, and what also distinguishes it from any of her others, is the intense experience of the frightened child that it manages to convey. Her loneliness, her sense of isolation and unworthiness – the particular details such as her fear that she has come too late, or that her clothes are too shabby – are the material of childish dreams we have all had. In Mechthild's case the action of the dream, on an emotional level, is to provide herself with a new family – which she would surely be craving if she had indeed just left her home to enter the beguinage. The tenderness of both the Mother and St John the Evangelist serve to reassure her that she is accepted, and loved, and will be safe. Also on the childish level is the spectacular aspect of the dream's wish-fulfillment: the pure earnestess of Mechthild's longing to join the heavenly elite, even as its smallest member, is beyond doubt – and especially moving as it is expressed with a child's vulnerability and trust.

Beyond this personal level there are further aspects to the vision of the Mass of John the Baptist, in which more universal mystical and theological truths are revealed. Generally, the allegory demonstrates that the mercy of the saints, and transformation through communion, are always accessible to the willing soul, no matter how poor or lowly, if it has faith, if – in the words of the maiden's cloak – it 'would gladly die of love'. There is reassurance here for all who fear that their sins are too great to be forgiven, or that the few good deeds they may have performed are insufficient. In this sense Mechthild's identification with the maid is one she would have us all follow, turning from the shadow of despair, and towards the affirmation of divine mercy.

Through the vision we get a glimpse of Mechthild's heaven, which is clearly ranked. Within the dream-church the groups are organized according to degree of sanctity. Those who died repentant, but with no good works, are less honoured than those who lived more actively according to God's law; still more highly placed are the ranks of maidens. On one side of the coin that Mary gives the child is an image of heaven hierarchically ranged into nine choirs, with the throne of God at the top (the tenth choir having been vacant since Lucifer's fall). However fervent Mechthild's commitment to the ideal of earthly, social equality, it does not qualify this traditional model of a heaven in which souls are rewarded according to their merit, and although all are saved, some are distinctly more holy than others. Here she replaces the world's false set of values, and its resultant false social and economic hierarchies, with the true one; the poor maid, by virtue of her purity and love, in fact belongs beside the saints in the choir. We recall Mechthild's desire to be scorned, and thus to be closer to Christ: the 'respect' of this world is without value, is itself to be despised.[5]

Mechthild's ranging of the heavenly choirs represents a convention first notably recorded by the fifth-century mystic known as Dionysius the Areopagite. In his *de Caelesti Hierarchia* (concerning the heavenly hierarchy), he described in minute detail the names and qualities of the inhabitants of the nine heavenly choirs, which were divided into three triads and included the familiar cherubim, seraphim and archangels.[6] Also profoundly influential during the middle ages was his *de Mystica Theologia* (translated into Middle English in the fourteenth century as *Deonise Hid Divinite*, the secret/mystical theology of Denis/Dionysius), in which he described the union between soul and God. His experience – now conventionally opposed to the more rational Augustinian version of mystical union – is paradoxical and ineffable, hingeing on a transcendence of will, a suspension of rational activity, a forgetting of self – a commitment to the *via negativa* – before union can occur. Frequently, while the soul waits in a kind of spiritual limbo for God, it experiences a painful trial – sometimes verging on despair – known as the 'dark night', in which it fears that it has been abandoned, that God has permanently withdrawn.

Mechthild's vision of St John's Mass reflects the Dionysian tradition, not only in her allusion to the celestial hierarchy, but also in her implied acceptance of the *via negativa*. First, her willingness to die of love indicates a spiritual readiness for the abandonment of self-will; then, the coin she plans to offer represents, as Mary explains, 'thine own will'. When she actually makes the offering (of her will) she is addressed by the voice of God, who leaves no doubt as to the nature of the exchange: 'If thou offer Me this coin so that thou will never take it back, then I will loose thee from the Cross and bring thee to Me in My Kingdom'. In the long run he

---

5 Mechthild seems more fully to have divorced herself from accepted class-dominated social hierarchies than Hildegard, who, we recall, believed that 'power and serfdom were derived from divine institution . . . [that] servitude (*servitus*) was a consequence of original sin' (Haverkamp, *op. cit.*, p. 198). Julian, in turn, appears to have transcended the notion of rank in her heaven.

6 The Dionysian triads are populated as follows (1) *seraphim, cherubim, throni*; (2) *dominationes, virtutes, potestates*; (3) *principati, archangeli, angeli*; their function *vis-à-vis* creation is to raise mankind to perfection through a process of purification and illumination. See Dionysius the Areopagite, *Opera Omnia, Patrologiae Graeca*, ed. J.-P. Migne, v. 3–4 (Paris, 1855), and *The Works of Dionysius the Areopagite*, trans. Rev. J. Parker, 2 vols. (Oxford, 1897). In a poem entitled 'Of the nine Choirs and how they sing' (1,6) Mechthild cites nine virtues to parallel the nine heavenly ranks: 'We praise thee O Lord,/ (1) That thou hast sought us in Thy humility,/(2) Saved us by Thy compassion,/ (3) Honoured us by Thy lowliness,/ (4) Led us by Thy gentleness,/ (5) Ordered us by Thy wisdom,/(6) Protected us by Thy power,/ (7) Sanctified us by Thy holiness,/ (8) Illumined us by Thy intimacy,/ (9) Raised us up by Thy love' (the numbering is mine).

is explaining the process of salvation; but in the short run he is allowing her the experience of immediate personal union-through-communion with himself, now. And this is what happens when John the Baptist lays the lamb on the mouth of the maid – Mechthild is joined with Christ: the 'pure Lamb laid itself on its own image'. At the moment of communion her likeness to God has, through grace, been absolutely restored, and they are as one.

Frequently Mechthild emphasizes the necessity of transcendence of self, but she is clear that this is not something that just 'happens'; it requires the active seeking of the soul. 'Three things make the soul worthy of this way', she says. 'Firstly, that it wills to come to God, renouncing all self-will' (1,27); and, 'Thou shalt love the naughting,/ and flee the self' (1,35). The pain experienced by the soul in the dark night may be devastating – 'How long must I endure this thirst?/ One hour is already too long,/ Should this continue for eight days/ I would rather go down to Hell/ Where indeed I already am!' (2,5) – but must be endured until God chooses to return. So, in the vision of St John's Mass the voluntary, active nature of the operation is made clear: paradoxically, the will must play a part in its own transcendence. A passive, painful waiting in the dark night may be required – 'Then, O Lord, I will wait with hunger and thirst' (2,6) – but active seeking and surrender is the first essential step: the maid must gladly offer the coin of her will, and must never ask its return.

A final noteworthy aspect of the vision of St John's Mass occurs at its culmination. Regaining God's likeness, the maid becomes one with the lamb; but she also fuses with the Mother, an identification fostered by Mary's consistently human maternal behaviour in the vision. John the Baptist lays the lamb on the maid's mouth, and thus the lamb lays itself 'on its own image'; it does this 'in the stall of her body, and suck[s] her heart with its tender lips'. The figure of the lamb in the stall explicitly evokes the nativity; and the dream-maiden's body-as-stall recalls the image of the Maiden Mary's body-as-hallowed habitation, in which the incarnate God was protected and nurtured before his birth. Within her body she gives suck to the lamb: 'it sucked her heart with its tender lips'. Thus Mechthild is transformed from child to mother; her heart's blood is the milk she offers. And in imitation of the Mother who has guided her to this apotheosis, her generosity multiplies itself, is limitless: 'The more it sucked the more she gave herself to it'.

Mechthild's later references to the Virgin maintain the image of maternal generosity. In a passage entitled 'Of St. Mary's prayer' (5,23), Mary is seen to play a key role in setting the process of redemption in motion. She prays, because (as a result of the Fall) salvation before the incarnation was impossible for anyone, no matter how holy their lives had been. 'Moreover, this maid drew our Lord down with the sweet voice of her soul';

after Gabriel explains that she will be the mother of God, 'she opened her heart with good will and all her might'.

> Then the whole blessed Trinity . . . entered into the being of her maidenhood and the glowing soul of her goodwill. The Trinity set itself in the open heart of her most pure body and united itself with all it found in her, so that her flesh was their flesh and that He, the perfect Child, grew in her body and she was the true mother of His flesh and remained a stainless virgin. And the longer she carried Him the more lovely, radiant and wise she became.

Elsewhere (1,22), the Virgin reveals that she has been the mother of 'many noble children':

> 'I was so full of the milk of compassion that I nurtured the wise men and prophets before the birth of the Son of God. After that, in my youth, I nurtured Jesus; later, as the bride of God, I nurtured holy Church at the foot of the Cross . . .'. Ah! blessed Mary! In thine old age thou didst nurture the holy Apostles with thy maternal wisdom and thy powerful prayer.

Mechthild then goes on to provide a long list of others mothered by Mary, which includes the martyrs, confessors, maidens and widows – and also the sinners. In other words, she is Mother to us all. Her mothering role will continue until the end of creation: 'thou must still nurture us . . . till the Last Day'; and beyond that, in heaven, the saved shall have eternal access to her as the perfect Mother:

> Then shalt thou see how God's children and thy children are weaned and grown up into everlasting life. Then shall we see and know in unspeakable joy, the milk and e'en the self-same breast, which Jesus oft as infant kissed.

In Mechthild's vision of heaven the Virgin is given a position apparently comparable to that of the Son (somewhat to the surprise of the archangels, who are not convinced 'that humans should be raised above them'): she is seen as standing at the left hand of the Father, while Jesus stands at his right; the sweet milk flowing from her breasts is the counterpart of the blood flowing from Jesus' open wounds (2,3).

But Mary's essential role in the process of redemption – which seems to elevate her to the level of the divine – is most dramatically reflected in Mechthild's discussion of who shall fill the spaces left in heaven by the fall of the rebel angels (3,1). 'By the throne of our Lady', she stipulates, 'no spaces shall be filled, for through her Child she has healed all the wounds of mankind to whom she herself granted grace . . .'. And finally Mechthild explicitly attributes divinity to the Virgin: 'Her son is God and she is goddess; no one can win like honour'. Mechthild incurred much criticism

for attributing divine status to St Mary, as she did by allowing John the
Baptist to perform the Mass (as a layman he was not considered by her
clerical critics to be properly qualified). But her own conviction as to the
truth of her revelations allowed her to dismiss such negative responses:
'No Pope nor Bishop nor Priest could speak the Word of God as John the
Baptist spoke it . . . Instruct me ye blind! Your lies and your hatred will
not be forgiven without suffering!' (6,36).

III

Despite these instances of Mechthild's identification with the figures of
child and mother, by far the most frequent role that she assumes in her
visions is that of lover; and Christ is her beloved. She makes unreserved
and explicit use of the language of erotic, human love. This fact has left
some readers, even twentieth-century ones, uncomfortable; the medieval
fear of the aroused female as a dangerous and sub-rational creature is still
with us. One critic, for instance, admitting that Mechthild's 'story . . . is
told with lyric genius', adds that 'there is a large element of pathology . . .,
far too much reproduction of the experiences reported in the Song of
Solomon, and unwholesome dialogues of love intimacies which mark
this type of amorous, romantic, cloistered mysticism'. A recent selection
of Mechthild's work, though twenty pages long, prefers evasion and
virtually ignores her erotic material.[1] Such views detract from the validity
of Mechthild's experience. The fact is that this passionate woman, page
after page, chapter after chapter, throughout her entire book, describes
her experience of union in ardent, glowing, unequivocally sexual language.

It needs to be pointed out that the use of love language had long been
considered a legitimate means of describing the soul's relation to God, the
spiritual love that leads to union. The Old Testament *Ezekiel* and *Hosea*
developed the theme of Israel as the ungrateful bride; later, Solomon's
Song was interpreted by Christians as representing the relationship between Christ and the church; and St Paul himself employed the metaphor
of church as Bride, Christ as Bridegroom. In the third century Origen
linked the marital relationship between Christ and church with that
between the Word and the individual soul; and Tertullian identified

[1] Rufus Jones (*op. cit.*), p. 49; John Howard, in Wilson (*op. cit.*), pp. 163–182.

virgins as brides of Christ, who were granted this special status for having consacrated their flesh to him.[2]

In the twelfth century, Anselm noted that he didn't think much of 'that kind of love between man and woman', and lumped these relations together with 'various other kinds of domestic attachment . . . ; being the work of instinct [they] were lower on the scale of friendship than the association of partners in business, or even in crime'.[3] Nonetheless, he found the erotic image most appropriate to describe his longing for God: 'My eyes eagerly long to see your face, most beloved, my arms stretch out to your embraces'; 'You have come; you have set me on fire; you have melted and fused my soul with yours'. And Bernard of Clairvaux was particularly active in reviving the imagery of the *Song of Songs* to express the ideal of mystical union. He 'saw the fact of sex [before the Fall as] God's very image stamped on man'; in the relations between the sexes, therefore, he found 'the best, the highest, the holiest and the most inclusive analogy that human experience knows for the relationship between Christ and his church, and – as a result of that – between Christ and the soul'. However, Bernard recognized that he was dealing with flammable material, and cautioned that 'you must bring chaste ears to listen to this Discourse of Love . . .; and, when you think about the Lovers in it, you must not understand by them a man and a woman, but the Word and the Soul'. His use of love language is cautious, explicating the sexual image as it is introduced: 'The Bridegroom calls the Bride "My love, my dove, my fair one" ', but, Bernard quickly adds, 'I think these titles answer to preaching, prayer and contemplation'.[4]

Mechthild, for her part, is unreserved in her use of the erotic image, and feels no need to qualify her accounts with Bernardine glosses; of course she is under no illusion that she is talking about literal, sexual intercourse between a man and a woman, nor does she perceive the least danger that the use of erotic language will result in physical arousal. Though she has been seen to recognize the body as an onerous impediment to spiritual liberation, it is explicitly left behind, in a state of sweet sleep, when her soul is carried aloft by God; were it not, there would by definition be no possibility of mystical union. (Mechthild elsewhere uses the image of inebriation to describe the supra-rational experience of

---

2 See Millet's introduction to *Hali Meiðhad* (*op. cit.*), pp. xl ff. and Woolf's 'The Theme of Christ the Lover Knight' (*op. cit.*), pp. 99 ff.

3 R.W. Southern, *St. Anselm and his Biographer* (Cambridge, 1963), pp. 71–73. The use of love language in the *Nun's Rule* and the *Wooing of Our Lord* has been discussed in the previous chapter.

4 St Bernard of Clairvaux, *On the Song of Songs*, trans. a Religious of C.S.M.V. (London, 1952), pp. 5, 16, 184. (We recall that Bernard favoured an end to double monasteries because he found the presence of the sisters distracting.)

union, but again there is obviously no question that she is talking about literal, physical drunkenness.)[5]

Mechthild's version of the mystical experience was of an intensely personal sort, involving immediate, intimate union with God. Her extravagant language probably seemed painfully dull to her as she endeavoured to express what had happened to her and where she had been, and to communicate to her readers, for the sake of their spiritual advancement, those divine revelations she had been charged to pass on; figurative language, however insufficient, had to be used if her ecstatic experiences were to be shared with others.

Certainly Mechthild's use of the erotic metaphor is far too insistent to be brushed over. It tells us something specific about her relation to her Creator, as Hildegard's more feudal vision did about hers. Much of the passionate language describing that relationship, and the explicitly sexual nature of the bond between the two participants, parallels that of the *minnesingers*, the German counterparts of the Provençal love poets. As an aristocratic young woman in thirteenth-century Saxony, Mechthild would certainly have been exposed to this body of courtly literature, and its associated social conventions, often both idolatrous and adulterous. The few references she makes to this influence are emphatically negative, as in her discussion of St Elizabeth:

'Elizabeth [explains the Lord] is and was a messenger I sent to unsanctified women who sat in castles and were so steeped in impurity, puffed up with pride and eaten up by vanity, that by rights they should have been cast down into the abyss.' (5,34)

In other words, Elizabeth was sent to rescue these ladies from the decadent clutches of courtly love. In Mechthild's vision of hell, she discovers the minstrel: he 'who [in life] can proudly awaken vanity weeps more tears than there is water in the sea'. And the only women who are condemned to the ghastly fate of standing in the flames of Lucifer's breath 'before the mouth of Hell / [are] princesses who with their princes / Loved all kinds of sin' (3,21). Mechthild not only rejects the literature itself, but recognizes it as an actively pernicious influence. Yet the evidence is there to suggest that it has affected the nature of her own religious experience.

---

[5] See, for example, *The Flowing Light*, 3,3: 'Wouldst thou come with me to the wine cellar/ That will cost thee much;/ ... If thou wouldst drink the unmingled wine/ Thou must ever spend more than thou hast,/ And the host will never fill thy glass to the brim!/ ... thy friends look askance at thee/ Who go with thee to the Inn/ ... they cannot dare such costs/ But must have water mixed with wine/ Dear Bride! in the tavern I will gladly spend all that I have,/ And let myself be dragged through the fires of love/ That I may often wend my way/ To that heavenly cellar'; also 1,44, 2,24.

The first book of *The Flowing Light* concludes with an extended allegory in which Christ appears as a beautiful youth, and the soul as his courtly mistress (1,44).

> 'I hear a voice [says the youth]
> Which speaks somewhat of love.
> Many days have I wooed her
> But never heard her voice.
> Now I am moved
> I must go to meet her,
> She it is who bears grief and love together,
> In the morning, in the dew is the intimate rapture
> Which first penetrates the soul.'

The lady's waiting maids, the five senses, warn her of her lover's approach; 'Lady!, Thou must adorn thyself!'

> 'We have heard a whisper,
> The Prince comes to greet thee,
> In the dew and the song of the birds!
> Tarry not, Lady!'

She attires herself in a shift of humility, a white robe of chastity , and a mantle of holy desire, and goes to the wood, where the nightingales sing, to await her lover. His messengers arrive first (Abraham, the Prophets, Mary and Jesus), and he finally arrives himself. He has prepared for her a dance, which he invites her to join. 'I cannot dance', she replies, 'unless Thou lead me'; but if he does, 'then will I leap for love', then 'will I . . . circle ever more'. Afterwards the youth praises the lady for her dancing, and invites her to join him at the riverbank:

> 'For thou art weary! Come at midday
> To the shade by the brook
> To the resting-place of love . . .'.

She waves away her waiting maids – 'Leave me! I must cool myself!'; the maids, reluctant to leave, suggest various remedies, including the tears of Mary Magdalene, the blood of the martyrs, and the wisdom of the apostles. The lady rejects all these comforts as inadequate: 'I am a full-grown Bride/ I must to my lover's side!' The maids now warn her of the fiery glory of God and the heavens; they cannot accompany her, for they will be blinded. But she is undeterred: 'I must to God – / His am I forever'.

Then the beloved goes in to the Lover, into the secret hiding place of the sinless Godhead . . . And there, the soul being fashioned in the very nature of God, no hindrance can come between it and God.

He adjures her to leave her 'self' behind, since she is 'by nature already mine!/ Nothing can come between Me and thee!'

> 'There is no angel so sublime
> As to be granted for one hour
> What is given thee for ever.'

He charges her to put aside her fear and shame and become a 'naked soul', retaining only 'that of which thou art sensible by nature'. At last the consummation takes place: 'Lord!' says the soul, 'Our two-fold inter-course is Love Eternal/ Which can never die.'

> Now comes a blessed stillness
> Welcome to both. He gives Himself to her
> And she to Him.
> What shall now befall her, the soul knows:
>   Therefore I am comforted.
>
> Where two lovers come secretly together
> They must often part, without parting.

The courtly, erotic image is effectively elaborated to describe the spe-cial communion, ecstatic and intimate, shared by Mechthild and her Lord. The account contains a few strategic signposts that establish the spiritual nature of the experience: the lady's clothes are taken from the wardrobe of Christian virtues – humility, chastity, holy desire; the mess-engers of the lover are explicitly biblical – the prophets, Mary and Jesus; the remedies offered by the waiting maids – tears of Mary Magdalene, blood of the martyrs, wisdom of the apostles – serve to reinforce the orthodox context of the vision. But even in these instances Mechthild does not intrude exegetically into her narrative to warn her readers of its allegorical nature, or seek to distance them from the ardour of the text. Quite the opposite: fear and shame, as obstacles to love, are to be cast off (as the lover bids his mistress to become a naked soul, divested of her robes). Mechthild's utter confidence in the power of love shines through; it is all that is required to unite lady and Lord. We are drawn in to the lyrical experience of the lovers, allowed to rejoice and take satisfaction in their consummation.

Aspects of Mechthild's narrative parallel to some extent the conven-tional material of the *minnesingers*' poetry. The enamoured lady preparing to receive her lover and departing for a sylvan dance appears, for in-stance, in this early thirteenth-century secular lyric:

> 'Now let me don
> My dress, for I am eager to be gone
> To join the dance and join the play . . .
> He will be there today.'
> Quicker than thought,
> From the press her gayest gown was brought.
> Swiftly was the girl arrayed.
> 'To the leafy linden tree my steps are swayed.
> My troubles are all allayed.'

The nightingales of courtly poetry appear with roughly the same frequency as dancing ladies; Wolfram von Eschenbach even compares himself to one: 'All the Maytime . . . The nightingale was never still . . . My song will seek your kindness,/Gentle lady'. The impatience of the lady awaiting her lover is common – 'I have these many evenings watched for my beloved/ From out my window over heath by road and shining meadow' – as is the vernal setting of the secret consummation:

> Under the lime tree
> On the heath
> There our bed was . . .
> There he made
> So rich and fair
> A bed from blooms . . .
> What he did with me
> Will be known to none
> Except the two of us unnamed . . .

But there are some key ways in which Mechthild has made this material her own. Courtly poetry is generally marked by an inequality of passion between the two lovers; the lovelorn knight begs on bended knee for his 'daungerous' lady's mercy, which she may or may not grant as the mood strikes her: 'Lady, wilt thou heal my smart,/ So let thine eyes upon me gaze . . ./ This way I soon must end my days/ I am so sick, so sore at heart'; 'So burn in me the flames her glances start . . ./ And her coldness to me wounds my heart'; 'Sweet lady, can my service have success,/ If your power to help me make me so content,/ That my grief will surely pass'.[6]

What is striking in Mechthild's description of the love between soul and God, both here and elsewhere, is its unqualified mutuality. The longing between the two lovers is equally ardent; there is no room for the

---

6 The lines cited are from poems by Neidhart von Reuental (c. 1180–1250), Wolfram von Eschenbach (c. 1170–1217), Walther von der Vogelweide (c. 1170–1230), and Heinrich von Morungen (d. 1222); see *An Anthology of Medieval Lyrics*, ed. Angel Flores (New York, 1962), pp. 426 ff.

bitter jealousy and resentment that so often lurks beneath the lines of the *minnesingers'* pleas. And this feeds into a much larger aspect of Mechthild's message and experience: God's meaning is love; we long to be reunited with him because we belong to him by nature; it is as natural for us to seek this reunion as it is for fish to swim and birds to fly. As the souls tells her maidens,

> 'Fish cannot drown in the water,
> Birds cannot sink in the air, . . .
> This has God given to all creatures
> To foster and seek their own nature,
> How then can I withstand mine?'

The soul's likeness to God can also be seen in the fact that it, too, is tripartite: 'Thou art threefold in thyself', explains Understanding to the soul, 'Therefore mayst thou well be in the likeness of God' (2,19). And when the beloved goes to 'the secret hiding place' with her Lord, nothing can come between them because of 'the soul being fashioned in the very nature of God'.

In a brief, early vision, Mechthild presents the soul as a modest but adoring maiden being received at court by her God:

> She is silent but longs above everything to praise Him. And He, with great desire, shows her His Divine heart. It glows like red gold in a great fire. And God lays the soul in his glowing heart so that He, the great God, and she, the humble maid, embrace and are one as water with wine. Then she is overcome and beside herself for weakness and can no more. And He is overpowered with love for her, as He ever was, He neither gives nor takes. Then she says, 'Lord! Thou art my Beloved! My desire! My flowing stream! My Sun! And I am Thy reflection!' (1,4)

The mutual longing of the partners, the reciprocity of their love, infuses this passage; the images of water and wine – which once mixed can never be separated – and of the Lord as sun and the soul as mirror, both seek to express the natural affinity between the two.

Mechthild elsewhere uses the image of fire and spark to explain this paradoxical relationship; although God is immeasurably greater, he and the soul are still of the same nature: 'So wilt thou burn inextinguishably as a living spark in the great fire of the living Majesty' (1,29). Consummation seems to involve a process of progressive transformation: 'Ah Lord!' she says, 'Love me greatly, love me often and long! For the more continuously Thou lovest me, the purer I shall be' (1,23). The more they love, the more she is able to recover her own true nature, and the more absolute the union.

Even beyond this, Mechthild cites love as the cause of the creation: if Lucifer had not fallen, God would still have desired to create the soul.

Here Mechthild diverges somewhat from Hildegard and her focus on the war against Lucifer and Antichrist – her heroic view of creation as being formed to restore the celestial ranks on high and defeat the forces of evil here below. While Mechthild agrees that the new souls will occupy the circle vacated by the fallen angels, she argues that this was not God's exclusive motive: it was rather the desire to love, and to be loved: 'As God willed no longer to remain in Himself, alone, therefore created He the soul and gave Himself in great love to her alone'. The soul then explains, 'I was created in love, therefore nothing can express or liberate my nobleness save Love alone' (1,22); and God responds, 'That I love thee continuously is My Nature . . . /That I love thee fervently is My Desire/ For I long to be greatly loved' (1,24).

Elsewhere, Mechthild reports a conversation between the three Persons of the Trinity, in which the Holy Spirit presents the plan of creation to the other two Persons: 'We will no longer be unfruitful! We will have a creative Kingdom' (3,9). The Father readily agrees, since 'Thou art one Spirit with Me; what Thou dost counsel pleases Me.' 'Even had the fall of the angels been prevented', he adds, 'man had to be created'. Then the Son speaks, agreeing with the plan, asking that in their created form the new spirits be fashioned after his pattern: 'My nature, too, must bear fruit.' 'Son,' replies the Father, 'I, too, have a great longing in My Divine heart and I hear the call of love. We will become fruitful so that man will love us in return. I will make myself a Bride . . . Then first will love begin';

> Then the Holy Trinity gave itself to the creation of all things and made us body and soul in infinite love . . . [and] the Son shared His heavenly wisdom and His earthly form with Adam.

Here again Mechthild affirms that the purpose of the creation is love – a particular love between God and the created soul. The personal, one-to-one bond between lovers serves to illustrate a special theological detail brought out by Mechthild: the souls that have been created are different from the angels, who are beyond time, and have never gone through life with its pain and joy. 'Human' souls are not only different, they are better, for they have been created out of God's desire to love and be loved. As the Lord says to the soul in her courtly vision, 'There is no angel so sublime/ As to be granted for one hour / What is given thee forever.' And elsewhere God explains to her that '[I have] chosen thee above all things! Thou art my Mistress! My Queen!' (2,42). Eventually, at the end of time, it is from the ranks of these favoured souls that the worthiest will be chosen to fill the tenth and highest celestial circle, to restore heaven to its pre-creation perfection.[7]

---

7 Appropriately, Lucifer's old place will be filled by Mechthild's favourite, John the Baptist.

IV

While Mechthild employs the conventional images and language of courtly love in her efforts to express the ineffable and transcendental, the system she describes is for the most part grounded in the Dionysian – and ultimately the Neoplatonic – tradition. According to this view God is the active, light-emitting Source, which flows sometimes through the angels, sometimes directly to creation. From the source, life streams out by a process of emanation; but it also exerts a counterflow whereby its creations are drawn back to itself.[1] So in Mechthild's system God's love is often seen in terms of light – the presence of the lover is marked by 'a light of utmost splendour/ [that] glows on the eyes of my soul' (2,5) – and the loving soul is drawn back to God.

Early in book one, for example, she explains that 'As He draws her to Himself, she gives herself to Him. She cannot hold back and so He takes her to Himself . . . She is engulfed in the glorious Trinity in high union' (1,5). Later, as the third book opens, the soul speaks to Desire, bids it go as messenger and and tell her beloved that she desires to love (3,1). 'Lord', reports Desire, 'I would have thee know/ That my Lady can no longer live thus – /If thou wouldst flow forth to her/ Then might she soar'. The Lord tells Desire to return: 'I cannot let thee in/ Unless thou bring Me that hungry soul/ Who alone delights Me above all things'. The soul joyfully begins her flight, and God sends two angels to speed her on her way; 'Then they took the soul between them and led her in with joy'.

Within this tradition the power of evil tends to be denied; it is merely non-existence, separation from God. As God is not only transcendent, but also immanent, every element in creation partakes of his being; simply to live is to be part of God. So Mechthild's work pays relatively scant attention to the question of evil. Lucifer's sins – hatred, pride and covetousness – are discussed, as are the lapses of the clergy (3,1; 6,21). But the focus of The Flowing Light is essentially on love. As in Hildegard's view, order is equated with good, each created thing longing to go where its nature impels it; as fish swim and birds fly, so the soul – unless disordered by sin – tends irresistibly towards its Creator; 'Therein', says Mechthild's soul, describing her divine encounter, 'have I seen the inexpressible ordering/ Of all things, and recognized God's unspeakable glory' (2,5).

Thus in Mechthild's courtly vision we encounter the peculiar arrange-

---

[1] See Parker (op. cit.); also the Encyclopedia Britannica, eleventh edition, vol. VIII (Cambridge, 1910), pp. 284 ff.

ment of the five senses as handmaidens to the soul. Were this a more conventional text we might well expect them to be leading her astray, away from her heavenly lover and towards an earthly one. But as Mechthild explains, 'It is a wondrous and lofty way in which the faithful soul walks, leading the senses after it as a man with sight might lead one who was blind' (1,26). The correct relation between the two is that the soul should control the senses, as the lady directs her serving women; properly governed, the senses present no danger to the soul.

Subsequently, in book two, Mechthild describes three heavens, perhaps the stages of a mystical journey; the first is 'made by the devil / With his false cunning . . . / There the soul remains uncomforted / And betrays the simple senses'. However, the second level is formed 'Of the holy longings of the senses . . . / In this heaven there is no light / The soul does not see God there, / But is conscious of an unspeakable sweetness / Which floods through its whole being': here the senses are seen as 'holy', playing a part in the process of mystical ascent. In the vision of John the Baptist's Mass we encountered the celestial hierarchy in the heavenly cathedral; the third heaven described by Mechthild is also 'vaulted and ordered / And irradiated by the Three Persons / Who thus commence the true greeting of God' (2,19).

To reject the ultimate power of evil, however, does not require denial of the devil's existence; rather he is robbed of his victory despite his attempts to trick and seduce the soul. Mechthild reports a visit from the devil, cunningly disguised 'so that I might think he was an angel' (2,24). She is not deceived, however, and so he returns (presumably aware of her Dominican compassion for the weak), 'disguised as a poor sick man'; this façade, too, is easily penetrated by the faithful and ever fearless Mechthild, who tells him that he has 'an eternal sickness' and should 'show thyself to a Priest or Archbishop', or better yet, 'the Pope'. The thwarted devil then reveals his true colours, 'became as black smoke and withdrew himself rudely and went away. But I was not afraid of him'.

Mechthild's autobiographical passage in book four makes even more explicit the fact that the devil is utterly under God's control. After she has had her first ecstatic experience, God gives her two angels, a seraphim and a cherubim, to care for her. But also he 'allowed two devils to come forward, great masters . . . from Lucifer's school', who devise various temptations for her; these trials are but a part of her spiritual growth, and God is confident that she will be able to withstand them. The first devil, also disguised as an angel, is summarily dispatched by the indignant soul: 'Thou wicked deceiver! While God stands by me / All thy wiles are in vain!' The second devil, who comes 'flying through the air', is horribly ugly: he has 'a short tail and crooked nose . . . a head as big as a barrel and fiery sparks surrounded by black smoke [coming] out of his nose'. He laughs in 'evil rage' and expresses his relish in the fact that so many of his earthly agents (presumably Mechthild's ecclesiastical adversaries) are able to torment her. Needless to say, she dismisses him as well: 'Thou hast by nature nothing good in thee; why dost thou make this long speech about thy wickedness?' And the defeated devil is finally forced to admit his powerlessness: 'God holds me so fast that I can do nothing unless He allows it' (4,2).

To the Dionysian/Neoplatonic celestial model Mechthild not only adds a devil but also a purgatory and hell that are strongly reminiscent of Dante – and may in fact have provided him with the inspiration for the structures of his underworlds.[2] Mechthild's purgatory is grim indeed: 'A bath was there prepared of fire and pitch, dirt, smoke and stench. A thick black cloud hung over it like a black skin. And therein lay souls like toads in filth' (3,15). Although these souls retain a human form, they have taken on the devil's likeness. The suffering they endure results from the fact that 'their flesh had blinded their spirits': in contrast to the paradigm in Mechthild's courtly vision, the senses of these souls, when alive, were not kept in their proper subordinate position. And so 'they stewed and roasted together . . . [and] a great troop of devils stood round about and tormented the souls in the accursed bath'. However, the power of divine mercy is felt in the midst of this ghastly vision. The visiting soul – Mechthild herself – begs her Lord to have mercy on these suffering creatures, and, when they have recognized him as the Truth, he agrees: 'Then out of His Divine heart our Lord fulfilled the desire of the poor souls and they rose up in love and joy'; he will lead them, he promises, 'to a hillside covered with flowers; there they will find joy greater than I can say'.

Mechthild, in this vision, attempts to reassure us as to the magnitude of divine forgiveness and the effectiveness of human intercession: in the course of time all the souls in purgatory will have made reparation for their earthly errors; but God is pleased to have their suffering both shortened and alleviated by others' prayerful intervention. Thus she approaches a reconciliation of the vexing paradox of divine mercy and justice which she later pursues by asking God directly for an explanation: 'If Thy righteousness companions Thy compassion/ How is Thy mercy so great? (3,22).[3] He replies that there are more in Holy Church 'who go

---

2   The question of Mechthild's influence on Dante is dicussed by Edmund Gardner in
    Dante and the Mystics (London, 1913); chronologically and geographically it is entirely
    possible for Dante to have had access to *The Flowing Light*. Gardner also examines the
    parallel between our Mechthild and Dante's Matilda, guardian of his Earthly Paradise
    (*The Divine Comedy*, Purgatory XXVIII ff). Mechthild's vision of the Earthly Paradise is
    to be found in 7,57.
3   In her Introduction to *The Flowing Light*, Menzies remarks that 'as the reader will see,
    theology was not Mechthild's strong point' (p. xxvii); in fact Mechthild does address
    the traditional knotty theological problems – such as the question of how to reconcile
    mercy and justice – but she chooses to 'explain' them through her revelations rather

straight to Heaven/ Than go down to Hell . . . My mercy forces Me yet further/ Than the ill-will of wicked men forces them;/ And my righteousness is greater / Than all the wickedness of the devil'. Elsewhere Mechthild is given further examples of this mercy. The unbaptized children, for example, are not consigned to limbo as they are in Dante's *Inferno*, but are admitted to the lower ranks of heaven (3,1); and 'although the home of sinners is obviously in Hell', Mechthild hints that redemption for some of them may be possible: 'God's compassion follows them there so that they are there today, but tomorrow perhaps in the company of the angels' (4,25).

But a hell there must be, however much Mechthild may wish otherwise, 'built in the deepest abyss'; and 'Pride was the first stone/ Laid by Lucifer' (3,21). Subsequent stones from which hell was constructed were contributed by other 'famous' sinners: Adam brought the heavy stones of disobedience, covetousness, gluttony and impurity; Cain brought the stones of anger, falseness and murder; Judas brought lying, betrayal, despair. Hell's cornerstones are the sins of sodom and false piety, and 'the whole place is upside down': its structure, the opposite of heaven's ascending pyramid, is that of a funnel, or inverted cone; Lucifer sits at the very bottom with sin, torment and infamy ceaselessly spewing from his mouth. As with the angels, the damned are ranked, with the sinful Christians at the lowest levels; the torments of the Jews and heathens are less severe since they did not have access to Christian teaching. Here, as in purgatory, the souls have taken on the devil's likeness and 'seethe and roast, . . . swim and wade in the morass and the stench among the reptiles and filth, . . . lie in sulphur and pitch'. And the punishments administered by Lucifer are determined by the nature of the sin: so 'he seizes the proud first of all, and crushes them under him';

All the Sodomites pass through his mouth and remain in his paunch . . ., when he coughs, they are coughed out. The false saints he seats in his lap and kisses horribly . . . The userer he gnaws ceaselessly . . . The robber he robs . . . The thief hangs by his heels as a kind of hanging lantern . . . Those who were unchaste together on earth must lie bound together before Lucifer . . . The murderers must stand before him covered with blood, beaten with a fiery sword by the devil . . . Gluttons and drunkards must suffer everlasting hunger and eat red-hot stones . . . There for sweetness sourness is given; there we see what we practised here.

Mechthild herself is devastated by her experience of hell: 'I, poor wretch,

than in a scholastic manner: the paradox of a triune One is frequently represented through lyric descriptions (i.e. 2,26; 3,1); the question of justification by faith has been addressed, as we have seen, in the vision of John the Baptist's Mass, as has the problem of how the flesh can be 'bad' if it has been created by God.

suffered so greatly from the stench and the subterranean heat that for three days I could neither sit nor walk nor use any of my five senses'. However she reassures us that she suffered no spiritual harm, and that perhaps she may even have brought some relief to the tormented souls: 'It is possible that a pure soul among these wretched creatures might be to them an everlasting light and comfort'. Mechthild's loving attitude towards the creation recoils from the thought of hell's suffering – 'Truly I cannot bear to think of their plight longer than it takes to say a Hail Mary' – and she takes no righteous satisfaction in the prospect of everlasting punishment for the wicked. The persistent trials visited upon Mechthild by her adversaries might have tempted a more vindictive spirit than she was to reserve spots for a few of them in hell. But except for Adam, Cain and Judas, she names no names – unlike Dante – and seems to be overwhelmed by compassion for each one of the unhappy souls below.

V

As we have seen, the persecutions endured by Mechthild eventually drove her to take refuge in a safer convent, where her seventh book was largely composed. The monastery at Helfta, 'the crown of German cloisters', was established in Saxony in 1229, and came to represent 'the highest level of feminine culture known to the Middle Ages'. The fast-growing community, twice forced to move to larger quarters, would have numbered 100 by the time of Mechthild's arrival. Gertrude of Hackeborn, who had been its distinguished abbess since 1251, believed that intellectual and spiritual activity were inseparable – 'if the study of letters should be neglected, soon the scriptures would no longer be understood, and monastic life would begin to decay' – and urged all of her nuns to be diligent in their studies, which included in some cases the *quadrivium* as well as the *trivium*. Aside from study and prayer, the activities within the convent would have included care of the sick and some manual labour – such as spinning, cooking, and the copying of manuscripts. Originally Cistercian, the convent reflected the influence of both the Benedictines and Dominicans; particularly, the Dominican monasteries, of which there were two close by, were under papal order to serve their convent-neighbours as spiritual directors. The Dominican presence must have helped Mechthild in her decision to relocate at Helfta – her friend Heinrich lived at nearby Halle – and it is possible that her brother Baldwin may have personally encouraged the move. Although the community was occasionally beset by problems, life there must have been considerably more stable than it had been for her in the beguinage, especially as she was now infirm and nearly blind; '[in the atmosphere of Helfta] the old beguine [found] . . . acceptance, . . . healing and refreshment'.[1] Her own gratitude for the care she received is fervently expressed in a prayer at the close of *The Flowing Light*:

> Lord! I thank thee that since in Thy love Thou hast taken from me all earthly riches, Thou now clothest and feedest me through the goodness of others . . . That since Thou hast taken from me the sight of my eyes, Thou servest me through the eyes of others . . . That since Thou hast taken from me the power of my hands . . . and the power of my heart, Thou now servest me with the hands and hearts of others. Lord! I pray Thee for them.
>
> (7,64)

Nonetheless, the transition cannot have been easy. The seventh book finds Mechthild, by now old, sick, and tired, capable of a gloom that would have been foreign to her earlier years, no matter how difficult their trials. 'Ah wretched creature!' she cries, 'Our childhood was foolish, our youth troubled; . . . Alas! now in my old age I find much to chide, for it can produce no shining works and is cold and without grace' (7,3); 'unworthiness censures me, indolence convicts me, inconstancy . . . reproves my changeableness' (7,6). She encounters her Lord in the guise of a pilgrim, lamenting the ingratitude of the church for which he has done so much: 'People drive Me out of My refuge in their hearts with their self-will and when I can find no resting place in them, I abandon them to their obstinacy' (7,13). Indeed, tired and worn out, Mechthild wonders why it is that she must remain alive. The answer to her plea that God take her soul is that he has more for her to do on earth: 'Thou shalt enlighten and teach and shalt stay here in great honour' (7,8).

These factors – her inclination to gloom and God's directive to instruct – partially serve to explain the different tone of the seventh book. There are few references to her personal ecstatic experiences; instead, she includes a greater proportion of 'useful' material – such as general prayers and explanations – capable of being shared with the others. Of course the fact that in her blindness she now had to resort to dictation may have meant that she was more reticent about describing her most intimate experiences of union. But the command to instruct was earnestly taken up, and was the more appropriate in a Cistercian house as it accorded with the Bernardine teaching that the duty of the contemplative was to

---

1 See Sister Mary Jeremy, O.P., *Scholars and Mystics* (Chicago, 1962), pp. 4, 17, 21 and *passim*; also Eckenstein (*op. cit.*), pp. 328 ff. and Menzies, who in her introduction to *The Flowing Light* describes Helfta as 'a cheerful place where a fragrant spirituality was combined with spiritual and intellectual work' (p. xxi).

'bring back from intercourse with God strength and food for other souls'.[2] Indeed she compares the soul to a vessel, constantly refilled by God's gifts, which should be poured out onto 'the imperfections of spiritual people':

> Great is the overflow of Divine Love which . . . pours forth, so that our little vessel is filled to the brim and overflows . . . Lord! Thou art full, and fillest us also with thy gifts . . . Even though we are as a small vessel, yet Thou hast filled it . . . We must pour out what we have received with holy desire on sinners . . . Again the little vessel is filled. Again we pour it out on the needs of poor souls who suffer in Purgatory. (7,55)

Thus does the aged Mechthild contrive to incorporate the active ideal of service to others into her cloistered, contemplative life at Helfta.

Still, many early themes are reworked in her final book. In book three, for example, Mechthild describes the passion and crucifixion of the individual soul, revealing that her spritual ordeal, insofar as it mirrors that of Christ, is a way of regaining the divine likeness and of achieving union. Thus the soul is betrayed, sold, seized, bound and overwhelmed; she is

> dragged before the Judge . . . and buffeted in the Tribune when devils assail her spirit . . . Taken before Pilate, . . . beaten and sore wounded, . . . scoffed at . . . She bears her cross . . . She is nailed so firmly to the cross by the hammer of Almighty Love that not all the creatures can release her. She thirsts greatly on the cross of Love and would fain drink the pure wine of God's children. (3,10)

As the soul is crucified, so does she rise and transcend her earthly limitations:

> Thus, in a holy end, she is taken down from the cross and says: 'Father, receive my spirit. It is finished'. She is laid is a sealed grave of deep humility . . . [and] rises happily on Easter Day . . . Then she ascends into Heaven . . . She is received into a white cloud of holy protection whence she is lovingly borne aloft and returns free from all care.

In the seventh book, Mechthild expands this image to apply to the actual physical trials endured by the entire community at Helfta – these may have been difficulties arising from the convent's poverty, or perhaps the disturbing effects of an assault by robber barons. In any case, she recounts that she was filled with pity for the troubles suffered by her community, and asked her Lord for his feelings about 'this prison'. In his reply he shows the greatest honour for her fellow nuns, for he makes clear that he

---

[2]   *The Flowing Light*, p. xx.

has shared their prison, and that their ordeal is to be equated with his: he too fasted and was tempted, and laboured with them; with them he was betrayed and sold, sought and seized, bound, mocked and buffeted; 'dragged before the judge [and] . . . scourged';

> I carried My Cross with them (when their burdens are too heavy they should think of Mine).
> I was nailed on the Cross with them (that they might suffer gladly and gladly bear all their troubles).
> I gave up My Spirit to My Father with them . . .
> I died a holy death with them . . .
> I was buried in an earthly tomb with them . . .
> I rose from the dead (as they shall also rise from death and from all their wants . . .)
> I ascended into Heaven in My Divine Power (thither they shall follow Me in the power and fear of God).

The personal focus of the earlier vision of one soul's crucifixion has here been broadened and transformed to apply to all of Mechthild's sisters. Now she refers not to the arduous spiritual experiences leading up to union, but to external hardships undergone by the community as a whole. Still the ideal of imitation of Christ applies; the courage of the women is praised, and they are given encouragement to persevere in the wake of their difficulties by Mechthild's first-hand account of Christ's words. Through her he assures them that he will never leave them, that their ordeal – their crucifixion – will assure their salvation. She is true to God's command to instruct, as she reveals to the others how their trials reflect those of Christ; at the same time she is able to share with them the experience of intimate communion with her Lord by recounting the conversation with him.

Back in the fourth book Mechthild recounts an encounter with a beautiful young woman – somewhat reminiscent of Hildegard's symbolic female figures – standing upon a great rock that represents Jesus. Her feet are adorned by jasper, a stone that drives out covetousness, 'excites heavenly hunger, . . . wipes away all darkness from the eyes', and represents Christian faith. In her right hand she holds a chalice, and in her left a fiery sword; she explains that with the sword she must threaten until doomsday, and with the chalice she must offer God's blood. In the maiden's heart is a spring of living water, to which are carried 'heathen children/ Leprous and blind'; and by the spring stands John the Baptist, washing the children, restoring their sight. When Mechthild asks the maiden's name she repies that she is Holy Church; 'And Oh! her countenance is so glorious that the more I look on her, the more beautiful she appears' (4,3).

Holy Church reappears in Mechthild's last book, 'a queenly maid of noble presence, fair skin and with the rosy bloom of youth' (7,48). Looking at her, she realizes that she knows her, 'for she had often been my dear companion'. They share an affectionate exchange, with Mechthild longing to repay the maid for all she has done, and offering her soul, and Holy Church ending by giving over all of her seventeen handmaids to Mechthild's service. Unlike the waiting-maids in Mechthild's courtly vision, these represent not the senses but a cluster of virtues essential to the Christian life: their names are Remorse, Humility, Gentleness, Obedience; Compassion, Purity, Patience; Holiness, Faith, Watchfulness; Moderation, Contentment, Peace and Stillness; Wisdom, Fear and Constancy. 'I thank thee', concludes Mechthild, 'That thou hast brought me so many helpers/ On my difficult way to Heaven'. Her earlier encounter with Holy Church served to infuse Mechthild, as an individual, with love for the maiden. And so does the account of her second appearance, as it describes her radiant beauty; but it also serves a didactic purpose, for the virtues that Holy Church consigns to Mechthild are crucial to the success of the monastic life, and in presenting them each by name, along with a list of the particular ways in which they will help the soul, Mechthild obliquely transmits to her sisters a spiritual code which will aid them in their own contemplative endeavours. Tactfully, she does not suggest that they might be in need of the assistance of these various handmaids; but by admitting how eagerly she – a revered member of Helfta – receives the offer of their service, she presents herself as a model for the others to follow.

The natural image still functions in book seven to express the soul's movements towards God; at the same time it reassures the others that in their efforts to transcend the physical they are following natural spiritual longings, and that with practice they are bound to meet with eventual success:

> The longer [a bird] flies . . . the more blissfully it soars, . . . hardly alighting on the earth to rest. So it is with the soul: the wings of love have taken from it the desire for earthly things. (7,61)

Important as the community was, the centre of Mechthild's life, the core from which her love for those around her flowed, remained her bond with her Creator. And interspersed amongst the gloom and didacticism of the seventh book is ample evidence that this incandescent, joyous relationship continued to the end:

> In her distress the soul became aware of the presence of her Love beside her in the guise of a youth of unspeakable beauty . . . she fell down at his feet and kissed his wounds; they were so sweet she forgot all her pain and was no longer aware of her old age . . . Then she stood up clad and adorned in unwavering courage. And He said, 'Welcome beloved!' (7,8)

It transpires that their shared suffering has served to bring the lovers yet
closer together (7,21):

> Now my sorrow and Thine
> Have rested in peace together
> Now is our love made whole . . .
> Risen from the dead
> Thou comest in to me,
> Comfort me, O my Beloved
> And hold me in Thy Presence
> In continual joy . . .
> In all ways I must die for love
> That is all my desire.
> Give me and take from me
> What thou wilt, but leave me this,
> In loving, to die of love!

The literary conventions of the *minnesingers* still serve to convey the soul's
passionate love for her Lord; communication through a go-between, in
this case Gabriel, is characteristic of the courtly tradition, as is the paradoxical image of the beloved as both enemy (he who inflicts the wounds)
and physician (he who alone can cure them):

> Holy Angel Gabriel, remember me!
> I commend to thee the mission of my longing;
> Say to Christ my dear Lord
> That I am ill for love of Him,
> That if I am ever to recover,
> He Himself must be my Physician . . .
> For He has wounded me
> Nigh unto death . . .
> He must lay Himself
> In the wounds of my soul. (7,58)

And the expressive figures – such as water and wine, spark and fire – that
represented the inseparable character of the bond between soul and God,
their twin natures, reemerge in this final brilliant image of union:

> The thoughts of God and of the loving soul mingle together as air is trans-
> fused by sunshine. In that sweet union the sun melts the frost and over-
> comes the darkness . . . Thus is it with Divine Love. (7,55)

Richard Rolle and the
Yorkshire Nuns

The fourteenth century witnessed a remarkable spiritual revival in England. Religious writing of all kinds flourished: manuals of instruction for parish priests, technical tracts dealing with questions of canon law, analyses of the finer points of moral theology, treatises on the vices and virtues, the ten commandments or the seven deadly sins and their remedies – all abounded.[1] But the most enduring of the religious literature produced during this period were the texts dealing with mysticism. Two of the central figures of the fourteenth-century English mystical movement pertain directly to our inquiry: Richard Rolle, hermit of Hampole (c. 1300–1349) and Julian of Norwich (1340–c. 1416). Rolle is relevant because, as a spiritual counsellor, he composed some of his most important works for women religious. And Julian, a self-effacing anchoress at Norwich who described herself as 'unlettered', wrote what is generally agreed to be the masterpiece of Middle English mystical literature, the *Revelations of Divine Love*.

The facts of Richard Rolle's life are made accessible to us not only by information from his own writings, but also by an *Office* that was prepared in the late 1300s in anticipation of his canonization;[2] but though he was enormously popular in the north, and amongst the poor, Rolle was never actually canonized. This failure may be attributable to certain similarities to the heretical Lollards, such as his emphasis on the spiritual aspect of religion, the love of Christ, and the 'individualist principle': in these respects he represented 'the best side of the influences that led to the Lollard movement'.[3] Perhaps because of the hagiographical impulse,

---

[1] For a more detailed account of these texts see W.A. Pantin, *The English Church in the Fourteenth Century* (Notre Dame, Indiana, 1963), Part III.

[2] The introduction to *Richard Rolle: The English Writings*, trans. and ed. Rosamund S. Allen, preface by Valerie Lagorio (Mahwah, N.J., 1988), provides a useful discussion of the biographical material about Rolle. See also Frances M.M. Comper's *Life of Richard Rolle* (London and Toronto, 1928), in which a translation of the *Office* appears (pp. 301 ff.).

[3] 'Richard Rolle', *Encyclopedia Britannica*, vol. XXXIII (*op. cit.*). The Lollards were the

the *Office* takes occasional liberties with strict fact – but its exaggeration is preferable to the frustrating lack of knowledge we have about the personal lives of Mechthild or Julian. And Rolle's personality was of the sort to lend itself to hyperbole: he was an eccentric, colourful character whose temperament was marked by emotional extremes and great religious fervour.

He was born in Thornton Dale, near Pickering, in the north riding of Yorkshire. The surrounding countryside, as 'one of the most extensive stretches of uninhabited country in England', would have been well-suited to a young boy of solitary ways; to the north were high moors, to the south lonely marshes.[4] So his anti-social and independent inclinations must have early been reinforced by his natural environment, as they were with the Brontë children five centuries later. Nonetheless he must have been seen as having scholarly potential, because he was sent to Oxford in his early teens, where his expenses were paid by a wealthy neighbour of his parents, Thomas de Neville. Richard's temper, however, did not lend itself to the abstract, academic pursuit of scholasticism, and after five years, when he was still only nineteen, he abandoned his university studies. Impatient with the frivolity of the moneyed class and with the corruption of the established church, he chose to reject the comfort and security that a career as a conventional member of the clergy would have ensured, instead committing himself to the life of a hermit. To this vow of poverty he remained true throughout his life, although the only rule to which he would subject himself was of his own design; he never joined an established religious order.

In considering Rolle's attraction to the solitary life, it is worth noting that the eremitic ideal within Christianity goes back to the third century, to Paul of Egypt, who lived in a desert cave and is popularly considered to be the church's first hermit.[5] Certainly there were solitaries in Celtic Britain, though the facts of their lives are mingled with legend. Amongst the Anglo-Saxon saints there were many hermits, of whom one of the best known is St Cuthbert (d. 687) who lived for many years in a stone beehive hut on the rocky isle of Farne. Those English hermits who dwelt on islands, or in the fens and forests, craved isolation; others preferred to mix their life of prayer with one of service to their fellows, and became

---

followers of John Wyclif (1328–1384), who like Rolle was born in the north riding of Yorkshire; his radical beliefs put him at odds with the church authorities – he rejected the notion of papal infallibility, attacked the doctrine of transubstantiation, believed that the Bible should be translated into English so as to be accessible to all. Although Wyclif escaped persecution, many of his followers were less fortunate.

4   See G. Home, *Evolution of an English Town: Pickering* (London, 1905), p. 266.
5   For this and subsequent information about solitaries I am particularly indebted to Rotha Mary Clay's *The Hermits and Anchorites of England* (London, 1914). See also the introduction to *Ancrene Wisse*, ed. G. Shepherd (London and Edinburgh, 1959).

ferrymen, or lighthouse keepers. In either case their commitment to the solitary life implied a mistrust of the creation, and more specifically the flesh, that set them in opposition to the Neoplatonic world view as we have seen it expressed by Hildegard or Mechthild, and placed a far greater emphasis on personal sin. They were universally revered, seen as 'living witnesses of the spiritual world'; and by the twelfth century in England the life of the recluse had come to be widely regarded as the state nearest perfection on this earth.[6]

Though associated with this tradition, Rolle always insisted on doing things his own way. In a bizarre episode described in the *Office*, he asked his sister to meet him in the woods with two of her tunics, together with his father's rainhood. Cutting the tunics so that they would resemble the garb of a hermit, he donned his new habit and fled, leaving his astonished sister with the impression that he had totally taken leave of his senses. He then proceeded to the home of a wealthy family, the Daltons, with whose sons he had become acquainted at Oxford. Odd as he must have appeared, Rolle evidently impressed them with his fervour; after he had preached an impromptu but edifying sermon in their church, Dalton invited him home, and having talked to him privately and satisfied himself as to Rolle's 'sanctity of purpose', invited him to stay:

> He, at his own expense, clad him according to his wish, with clothing suitable for a hermit; and kept him a long time in his own house, giving him a place for his solitary abode and providing him with food and all the necessaries of life.

Thus Rolle was able to pursue his calling as a hermit without having to go through any of the ordinary channels; here at the Daltons' he remained for several years, and here he experienced his spiritual awakening and his first temptation by the devil.

For Rolle, there were no halfway measures. His religious life was intensely emotional, involving a total spiritual tranformation, 'a concentration of the affections, and a resulting experience of celestial joy'.[7] His particular version of the mystical experience is marked by its evidently sensual nature, perceived as it is in terms of *calor, canor* and *dulcor* – heat, song and sweetness. As described in his *Incendium Amoris*, the *Fire of Love*, it first manifests itself as a pleasant warmth that grows increasingly hot and more intense, then as song – as heavenly melody – and finally as a consuming inward sweetness. Conversely, the soul without love is

---

[6] Clay (*op. cit.*), pp. xvi, *et seq.*
[7] *Writings Acribed to Richard Rolle, Hermit of Hampole*, ed. Hope Emily Allen (London and New York, 1927), p. 6.

described as cold, frozen – though it may be susceptible to a false fire that can lead it astray.

It is perhaps not surprising in someone with as evidently a sensual nature as Rolle's that the world and its delights should have been seen as presenting a serious threat: the creation was to be admired only for God's sake, and not its own; life on earth was a wretched exile, and the very business of being alive necessitated contact with evil. Like Mechthild of Magdeburg, Rolle's religious and political ideology converged; he, too, was outraged at clerical decadence and recoiled from a social system based on wealth and rank. But for him the world itself was a far more sinister place, best avoided through a life of solitary withdrawal; consequently holiness was not to be measured by charitable deeds, but by inner joy.

Rolle's spirituality is noteworthy, too, for its resolutely anti-intellectual character. Far more important than any 'knowledge' is the fire of love; in fact the desire to know God is the result of excessive pride, and to recognize his incomprehensibility is to show true love. Earthly temptations are not overcome by reason or learning, but by love; and exclusion of the intellect is to be sought, so as to permit a more effective identification between lover and beloved. Constant meditation on the crucifixion and the name of Jesus is the means of attaining the heights of contemplation; thus Rolle composed, for example, many lyrics on the passion, and a piece entitled 'On the Vertuz of the Haly Name of Ihesu'.

In his younger years, however, Rolle did not always seem to be infused with the love he so advocated. He was often brittle and harsh; there was only one way to be right: his way. If you did not love God absolutely you did not love him at all – there was no middle ground. His belief in the special sanctity of hermits seemed suspiciously to smack of the same pride he decried in others. His denunciation of his enemies, the monks (whom, like Hildegard, he despised for being lukewarm), was distinctly uncharitable; indeed, he seemed bent on proving to them that 'his spiritual gifts were superior to theirs'.[8] And his attitude towards women was decidedly negative: his first devil chose the guise of an alluring female – a young woman of his acquaintance, who tried to seduce him – as the most dangerous of temptations, and more generally he held women responsible for much of the world's corruption.[9]

When he left the Daltons, probably after a stay of four years, he travelled about the countryside as a hermit for a number of years, during which time his activites and whereabouts have not been established. He

---

8   H.E. Allen (op. cit.), p. 125.
9   See the Office in Comper (op. cit.), p. 305. As late as the early 1340s Rolle was to warn that it was better to avoid women altogether than 'face their immoderate love or scorn'; see The Fire of Love, trans. Clifton Walters (Harmondsworth, 1972), ch. 12.

may even have gone as far as Paris and studied at the Sorbonne. Towards the end of his lifetime – which was cut short by the plague – he surfaced again, having evidently undergone a significant change. He seems to have mellowed and become less egocentric. His intransigence has softened to allow him to admit that there are degrees of love; and his anti-feminist position has been modifed. We now find him acting as a kindly spiritual advisor to individual women who have undertaken the religious life, and even to an entire community of nuns at Hampole, amongst whom he died and was buried. The three Middle English epistles that he addressed to his female protégées – *Ego Dormio*, *The Commandment*, and *The Form of Living*[10] – written in the 1340s, are the product of the greater benevolence of his mature years.

Evidence exists to suggest that Rolle's spiritual guidance met a significant need; the morale of Yorkshire nunneries in the first half of the fourteenth century was grim indeed. There were 27 of them, a considerable number, but they tended to be small and poor. Their poverty was exacerbated by the frequent raids of both English and Scots as they pursued one another back and forth across the border. This disruption, which left their lands ravaged and often led to the nuns actually having to flee their convents, was obviously inimical to a life of quiet prayer and contemplation; we recall from Hildegard's experience how crucial was the dependable order of the convent to the growth and sustenance of her spiritual life: if such immediate questions as where the next meal is coming from become too pressing, it is difficult to concentrate entirely on matters of the spirit.

Poverty and disruption were not the only causes of the convents' problems; evidently the young women of Yorkshire were not of a naturally submissive temperament – 'they schooled their hot blood with difficulty to obedience and chastity'.[11] Instances of 'fleshly sin', of apostasy, of disobedience were rife, often leading to the expulsion of the guilty nuns. Between the years of 1280 and 1360, 19 of the 27 houses were investigated by the archbishop for these and similar offences. At the Benedictine house of Basedale, for example, the Prioress Joan de Percy was 'deprived for dilapidation of the goods of the house and perpetual and notorious misdeeds' – she responded not with contrition, but by leaving the convent, 'taking some of her partisans among the nuns with her'. In the same year,

---

[10] See R.S. Allen (*op. cit.*), pp. 133 ff. for modern English translations of these letters; all quotations in the following discussion are taken from this text; italics are mine. The Middle English texts are printed in H.E. Allen's *English Writings of Richard Rolle* (Oxford, 1931) and C. Horstmann's *Yorkshire Writers*, I (London, 1895).

[11] See 'The Moral State of the Yorkshire Nunneries in the First Half of the Fourteenth Century', in Eileen Power, *Medieval English Nunneries* (Cambridge, 1922), pp. 597–601. Power has combed convent registers and other contemporary Yorkshire records for her comprehensive data.

1307, another nun at the same convent 'confessed that she had on three separate occasions allowed herself to be deceived by the temptations of the flesh'. In 1315 at Kirklees, a Cistercian house, three of the nuns, Elizabeth de Hopton, Alice Raggid and Joan de Heton, were apparently 'wont to admit both secular and religious men into the private parts of the house and to hold many suspicious conversations with them'. At Keldholme, beginning in 1308, there was a ferocious battle between Emma of York and Joan of Pickering as to who would be elected to the position of prioress; numbers of nuns were expelled in the course of this struggle, some for disobedience and some for immorality. In 1300 a nun named Cecily, from the Benedictine house of St Clement's, was met at the gate one night by several men leading a saddled horse; according to the archbishop's account, she threw off her nun's habit, 'put on another robe and rode off with them to Darlington, where Gregory of Thornton was waiting for her and with him she lived for three years and more'.

These are but a few of the more extreme examples of misbehaviour amongst the Yorkshire nuns. Lesser offenses included an inappropriate interest in 'newfangled clothes', which were often bequeathed to the nuns and 'against which their bishops waged war in vain'. These 'cheerful secular garments' included colourful tunics, girdles and shoes in the latest style, and led to the regular admonition of the northern houses.[12] But none of this is to suggest that all of the houses were corrupt, or that there was no serious commitment amongst these women religious. That 27 houses existed in Yorkshire itself attests to a strong local attraction to conventual life. The fact that time and again, after being expelled, these women sought to be readmitted to their houses indicates that in the long term this was the vocation they truly wanted to pursue. The very attributes of passionate independence and sensuality have of course been seen to exist in Rolle himself, and their taming to have presented something of a challenge to him. However the result of his struggle was a greater spiritual maturity and a particular ability to speak to the more earnest of these sisters in language they would be able to understand.

The earliest of the three epistles, addressed to 'my dere syster in Christ', opens with the words 'Ego dormio et cor meum vigilat', 'I sleep but my heart is awake'. This quotation from the Song of Songs (V, 2) sets the stage for the rest of the letter. The contrast between physical dormancy and spiritual wakefulness is established: the world and its pleasures must be ignored if the life of the soul is to flourish. The ardour of the Canticle, too, is appropriate to Rolle's message; in the first paragraph he warns the young novice that love must never be halfhearted,

---

12 Ibid., pp. 329, 587. One wonders whether these bequests of clothing were made out of consideration for what must have been the punishing cold of the convents during the long northern winters.

that the lover must meditate constantly on this love, 'frequently even dreaming of it'. Rolle proceeds to develop the erotic metaphor of his opening quote by introducing himself as the go-between, who wants to bring the two lovers together: 'Because I love you I am courting you . . . not for myself, but for my lord! I want to . . . lead you to the bed of the one who has set you up and paid for you, Christ, son of the king of heaven'.

As he develops the appeal to his disciple, Rolle briefly makes use of a pair of hidden persuaders that recall the *Nun's Rule* – desire and fear. First, she has been chosen by Christ, the prince, because he 'desires the beauty of [her] soul'; she is the best beloved of the most desirable suitor. And the more ardent her love for God, the higher shall be her rank amongst the angels; Rolle explicitly states that his goal is 'to set [her] heart alight to crave the companionship of angels', preferably the seraphim – to which order 'are admitted those who want least from this world and, feeling most sweetness in God, have hearts which are most burning in love':

> It is the case that if you are resolute in burning love for God while you live here, there can be no doubt that your seat can be allotted for you very high up and most happily, close to God's presence among his holy angels.

On the other hand, the fate that awaits her should she choose to indulge in 'earthly entertainments' is presented in unequivocally repulsive terms:

> [The wealth of this world] withers into wretchedness,
> Robes and riches rot in the ditch, . . .
> Luxuries and love-tokens very soon will stink,
> Their wealth and their possessions will pull them down to death . . .

But Rolle is not interested in dwelling on the standard clichés. Amongst the conventional references to the dangers of wordly delights, he alludes to the difficulty his friend will have leaving behind her loved ones, and here he reveals the sympathy he has for her as an individual. He writes to her 'because I detect in you more integrity than in others'; she is at least as likely to mourn the severing of her emotional bonds as the loss of physical luxuries, so he takes particular care to reassure her that she will find 'merriment, joy and music in the song of angels . . . if you abandon everything which you derive human pleasure from and cease to be preoccupied by your friends and relations'.

The core of *Ego Dormio* describes three stages of love through which the soul may pass on her way towards the perfect love of God. We recall Rolle's earlier intransigence; he now does not require that the heights of mystical ecstasy be achieved – to labour earnestly at progressing from one stage to the next is a worthy act of love. Aside from a greater tolerance, we begin to see the working of a genuine charity in this letter: his motive in writing is not to make himself look holy, but step by step, gently and gradually, to help this young woman along the way to her spiritual goal. So the first step as he describes it is easily understood: she must follow the ten commandments, and keep herself from the seven deadly sins – which separate the soul from God; in other words, simple obedience to God's rules qualifies as a degree of love. It is not hard to see how useful a piece of advice this would be for someone who was lonely and uncertain about her spiritual direction – these are solid signposts to hold on to throughout the early periods of doubt, which if adhered to will lead automatically to the next degree of love. The second stage explicitly involves the renunciation of family – 'your father and mother and all your relations'. Again Rolle is specific as to the course of spiritual action that must be followed, though now a more active effort than simple obedience is required of the soul: she must follow Christ in poverty, being pure of heart, chaste of body, dedicated to the virtues of simplicity, endurance, patience, tolerance.

> In this way you will experience peace, interior and exterior, and come to spiritual life, which you will find sweeter than anything on earth.

The renunciation of the world, he assures her, will be followed by the desire for solitude, the better to feel the sweetness of spiritual love. Control of the mind is of major importance at this stage, to keep the thoughts from straying back to the outside world; thus Rolle provides a number of concentration techniques – earnest repetition of the Our Father and the Hail Mary, the fixing of the heart on Christ, and perhaps most important, meditation on the name of Jesus ('nothing pleases God so much'). While she is at the second stage, he warns her that she will be confronted with three enemies: the body, the world and the devil; but he is careful to spell out how each of these foes shall be defeated. The body can be overcome through chastity, and the world by a yearning love of Christ, a devotion to his name and a desire for heaven. The devil must be conquered by 'standing firmly against all his temptations in honest love and humility'.

At this point of his epistle, before he moves on to the third degree of love, Rolle includes a lyric entitled 'Meditation on Christ's Passion', which is to serve as an aid in contemplation:

> If you meditate on this every day, you will find great sweetness, which will draw your heart upwards . . . above all earthly things, so that the eye of your heart may gaze into heaven.

The poem is noteworthy for its emphasis on Christ's humanity, and on his suffering. The first four verses concentrate on the physical agonies accompanying the crucifixion: he was 'most sorely beat [by the scourges] till his own blood ran wet'; the thorns from his crown pricked deep into his head; 'nailed were his hands and nailed were his feet,/ And pierced was his side'; 'Naked his white breast and red his bloody side; 'nailed on to a tree . . . he who is our soul's good,/ [was] defiled just like a fool'. Rolle's aim here recalls *The Wooing of Our Lord*: to engage the sympathy of the nun for this beautiful, suffering hero – who might have saved himself, but out of love has chosen to take on this pain – and to inspire her with the desire to be united with him as completely and as soon as possible; significantly, he phrases the closing sequence in the voice of the woman herself, as she contemplates the passion:

> Jesus, receive my heart, and to your love me bring; . . .
> Save you, I yearn for nought; this world therefore I flee;
> You are what I have sought; your face I long to see . . .
> How long must I be here? When may I come you near . . .?

The third degree of love, called 'contemplative life', cannot be reached without grace; it is marked by delight, comfort, the 'wisdom and discernment to live according to God's will'. The heart must be absolutely given to Jesus at this stage, and when this occurs no earthly hardship can affect the soul. Although Rolle does not use visual imagery to communicate the experience of ecstasy, his description is reminiscent of Mechthild's: 'when you first reach it', he says, 'your spiritual eye is carried up into the glory of heaven and there is enlightened by grace and set ablaze by the fire of Christ's love'. In this stage Role's *calor, canor* and *dulcor* recur: the soul will feel the burning of love in her heart, she will be filled with love, joy, and sweetness.

> And then . . . your prayers turn into joyful song and your thoughts into sweet sounds. Then Jesus is all your desire, all your delight, all your joy, all your consolation, all your strength, so that your song will always be about him, and in him all your rest. Then may you indeed say, 'I sleep and my heart wakes'.

Rolle concludes *Ego Dormio* with a passionate love lyric, '*Cantus Amoris* – A Song of Love'. As in the 'Meditation on Christ's Passion', Rolle departs from his stance as benevolent counsellor. Instead, he speaks with the voice of the lover overcome with longing – and in so doing, provides a love song with which the nun can herself address her beloved.

> My song is in sighing, my life is in longing, . . .
> When will you come, Jesu my joy, . . .
> Now I grow pale and wan for the love of my dear man . . .
> Jesu, God yet human, . . .
> I sit and sing of love-longing which in my heart has bred . . .

Jesu, Jesu, Jesu, for you it is I yearn . . .
Jesu, my dear and my bounty, . . .
Jesu, my mirth and melody, . . . Jesu my help and my honey, my
health, my comforting,
. . . ever to my Love I cleave: may love my grief relieve,
And to my bliss me bring and grant all my yearning, Jesu, my love,
my sweeting.

With the provision of this final song Rolle performs a crucial act: he turns over to his friend the care of her own spiritual life. She has her letter – which he obviously expects her to be able to read and re-read herself – explaining the importance of renouncing the world and the stages that must be followed in order to achieve a perfect love of God. It describes the sweetness of the ecstasy that the soul will experience when united with God, and provides the lyrics she may use as 'scripts' in the course of her meditations. From this point she is on her own. The implication of trust is unmistakable: far from seeing her as a wanton daughter of Eve who will eagerly indulge in the first carnal opportunity that presents itself, Rolle is confident that his friend now has all the equipment she requires to proceed safely along her chosen path. While *Ego Dormio* may at first seem patronizing in its simplicity, it soon becomes clear that what Rolle wants is a tight, practical document that will enable the sister to be free, to be her own guide. He is confident of her ability to maintain this independent course; she does not need more detailed descriptions of what her spiritual experiences will be like, because she will be having them herself.

In Rolle's epistles we see, in addition to a new respect for women's spiritual potential, a coming together of other important political/philosophical strands. The anti-intellectualism that drove him from Oxford is evident in the lack of authoritative citations. Although Rolle himself has become theologically well-read – if largely self-taught – in the course of his life, he chooses not to bolster his arguments with scholastic references. Instead of relying on the power of intimidation that such authorities would have, he encourages the novice to trust in her own reactions, to trace her own progress through a process of self-examination, a turning inward – away from the world and its hierarchies, towards the pure life of the spirit. Further, he turns away from the traditional application of guilt as a cudgel – used, as we have seen in the *Nun's Rule*, to keep female religious in line; there are no references to Eve as the cause of all our woes, to the pretty faces that have dragged men down to the depths of bestiality, or to white hands that should be scraping the earth out of their own graves. He rejects these manipulative approaches because what he wants for his correspondent, as for himself, is freedom.

Ego Dormio was written for an unnamed nun, probably one who had just entered the religious life, at the convent of Yedingham, near to the

Daltons' manor on the border of the north and east ridings of Yorkshire. Doubtless this house would have been known to Rolle since the time of his stay with that family. The second and third of the English epistles – *The Commandment* and *The Form of Living* – were composed for Margaret Kirkby, a member of the Cistercian community at Hampole. Founded about 1170 for 14 or 15 sisters, Hampole stood in a pleasant vale on the banks of a stream, in the south part of the west riding, near to the city of Doncaster.[13] Rolle was unofficially attached to the house at Hampole during his last years; he is said to have occupied a cell in the woods nearby, but it is also possible that he had friends in the neighbourhood with whom he stayed; obviously he would not have been able to live within the confines of the convent. The region around Hampole had become a centre of sorts for solitary life, and this may have been what first attracted Rolle; it was also the case that the confessor at Hampole was a Franciscan friar, with whose commitment to apostolic poverty Rolle would have felt an important kinship.[14] The convent itself, in spite of its long tradition of poverty, offered frequent haven to nuns who had been forced by the raids of English or Scots soldiers to flee their own houses. And despite their contact with the outside world – they owned lands and produced wool – the nuns at Hampole seem to have been relatively free of the corruption that occurred in some of the other Yorkshire houses; there *were* two nuns found guilty of 'unchastity' – but only two, and those a generation apart, in 1324 and 1358. Other lapses included such minor misdemeanours as eating in the guest house, or in private rooms; or of having children over five as visitors within the convent – not terribly pernicious.

The relationship between Margaret and Richard, her spiritual advisor, was a very special one, recalling that of two twelfth-century English solitaries – Roger, a monk of St Alban's, and Christina of Markyate. As Christina was one of the first known female recluses in England, her story bears repeating. Roger had established his hermitage by the side of a road in Bedfordshire, on a spot to which he was said to have been led by a company of angels, and was renowned as a hermit. Though vowed to virginity, Christina – whose original name was Theodora – was forced into marriage; left with no choice, she fled with the help of a friend, 'Edwine an Ermite', who brought her to Roger's dwelling. Her husband Burfred was thus convinced of her unalterable commitment to the

---

[13] See Comper (*op. cit.*), p. 187. It is not altogether certain that *The Commandment* was composed for Margaret, but at its conclusion MS Dd. 5.64 reads *'Explicit tractatus Ricardi Hampole scriptus cuidam sorori Hampole'* – that is, it was written for a sister of Hampole, and as Rolle was her particular advisor, this is most likely to have been Margaret.

[14] See H.E. Allen (*op. cit.*), pp. 511 ff.

An anchoress is enclosed, perhaps by a bishop; henceforth she will be considered as one dead to the world, and will remain in her cell, dedicated to a life of prayer and meditation. Initial letter from Office of fourteenth-century Pontifical. British Library Landsdowne MS 451, fol. 76v.; by permission of the British Library.

religious life, and coming to the hermitage along with the priest who had married them, released her from the marriage. She remained with Roger as his devoted disciple until his death, often subjecting herself to terrible physical stress – for her first four years as a recluse she lived in a tiny corner of Roger's hut, in which she was closed up by a heavy wooden panel, and from which she was released only once a day; these quarters must have been considerably smaller in dimension than a closet, for we are told that she had to huddle on the stone floor, and that her corner was so narrow there was no room for her to wear extra clothing in winter. Upon Roger's death in 1122, Christina became 'heir' to his hermitage, and was widely regarded as a prophet, being particulatly gifted in her ability to read the thoughts of others and see what was taking place at a distance. It is a testament to the respect in which she was held that a pair of sandals 'exquisitely embroidered by Christina' was proudly presented by her abbot to the English pope, Aidan IV, in the hopes of winning his favour.[15]

In the two centuries following Christina's life the institution of female recluses, specifically ones who were strictly enclosed, became firmly established. These enclosed women – whose ranks Margaret Kirkby eventually joined – came to be known as anchoresses, from the Latin (and originally Greek) word *anchoreta* (=one who has withdrawn). Their cells were often attached to churches, and might have two windows, one, hung with a black curtain, through which they could communicate with the outer world, one from which the altar and divine service were visible. Aspirants to the life of anchoress were closely examined to ensure that their motivation and fortitude were sufficient to survive this particularly arduous life, and permission of the bishop was required before it could be undertaken. The service of enclosure was supremely solemn, as it was essentially the counterpart of the mass for the dead. That is, the anchoress was henceforth to be considered as one dead to the world: the words of the service referred to her cell as a grave; the last rites were administered; earth was 'cast upon [her] and she was prayed over as a corpse'.[16]

There was some variety as to the extremes of asceticism in the lives of these women. As they were enclosed, they could not provide for themselves, and thus had to rely on others for their food. Some seem to have lived quite comfortable, if austere lives; some even had maidservants – as for example the sisters for whom the *Nun's Rule* was originally composed. As was the case with *Ego Dormio*, the extremes of penance were discouraged, since physical discomfort tended to distract the anchoress from her spiritual pursuits. There was no regulation dress for these solitaries, though a pilch made of skins was recommended for winter, and a black gown and mantle for summer. Their diets tended to be vegetarian,

---

[15] See Clay (*op. cit.*), pp. 21 ff., 119, 150.
[16] See Shepherd (*op. cit.*), pp. xxxiv–xxxv and Clay (*op. cit.*), pp. 93 ff.

consisting of soups made of beans or peas, puddings flavoured with butter or herbs, and occasionally fish. But they were to have no belongings: 'to forsake all was the initial step of the hermit's career'.[17]

Aside from the fact that she was a nun, and eventually became an anchoress, the information about Margaret Kirkby is scant. Evidently Rolle, as her advisor, wrote his third epistle, *The Form of Living*, to prepare her, and for her to take with her, when she was enclosed in 1348. Earlier he had written other pieces for her – *The Commandment*, about 1343, and another vernacular piece, *The English Psalter*, as early as 1338. Armed with the much longer *Form of Living*, she may have decided to leave *The Commandment* behind for the benefit of her sisters at Hampole when she moved to her cell. It is possible that Margaret came from a family named LeBoteler, who lived at Skelbroke, a mile and a half north of Hampole, in the parish of South Kirkby. These LeBotelers founded a chantry in the Skelbroke chapel, 'where arms bearing covered cups, as was common with "Botelers", are still to be seen over the porch'.[18] We know that she lived until the turn of the century, between 1401 and 1405, and that Richard would probably not have made her acquaintance until she entered the convent at Hampole. If we assume that the *English Psalter* was written for her in her first year as a nun, and that she was then 16 – the usual age of profession – this would put her birth date back to 1322, and mean that she lived to be at least 79, if not into her 80s. Since the year of her enclosure as an anchoress was 1348, she would have been 26 at the time; thus she would have belonged to the Hampole community for ten years before assuming the solitary life. As a recluse, her first cell was attached to the chapel at East Layton – 'capelle de Estelaton' – which was twelve miles from Rolle's cell. Thus, as her 'sponsor', he would still have been able to visit her. Rolle's proximity may explain her choice of the East Layton chapel, which was evidently unsatisfactory in other ways: from her cell she could neither see the altar nor hear the service, and in 1356 she asked and was granted permission to move to another church, at Ainderby.

In the *Office* there is a dramatic account of one of Rolle's visits to Margaret, which provides us with the only personal information we have about her. In April of 1349, that is five months after her enclosure, she was overcome by a 'grave attack of illness', so that 'for thirteen days continuously she was utterly deprived of the power of speech'. Moreover, this

---

[17] Clay (*op. cit.*), p. 104.
[18] See H.E. Allen (*op. cit.*), p. 509, and pp. 502 ff. for further discussion about Margaret. The decree issued by the abbott of Eggleston on her enclosure in December 1348 makes specific reference to 'Margaretam la Boteler sororem domus monialium de Hampole'. The dates of Margaret's life are necessarily uncertain; I have based my reconstruction on the evidence supplied by H.E. Allen.

illness caused her such pain that she was unable to rest in any position. Richard was sent for, 'and when he came to the recluse he found her unable to speak and troubled with very grievous pains'. He stayed with her, sitting by the window of her cell as they attempted to share a meal, at the end of which Margaret was oppressed with sleep, and she rested for a time, leaning gently upon his shoulder. Suddenly she was seized with convulsions so violent that she seemed about to break the window, in the midst of which she regained the power of speech, and burst forth with 'Gloria tibi domini', to which Richard added, 'Qui natus est de virgine'. This pattern again repeated itself, with the second round of convulsions so terrible that Richard attempted to hold her, 'lest she should rend herself or strive in any way to injure the house'. Slipping from his grasp, she fell to the floor and awoke, relieved of the convulsions and with her speech restored. He promised her at this time that she should never again be so afflicted as long as he lived. The next, and last, time her illness recurred, she sent a messenger to inquire after him, 'for she doubted not that he had passed from this world'; the messenger returned with the news that, indeed, 'the aforesaid illness had returned to the recluse shortly after the hour of Richard's departure'.[19]

All we know about Margaret beyond this is that she asked once more for permission to move her cell, around 1380; this time she returned to her original house, Hampole, as a recluse, and it has been suggested that she may even have taken up occupancy in Richard's old cell – he had by then been dead for 30 years. Though Rolle had for some time been a local favourite, especially amongst the poor, his cult began to flourish in earnest soon after Margaret's return. Numbers of miraculous events occurred which were taken to be evidence of his sanctity, and which are recorded in the *Office*: Roger, a householder, is preserved from being crushed by falling rock; Joan, possessed by cruel demons, is freed by the saint's intervention; the saint appears to the bedridden Thomas Bell, and heals him by a touch; a drowned boy is restored to life after an offering is made at the saint's tomb; many others – deaf, blind, dumb – are cured of their afflictions by the intervention of the saint.

Considering the extreme poverty of the convent at Hampole – in 1353 it was actually in a state of collapse and was threatened with dispersion[20] – the growth of Rolle's cult was opportune to say the least, and led to new prosperity for the house. Despite the fact that he was not canonized, his popularity continued unabated until the dissolution of Hampole in 1539. A count of surviving manuscripts provides eloquent testimony: *The Form of Living*, perhaps first recopied by Margaret herself in her cell, survives in 38 manuscripts; 42 copies of the *Incendium Amoris* remain, while the Latin

---

[19] The *Office*, reprinted in Comper (*op. cit.*), pp. 307–8.
[20] H.E. Allen (*op. cit.*), p. 515.

and English versions of his *Emendatio Vitae* together total an astonishing 109.[21]

So in all probability one of the most important aspects of Margaret's life was her relationship with her mentor – not only between the ages of 16, when she met him, and 27, when she was separated from him by death, but long after, when at 58 she returned to Hampole and helped encourage the growth of his cult, and up to her death, still an anchoress, at 79. Perhaps by looking at the particular points that Rolle sought to pass on to his disciple, we can find out more about her. One of the more notable features of *The Commandment* is that he now gives names to the three stages of love: insuperable, because it cannot be overcome; inseparable, because the 'thoughts and inclinations' cannot be separated from Jesus; and singular, because all delight is now in Jesus. Already we can infer that he has a good opinion of her intelligence, as he both names and cogently defines the degrees. As in *Ego Dormio*, Rolle presents Jesus as the best lover – that is, the most handsome, rich and intelligent – but now he passes over this quickly; the emphasis is rather on encouraging the development of self-sufficiency. Reliance on earthly friends is discouraged – the angels and saints will stand her in better stead – as is flippant chatter between fellow nuns. The approach suggests that Richard has great confidence in Margaret's independence, and considers neither the thought of lost lovers or friends to be a serious trial for her.

Silence, he goes on to point out, is an essential prelude to concentration, which in turn is necessary if her soul is to approach the joy of union. Yet this silence does not suggest passivity – indolence and lukewarmness are antithetical to spiritual growth; beneath the quiet exterior an effort to fulfill God's will must always be in progress. The mind's activity must be regulated through prayer (which 'consists in looking and asking day and night for the love of Jesus Christ') and meditation; the distractions of the world will be avoided by this ongoing inner busyness:

> look for him inwardly, in the faith, hope and love of holy church, tossing out all sin and abhorring it with all your heart . . .

Richard does not neglect the role of grace, of course; but he does describe the love of the soul for God as an intensely active process, involving not so much the surrender as the energetic cooperation of the will, the voluntary direction of thought towards God. His confidence in Margaret's ability to regulate her own mind, and inwardly to pursue the love of God, looks forward to his confidence in her ability to flourish in the enclosed life.

The Commandment provides Margaret with specific instructions to

---

21 Pantin (*op. cit.*), p. 245.

enable her to accomplish her goals; as in *Ego Dormio*, Rolle assumes the sister will be reading the text herself, and will largely be in charge of her own growth. 'Decorate your soul prettily', he urges, with the virtues of chastity, humility, courtesy and submissiveness ;

> construct inside it a stronghold of love for the Son of God and make your will eager to receive him . . . Wash your thoughts clean with tears of love and burning longing . . .

She should focus on the vision of Christ's beauty:

> In everything you do, concentrate . . . on arriving at the vision of his beauty, and place all your resolve on this . . . While we are living here we should constantly be yearning for that vision with our whole heart . . .

Meditation on Christ's passion and wounds will bring about compassion; and 'where tears well up there will be kindled the fire of the Holy Spirit', which will purify the heart and fill it with love. Richard reassures Margaret with the reminder that love acts to purge the soul – its fire burns away the rust of sin, 'as refined gold is tried in a furnace' – and thus there is no need to dwell on guilt or self-loathing: purity follows love naturally, and the purer the heart, the more joy Christ places in it.

Richard does not try to inspire fear in his disciple, but points out that if separation from the world seems too hard, she should turn her thoughts to the torment of those who have lost eternal joy through brief indulgence in physical pleasure. The name of Jesus is a far more efficacious means of perfecting love in this life, and being taken into the angelic orders after death, 'to behold in unending joy him whom [she has] loved'.[22]

The Form of Living covers many of the same themes as *The Command-ment*, though in a much expanded form; presumably Rolle has gone into greater detail because Margaret will henceforth be enclosed, and as a solitary will have all the more need to be able to govern her own spiritual growth and fend off the various attendant dangers. The epistle divides itself into two halves, chapters 1–6 and 7–12,[23] with the first part concentrating on renunciation of the world. As we know, this is a frequent topic for Rolle, but in *The Form* he gives it a particular focus: the importance of rejecting earthly praise in favour of God's approbation. A desire to impress those around you, or an attachment to the opinion of others, can lead to a number of grave errors: pride in intellectual superiority, pride in

---

[22] See *The Commandment*, in R.S. Allen (*op. cit.*), pp. 143–151.

[23] See the *Form of Living*, in R.S. Allen (*op. cit.*), pp. 153–183. Chapter 11 was probably not in Rolle's original version, and may have been an earlier composition that was later added to *The Form*.

self-denial and good deeds, pleasure at praise, resentment at criticism. These faults are especially dangerous because there is no realization of wrong being done, and any of them can lead to hypocrisy, the cultivation of a false exterior of piety which cloaks an inner malevolence: if anything, he warns Margaret, you should 'try to be better than you appear'. Further, Rolle points out that the desire to impress others can lead to an abuse of the ascetic ideal. It hardly needs repeating that she should not overeat or pamper her flesh; but to err in the opposite direction is equally dangerous:

> Many who were ardent at the beginning...have harmed themselves by excessive self-denial and made themselves so weak that they are not able to love God as they should.

Lukewarmness is as much an obstacle to the love of God as is the active indulgence of physical desire.

What Richard is alerting Margaret to is the kind of sin by which she is likely to be threatened in her solitary hours: pride in seeming to be 'holier' than others; spiritual torpor – which is a kind of sloth – as the result of physical exhaustion. To warn her thus is not to suggest that she is weak or prone to vice, but that anyone who undertakes the solitary life should occasionally expect to be beset by these difficulties.

Along with the spiritual perils that may await the solitary, Rolle warns Margaret of the danger of aggressive temptation by the devil – who is particularly interested in catching those who have turned to God; thus he devises

> a thousand tricks which he uses to discover in what way he can deceive them . . . He will trick lots of them so stealthily that many a time they are not aware of the cage he's trapped them in.

> Sometimes, as well, the Devil tempts men and women who are solitary and alone in a way which is ingenious and sly. He transforms himself into the appearance of an angel of light,

and claims that he has come to conduct the soul to heaven. He may try to stir up pride, to deceive 'through vainglory, . . . or with excessive desire and pleasure for food . . . [or] by overdoing abstinence from food' – and here he will be trying to exploit what he knows to be an area of susceptibility. Thus the anchoress must be constantly alert to the possibility of diabolically inspired temptation, and must adhere to 'the good middle way', avoiding excess.

But Rolle does not leave Margaret alone with the threat of the devil's trickery; he explains that God permits the temptation of 'good men for their benefit, so that they can be crowned in a more exalted manner'.

126

Temptation does not mean that God has forsaken her, but that greater rewards are in store: and she must never forget the reassuring fact that the devil is in God's power, that 'he can do no more than God gives him permission to do'. Jesus 'rescues [his lovers] from the appetites of flesh and blood'; and when

> you have abandoned the comforts and pleasures of this world, and devoted yourself to the solitary life for the love of God, . . . the consolation of Jesus Christ . . ., with the fire of the Holy Spirit . . ., shall be in you and with you, leading you and instructing you.

Rolle concludes the first half of *The Form* with a complex discussion on sin, on how to achieve and maintain purity, and on how the soul is to bring her will into conformity with God's.[24] Richard's discussion is elaborately structured, again reflecting his confidence in his disciple's intelligence. Each of the four major sections of his discussion is divided into three sub-units: for example, in his treatment of sin he describes the sins (1) of the inner feelings (2) of speech (3) of action. Each of these headings is followed by a long paragraph which provides an exhaustive list of examples; he mentions over fifty specific sins of the inner feelings – harmful thoughts, consent to sin, desire for harm, and evil disposition, to name but a few. Rolle's treatment of the other three subjects – how to achieve, and maintain purity, how to subordinate the will to God's – is similarly comprehensive. His thoroughness is a measure of his determination that Margaret at the very least be able to remain secure, on her own, in the first degree of love – a love that is 'robust in the face of all temptations, and constant, whether you are in easy circumstances or in anxiety'. The object then, as he says, is to 'love your Jesus Christ more than you have been doing', and to work towards the second degree, inseparable love,

> when all your heart and your thought and your strength are so wholly, so entirely and so perfectly fastened, fixed and confirmed in Jesus Christ that your thought never slips away from him . . . When you are not able to forget him at any time, whatever you do or say . . .

Again, the tools are supplied which will allow the anchoress independence, and allow her to progress from one stage of love to the next.

The second part of *The Form of Living* presents to Margaret the 'particular details of the love of Jesus Christ and of the life of contemplation', and once more Richard can be seen to gear his approach to the special

---

[24] This chapter seems to be an elaboration on *Ego Dormio's* discussion of the first stage of love, in which adherence to the ten commandments and avoidance of the seven deadly sins are urged.

situation of the solitary. He emphasizes that there is a hierarchy of reward – the most ardent lovers of Christ 'are destined for the highest state of advancement in heaven'. This information may act as a positive goad should her determination flag, as proof against lukewarmness. Within this life, the third degree, singular love, is 'the highest and most wonderful to attain':

> Other delight and other joy [the heart] does not desire, for in this degree the sweetness of [Jesus Christ] is so envigorating and so enduring, his love so buring and cheering that he or she who is in this degree can as easily feel the fire of love burning in their soul as you can feel your finger burn if you put it in the fire.

In this degree the soul will experience, in addition to *calor*, the song and sweetness – *canor* and *dulcor* – that Rolle described as central to his own earliest mystical experiences. Thus he encourages his disciple with the assurance that singular love is as accessible to her as it has been to him.

Emphatically, Richard comes back to the value of independent judgement for the solitary; as he remarks, no outside observer is capable of ascertaining another's spiritual state:

> *No act which I perform externally is proof that I love God.*

Thus he reaffirms the importance of rejecting the world's opinion, but now it becomes clear how fundamentally misdirected is the effort to impress others through a pious exterior:

> *no one except God knows whether my heart is loving my God, so no one knows enough to inform me if I love God.*

Margaret must, essentially, become her own spiritual director. What is in her heart is all that matters, and only she can have knowledge of this:

> *Accordingly, love really is in the motivation not in the action.*

This simple sentence is a powerful reflection of the trust he places in her as she withdraws from the world, and of his fervent belief in the superiority of the arduous life she has so courageously undertaken. Once more in his final chapter Richard reiterates this conviction:

> Contemplative life is largely interior and for that reason is more enduring and secure, more delightful, more lovely, more rewarding, because it rejoices in God's love, and relishes the life which lasts forever . . .

But the real climax of *The Form of Living* is to be found in the tenth chapter, where Rolle asks, 'What is love?', and answers with what must surely be one of the most passionate and lyrical passages in the English language:

> Love is an ardent yearning for God, with a wonderful delight and security ... Love is one life, coupling together the one loving and the one beloved ... Love is the beauty of all virtues ..., a device through which God loves us and we God and each of us one another. Love is the desire of the heart, ... a yearning between two people, ... a stirring of the soul to love God for himself and all other things for God ... Truth may exist without love, but it cannot be of any use without it. Love is the perfection of scholarship, the strength of prophecy, the fruit of truth, the spiritual strength of the sacraments, the confirming of intellect and knowledge, the wealth of the poor, the life of the dying.

In Rolle's own life we have seen the transforming power of this love; the erratic, arrogant misogynist has grown into a loyal friend who will rush to the cell of his afflicted disciple and stay by her as long as her anguish endures; who will patiently spell out in his epistles not only the stages of love, but the technical means of achieving them; and will leave her with the greatest gift of all – self-reliance, freedom from dependence on a flawed world, the ability to look within herself, understand the state of her own soul, and move confidently towards a state of singular love with her God.

As for Margaret, we can surely conclude that she was strong, courageous, intelligent, purposeful – deserving of the great esteem in which she was held by her dear friend and advisor. Her life as a contemplative, and her pursuit of the three degrees of love, must have brought her fulfillment, as she remained enclosed for over 50 years, until her death. And we can also infer that the bond of love between Margaret and Richard was one of mutual benefit: as she was helped along her spiritual path, so was he able to attain a degree of tenderness and generosity that on his own might not have been possible. For him, to love God perfectly was not so difficult as to love another soul well; in this respect, perhaps Margaret was the leader, and Richard the disciple.

Julian of Norwich

I

Julian, an anchoress at Norwich, is surely the most glorious individual representative of the solitary life in medieval England. Paradoxically, because she was so thoroughly committed to her solitude, we know very little of real interest about her, though it is possible to get a faint outline of her life by stringing together a few facts and a few conjectures. We do know that she was born in 1343, and almost certainly lived until after 1416, when she would have been 73; in her thirty-first year, 1373, she experienced a series of sixteen revelations which form the basis of her writings. Probably she was still living at home with her mother when she had her visions: Julian explicitly refers to her being at her bedside during her illness. After receiving the revelations Julian may have joined a religious order, but there is no solid evidence to confirm this supposition. Eventually she did become an anchoress, but she could have done so as a pious laywoman.

Julian refers to herself as 'unlettered', but by this she probably meant that she did not know much Latin; her writing suggests that she was well-read, if not formally educated. There was a community of Benedictine nuns nearby at Carrow, with which she may have been informally connected; they ran a school for young girls, and it is possible that Julian was a student there as a child. Her writing indicates that as an adult she was familiar not only with the scriptures, but also a range of contemporary spiritual texts – including, perhaps, the Nun's Rule and Rolle's epistles – some of which she could have borrowed from the library of an Augustinian house across the road from her anchorhold. She possessed an easy familiarity with a range of rhetorical 'colours' with which she enhances her style. Norwich – at this time a wealthy city with a population second only to London – had a thriving intellectual atmosphere which could in itself have encouraged Julian in her desire to pursue her own studies.[1]

---

[1] See F. Reynolds, 'Some Literary Influences in the Revelations of Julian of Norwich', *Leeds Studies in English and Kindred Languages* 7 (1952), pp. 18–28, and Norman Tanner,

That she was well known and respected during her lifetime is indicated by the fact that she is cited in a number of late fourteenth and early fifteenth-century wills. Unfortunately, this sort of biographical material is largely conjectural. We do not even know for certain what her name first was, since 'Julian' would likely have been the name she assumed when she entered the anchorhold at St Julian's church.

One certainty is that as an anchoress she was visited by those in search of spiritual advice and consolation. Her most celebrated visitor was Margery Kempe, who has fortunately left us an account of a visit with Julian by which she was much consoled; through Julian's words we can glimpse her extraordinary tact and sensitivity. Margery was notorious for her hysterical fits of violent weeping – hardly Julian's style – but still she was anxious to reassure her visitor on the question of these cryings. 'St Jerome', the anchoress pointed out, 'says tears torment the devil more than do the pains of hell'; and 'St Paul says that the Holy Ghost makes us seek and pray with mourning and weeping so plenteous that the tears may not be numbered'. To console Margery for the contempt in which she was often held, Julian reminded her that 'the more spite, shame and reproof you suffer in this world, the greater is your merit in the eyes of God'.[2]

Julian has long been a sentimental favourite of English Christians; the 1901 translation of the *Revelations of Divine Love* went into its fourteenth printing in 1952, and since then several other translations from the Middle English have appeared.[3] Recently the theological content of her work has come to be taken more seriously, and has been the focus of a number of excellent studies. Although she has never been canonized, a 'Julian of Norwich' day has been entered into the Church of England calendar, and she is now often the main attraction at conferences on women's mystical writing. All of this attention would certainly have embarassed Julian; she saw herself as undistinguished, unworthy – even a

'Popular Religion in Norwich with Special Reference to the Evidence of Wills, 1370–1532', PhD. dissertation (Oxford, 1973); also *A Book of Showings to the Anchoress Julian of Norwich*, introduction, ed. E. Colledge and J. Walsh (Toronto, 1978).

2 *The Book of Margery Kempe*, ed. S.B. Meech and H.E. Allen, EETS OS 212 (London, 1961), pp. 42–3; the translation is mine.

3 By Julian's time the tradition of composing spiritual treatises in the vernacular was widespread. The modern translations of her works include *Revelations of Divine Love*, trans. Grace Warrack (London, 1901); *Comfortable Words for Christ's Lovers*, trans. Dundas Harford (London, 1911); *Revelations of Divine Love Shewed to a Devout Ankress by Name Julian of Norwich*, trans. Roger Hudleston (London, 1927); *A Shewing of God's Love: The Shorter Version of Sixteen Revelations by Julian of Norwich*, trans. Frances Reynolds (London, 1958); *The Revelations of Divine Love*, trans. James Walsh (London, 1961); *Revelations of Divine Love*, trans. Clifton Wolters (Harmonsworth, 1966); *Revelations of Divine Love*, trans. M.L. delMaestro (New York, 1977), Classics of Western Sprituality Series.

'wretched creature', who had nonetheless been blessed with a sequence of visions revealing God's love for humanity. She felt keenly her responsibility to share these experiences, but insisted that they were not a particular sign of God's favour towards her. In her words, the visions are 'general and in no way special', 'common and general as we are all one': 'If I look at myself singularly, as an individual, I am as nought', she asserts, 'but in general I am in oneness of charity with all my fellow Christians'.

Julian composed two versions of the *Revelations*, one in 1373 and one some twenty years after; the later version is several times longer, and includes the fruits of her meditations upon the experiences recorded in the earlier text.[4] It seems possible that Julian would have undertaken the 'revision' in her cell, after becoming an anchoress; this might in turn suggest that she did not have a scribe, but, like Mechthild, was doing the writing herself. Considering her reputation within her lifetime, it is perhaps odd that so few of her manuscripts have survived. Of the early, short text there is but one, from the fifteenth-century, evidently quite close to the original. Of the later version there are only three complete manuscripts, all post-Reformation; the first printed text was published in 1670.[5]

The short text is the more immediate and personal of the two accounts; in its brevity it is also clearer, and for these reasons it is a good place to begin a study of Julian. Her goal in writing is to share her revelations, and thus to help her fellow-Christians in their spiritual progress; generally her humility is such that she would not consider herself an object worthy of attention, but – fortunately for us – some information is necessary to clarify the context of her visions. And so she is obliged to begin with a few key personal details. These are extraordinary in their beauty and the clear intensity of their telling. Her fine intelligence, her honesty, her utter devotion to her Lord, are all evident in these opening passages.

Julian first tells us that earlier in her life, some years before she experienced her visions, she had asked God for three gifts, or graces: the first was for a better understanding of Christ's passion; the second was for a

---

[4] See Appendix for the sixteen revelations as listed at the start of Julian's 'second edition'. The Middle English version of the long text has been edited by Sister Anna Maria Reynolds (*Sixteen Revelations of Divine Love*, Doctoral thesis, Leeds University, 1956), by Edmund Colledge and James Walsh (*A Book of Showings, op. cit.*), and by Marion Glasscoe (*Julian of Norwich: A Revelation of Divine Love*, Exeter, 1976); and the shorter version by Frances Beer (*Julian of Norwich's Revelations of Divine Love*, Heidelberg, 1978). The few known facts of Julian's life, and the more numerous conjectures, can be found in the Introductions of both translations and Middle English editions.

[5] The absence of MSS may indicate that Julian was not attached to any particular house or order; if she had been, the recopying of her work would probably have been a prime undertaking for her sisters.

bodily sickness; and the third was to have three wounds. For the first grace,

> I wished I had been with Mary Magdalene[6] and the others who were Christ's lovers, that I might have actually seen the passion of our Lord, which he suffered for me; and that I might have suffered with him as did the others who loved him . . . I desired a bodily sight wherein I might have more knowledge of our Lord and Saviour's physical pain, and of the compassion of our Lady, . . . for I wished, as a result of this shewing, to have a truer understanding of the passion of Christ. (I)[7]

The second wish was for a physical illness so severe that it would bring her to the point of death:

> In this sickness I desired to have all of the physical and spiritual pains that I would have if I were to die, all the fears and trials brought about by fiends . . . I hoped these might be a help to me when I did die, for I wished to be soon with my God. (I)

Julian's third wish resulted from hearing an account of the martyrdom of St Cecila – who received three wounds in the neck, from which, after lingering several days, she eventually died:

> Inspired by this, I conceived a mighty desire and prayed that our Lord would grant me three wounds in my lifetime, . . . the wound of contrition, the wound of compassion, and the wound of willing longing for God. (I)

When Julian was part way through her thirty-first year – 'when I was thirty and a half winters old' – her second wish was granted. She was struck down by a terrible illness in which she lay three days and three nights, and from which no one expected her to recover. On the fourth night the last rites were administered, in anticipation of her death. She hardly expected that she would last until day, but lingered on another, and another day, until the seventh night, when those about her thought she must surely die; and so did she. Yet she was not ready:

---

6 Mary Magdalene, as the representative of the contemplative life, was commonly considered to be the greatest of Christ's lovers. Her presence at the crucifixion is attested by Matthew (XXVII, 56), Mark (XV, 40) and John (XIX, 25); see also Luke (VII, 47 and X, 42).

7 The translations from the short text, in which I have stayed as close to Julian's original as possible, are mine, based on British Library Additional MS 37790; the roman numerals refer to the chapter divisions within the manuscript; where italics occur, they are mine.

In this I was right sorry, not because there was anything on earth I wanted to live for, nor because I was afraid, . . . but because I wanted to live so that I might come to love God better, . . . and have the greater knowing and loving of God in the bliss of heaven. (II)

She understood, and accepted 'with all the will of my heart', that she was to die; and by daybreak her body was dead 'from the midst downwards'. Then was she anxious to be set upright, and asked those about her to prop her up, so that she might have 'the more freedom of my heart to be at God's will, thinking of him while my life would last'. The parson was sent for, 'to be at my ending'; he came, with a child, and bringing a cross: 'By then I had set my eyes and might not speak'. Nonetheless, he bid her behold the cross 'in reverence of him that died for thee and me.'

Julian confides to us that she thought she was doing quite well, since she was looking upwards towards heaven 'where I trusted for to come', but nonetheless she assented to the parson's request and 'set my eyes in the face of the crucifix'. Again death seemed imminent:

After this my sight began to fail, and it was all dark about me in the chamber, as murky as if it had been night – except in the image of the cross, where a common light remained, though I knew not how. Everything but the cross was as ugly to me as if it had been occupied with fiends. (II)

The upper part of her body began to die; her hands dropped down, and her head fell to one side. The only pain she felt was a shortness of breath and a failing of life, and she imagined that she was finally at the point of death. But suddenly all her pain was gone; 'I was as whole . . . as ever I was before or after'; she recalled her wish for the second wound – compassion – and the first revelation began.

This first shewing – and a number of others – involves a kind of 're-enactment' of the crucifixion, in which the ordeal experienced by Christ is presented in minute detail. The effect of the re-enactment, however, is not in the least morbid, but instead (like the actual crucifixion) serves as irrefutable evidence of the infinite love God has for all those who love him: because of the greatness of his love, Christ's suffering as man was a great as it could have been – in other words, if he could have suffered more for us, he would have – and so it must be shown. The visions' purpose is not to inspire fear or guilt, but rather reassurance; they are described as 'comforting and greatly stirring words for all those who desire to be God's lovers'. The journey to oneness with God is bound to be fraught with frightening experiences – personal doubt, the trials inflicted by a jealous devil; but the message of the revelations is that we are always protected and kept secure by the absolute power of divine love.

And this is a love that is wholly egalitarian: in Julian's understanding there is no hierarchy.[8]

Thus it becomes clear that in the course of the revelations all of Julian's three requests are granted. She is given a greater understanding of the passion; she experiences the physical illness that brings her to the point of death; and she receives the three wounds – of contrition, compassion, and longing for God. Through her own bodily pain and spiritual wounds, achieved with grace through contemplation of the crucifix, she is brought to an identification with the suffering Christ that unites her with him:

> Here I saw a great oneness betwixt Christ and us, for when he was in pain, we were in pain. (X)

Through this identification the effects of sin are effaced, and the divine likeness regained.

II

The first shewing is of Christ's crowning with the garland of thorns, and in it the crucifix that has been set before the dying Julian seems literally to come to life:[1]

> Suddenly I saw the red blood trickle down from under the garland, all hot, fresh, and plentiful, as lifelike it seemed to me as it was when that garland of thorns was thrust on his blessed head . . . (III)

But in addition to this dramatic bodily sight, her vision includes a

---

8 In the sixth revelation Julian describes the three graces that 'every soul shall have in heaven who willingly has served God in any degree here on earth' – though God is particularly grateful to those who devote their youth to him. In her later revision Julian adds, 'I saw that if a man or woman was genuinely turned to God for however long or short a time, even if it were for a single day of service, . . . he should experience all three degrees of delight' (Wolters, *op. cit.*, pp. 85–6); cf. St Matthew's parable of the workers in the vineyard (XX, 1–16), re-told in the fourteenth-century *Pearl*, vv. 42–8.

1 Catherine Jones points out that the city of Norwich was the 'seat of the East Anglian school of art, which was at its height during this period', and that Julian may partially owe her pictorial ability to its influence (in Wilson, *op. cit.*, p. 272). Julian seems to lend strength to this conjecture by her own reference: 'I believed steadfastly in all the pains of Christ as they were shown and taught by holy church, and also the paintings of crucifixes that are made according to holy church's teaching' (I). See also Margaret Rickert, *Painting in Britain in the Middle Ages* (London, 1954).

number of profound spiritual truths that form the basis for the subsequent fifteen revelations. She realizes immediately that this shewing has been given to her directly by God, without intermediary, and she is filled with wonder that he would be so intimate[2] with her, a 'sinful creature living in this wretched flesh'. She sees that she has been given the shewing as a comfort, to help her through the difficult time that lies ahead: for before her ordeal is over she will be assailed by the devil, trying to undermine her faith when she is at her most vulnerable.

> I saw that [this sight of his blessed passion] was strength enough for me, yea, and for all living creatures, who shall be safe from all the fiends of hell and from all spiritual enemies. (III)

It is an essential part of her understanding that this temptation will be permitted by God, who will protect her throughout the ordeal. Here, in this echo of Rolle, lies a crucial element of Julian's overall message: any power that the devil seems to have is in reality allowed by God; if we suffer it is because God – not the devil – wills us to suffer, and thereby to come closer to him.

Within the first vision the spiritual, or ghostly, revelations continue, and in them we get the first instances of Julian's astonishing capacity to use and interpret imagery.[3] In a sight of God's matchless love Julian sees that he is all things that are good and comforting,

> he is our clothing, for love wraps us and winds us, embraces and encloses us, hangs about us for tender love, that he may never leave us. (IV)

And to help in her understanding of love, at once so vast and tender,

> he shewed me a little thing the size of a hazel nut lying in the palm of my hand, . . . as round as any ball. I looked at it and thought, 'What may this be?' (IV)

She is answered that it represents the creation – all that is made – and that the only reason, in its littleness, it endures is because God cares for it:

> 'It lasts, and ever shall, because God loves it, and so through the love of God, does every thing have its existence.' (IV)

---

2 Julian's word is 'homely', by which she means friendly, familiar, comfortable, personal, at home with – as well as intimate. All of these connotations are important in understanding the special nature of her relationship with her God. Unfortunately this sense of 'homely' been lost to us, and there is no satisfactory modern equivalent.

3 Wolfgang Riehle (*op. cit.*, p. 11) comments on Julian's ability to 'blend concrete imagery with thought processes which are often very abstract'.

God is the maker, the lover, and the keeper; this, too, is a point that Julian makes repeatedly throughout the *Revelations* – he is splendidly omnipotent, the Creator of all, but at the same time he is profoundly gentle and caring, personally tending each of his creatures, no matter how small or unimportant they may seem.

Julian is then granted a vision of the Virgin Mary, who appears as a simple maiden, at the age she was when she conceived; and through this aspect of the vision Julian is brought to a clearer understanding of the apparent paradox of divine power and tenderness – for even Mary is astonished by the Creator's 'homeliness':

> She beheld our God that is her Creator, marvelling with great reverence that he would be born of her that was created . . . Knowing the greatness of her maker, and the littleness of herself that was made, caused her to say meekly to the angel Gabriel, 'Lo me here, God's handmaiden.' (IV)

In the next part of the revelation, which looks back to the image of the hazel nut, Julian is shown that anyone who desires to succeed in the contemplative life must recognize the insignificance of the creation. The cause of human anxiety and dissatisfaction is a wilful preoccupation with earthly matters; those who 'love and seek their peace in this thing that is so little . . . and know not God who is all mighty, all wise, and all good', can find no ease of heart or soul.

Julian realizes that she will never have true peace until she is, through his mercy and grace, fully joined to him – until no part of the creation stands between her and her God. A transcendence of this world is necessary, not because it is to be feared or hated, but because it is an obstacle to oneness, and immeasurably small in relation to its maker:

> God will be known, and it pleases him that we find rest in him. For all that is beneath him is insufficient to us. And this is why no soul is at peace until it has set at nought all that is made: when it is noughted through love . . . then is it able to receive spiritual peace. (IV)

This apparently simple passage is an example of Julian's ability to weave familiar strands from the medieval mystical tradition into her own particular pattern. (1) Great as he is, God is nonetheless pleased by our love for him: in this Julian recalls Mechthild's understanding that God's purpose in making the world was love – the desire to love, and to be loved in return. (2) All that is beneath God is insufficient: here Julian echoes the teaching of St Bernard's *On the Love of God* – cupidity, which results in sin, is nothing more than misdirected love; earthly objects are bound to dissatisfy, because as vessels they are insufficient to contain that love which is meant for God alone. (3) The soul must be 'noughted' before it can find peace: this notion recalls the ideal of the *via negativa* – the transcendence of personal will, the forgetting of self that Dionysius held to be an essential prelude to mystical union.

But these three themes, traditional as they may be, are brought together in a way that ends by affirming the originality of Julian's particular message (and incidentally suggest that she was familiar with quite a range of spiritual texts before she first experienced the revelations). In contrast to Mechthild, Julian makes no use of the erotic image; the comfortable friendliness between her and her God seems to minimize the need for metaphor. And the Bernardine and Dionysian themes, as she introduces them, serve to underscore the personal nature of the bond between the soul and God, to point us towards the fact that this love is the only source of safety and rest.

We can also see in such a passage how deceptive is the apparent simplicity of Julian's style. Clarity is of course her goal, and she is always controlled by her deep humility; both factors commit her to the use of accessible language. But however little she might like to admit it, she is possessed of a formidable intelligence which makes her capable of great theological density and complexity, and means that her work requires and rewards the most careful and detailed of analyses.

She concludes her account of the first vision with a summary of its contents, again for the sake of clarity; recognizing its complexity, she wants to be sure that no aspect of the divine truth should be lost in the process of transmission. In this recapitulation she reminds us that within the first revelation she was shown six things:

> The *first* is the tokens of the blessed passion and the plenteous shedding of his precious blood. The *second* is the maiden, . . . his dear mother. The *third* is the blissful godhead that ever was and is and ever shall be: all mighty, all wisdom, and all love.
> The *fourth* is that all he has made . . . is great and fair and large and good, but the reason it seemed so little was because I saw it in the presence of the maker. The *fifth* is that he made everything that is created because of love, and through the same love it is protected . . . The *sixth* is that God is all things that are good, and the goodness that any thing has is God. (V)

And all the while that she receives these spiritual shewings, the 'bodily sight of the plenteous bleeding of the head' persists; and the five spiritual truths proceed from the 'tokens of the blessed passion'.

At the conclusion of the first revelation, Julian informs us that this and all of her subsequent visions were shown in three ways: by bodily sight, by words formed in her understanding, and by ghostly sight. These categories can be seen largely to correspond to the three stages of mystical ascent first described by St Augustine in the fifth century: corporeal, imaginative, and intellectual. According to this 'classical' scheme, adhered to throughout the Middle Ages by writers attempting to describe the mystical process, 'corporeal' visions are perceived by the external senses, and 'imaginative' ones by the interior senses; 'intellectual' visions are purely spiritual.[4] So Julian's first revelation could be said to have begun with the first of these stages, the 'corporeal' sight of the bleeding head having been stimulated by the actual physical contemplation of the crucifix at her bedside. The subsequent sights of the little hazel nut and the Virgin Mary, insofar as they were visual and yet perceived by the internal senses alone, would seem to qualify as 'imaginative'. And the remaining ghostly truths – that the godhead is all mighty, all wisdom, and all love; that the creation was made and is protected out of love; that God is all that is good – could evidently be classified as 'intellectual', as they transcend sensory perception of any sort. The second category described by Julian – that of the words formed in her understanding – would also correspond to Augustine's 'imaginative' type of vision; Julian 'hears' the words of God, as he speaks to her in a number of revelations, but clearly not with her external ears. These 'words' do much to establish and sustain the intimate, friendly nature of the relationship between Julian and her Creator; but before turning to them, the rest of the bodily, or 'corporeal', sights will be examined.

III

In addition to the first shewing, there are three revelations in which Julian is shown Christ's actual suffering on the cross: the second, fourth and eighth visions. In the second she continues to see 'with bodily sight the face of the crucifix that hung before me':

> I beheld . . . scorn, spitting, defiling of his body, and buffeting of his blessed face; many more sorrows and pains than I can tell, and often times a changing of colour, and his blessed face entirely covered with dry blood.
>
> (VIII)

> And after this [in the fourth revelation] I saw the body plenteously bleeding, hot and freshly and as lifelike as I had before seen [it flowing] from the head, and this was shown me in the wounds of the scourging, and it ran so

---

4   See J. De Tonquédec, *Apparitions*, in Dictionnaire de Spiritualité (Paris, 1937 ff.), I, cc. 801–9; Paul Molinari discusses in some detail the question of the correspondence between Julian's and Augustine's schemes in *Julian of Norwich: The Teaching of a 14th Century English Mystic* (London, 1958), pp. 60 ff.

plentously . . . that if it had been so in nature for that long it should have covered the bed with blood, and continued on overflowing . . . (VIII)

After this Christ showed me [in the eighth revelation] a part of his passion near his dying. I saw that sweet face as it were dry and bloodless, pale with dying, . . . then more deathly pale . . . becoming blue, and then more blue, as the flesh became still more deathlike. For all the pains that Christ suffered in his body were shewn me in the blessed face, . . . especially in the lips . . .; and also the nose clogged and dried . . .

   It seemed to me that the drying of Christ's flesh was the greatest, and the last, pain of his passion. And in this dryness I was reminded of Christ's words, 'I thirst'[1] . . . The blessed body dried a long time with the wringing of the nails, the hanging of the head, and the weight of the body; with the blowing of wind from without that dried him and pained him with cold more than my heart can think . . . (X)

These passages invite comparison with the portrayal of the crucifixion in the *Wooing of Our Lord* and in Rolle's lyrics on the passion. We encounter a similar concentration on the physical suffering – specific parallels are with the *Wooing*'s detailed account of Christ's bearing of the cross, his scourging, the stretching of his limbs as he hangs on the cross, the paining by cold; and with Rolle's description of the crown of thorns tearing Christ's head, the nails piercing his hands and feet, his side red from the blood of its wound. Such close parallels may indicate that Julian was familiar with these works; certainly she shares with them the belief that meditation on the crucifixion will effect an enhancement of compassion – literally, of a suffering *with* Christ – which plays a complex role in speeding the soul towards a closer bond with God. It reinforces our understanding of the ordeal willingly undertaken by Christ, and therefore of the greatness of his love for us; and by allowing us to identify, through his human pain, with Christ, our souls can begin to be restored to their divine likeness.

   As it includes descriptions of the spitting and buffeting, the wounds caused by the scourging, and the tearing of the nails, Julian's account is linked with other earlier literary treatments of the crucifixion as well. One representative sequence of thirteenth-century lyrics, *My Lover on the Cross*, depicts Christ as 'hewed all about, pricked with thorns; his fair hands and feet are pierced with nails'; 'his back is beaten with rods, his body whipped with scourges, and his side stabbed by a spear'. Elsewhere, pathos arises from the coldness endured by Jesus on the cross, the changing of his colour, and the profuseness of his bleeding: 'I see his cold body, and his face that has turned all blue; . . . high upon the cross he

---

[1] *John*, XIX, 28, 30: 'After this, Jesus knowing that all things were now accomplished, that the scripture might be fulfilled, saith, I thirst . . . When Jesus had received the vinegar, he said, It is finished: and he bowed his head and gave up the ghost'.

hangs, all covered with blood; . . . alas my sweet Jesus, you bleed too long
. . . the very stones grow wet'.[2]

Yet despite these traditional echoes, each of Julian's 'bodily' visions
emerges as intensely personal. Her attention to detail reminds us of
Hildegard's careful descriptions, and enhances the particular realism of
her account. 'The shewing of Christ's pains', she recounts, 'filled me full
of pain'; 'no bodily pain could have been worse: for how might my pain
be greater than to see him suffer that is all my life, all my bliss, all my
joy?' But nowhere does she allow her distress to impede the faithfulness
of her telling. We can hardly help but believe in her, as she endeavours to
share her experiences and make the crucifixion take place before our eyes
as well.

Her credibility is due to more than her precision, though her focussing
on such details as the drying of Christ's lips, or the clogging of his nostrils, is surely extraordinary. Each of her physical sights is marked by the
fact that it describes the crucifixion not as a *fait accompli*, but as it is in the
process of happening. She has made the transition from the object con-
templated – the literal crucifix before her – to the transcendental reality of
Christ's sacrifice. The images she shares are not static 'stills' – if it is
possible to draw a modern comparison – but film-like, moving pictures.
Thus the verbs she uses are all verbs of continuing action; she speaks of
defiling and *buffeting*, the *changing* of colour; the *flowing* of the blood, the
drying of the flesh.

And from each shewing of Christ's pain she extracts the message of
love. She understands, for instance, that the bleeding of the head is revealed because 'our Lord Jesus, through his courteous love, would show
me comfort before the time of my temptation'. She sees that the plenteous
bleeding of the body is a kind of foreshadowing of the cleansing effect of
communion:

> Out of tender love for us God has made the waters on earth plenteous for
> our service and physical ease; yet it pleases him better that we take his
> blessed blood to wash away our sin; there is no liquid that is made that he
> so likes to give to us, for it is so plenteous and of our own nature. (VIII)

The fourth shewing, of the physical defiling of the body and the buffeting
of the head, emerges from the reassurance of the third, in which Julian
has seen God in a point, 'that is in my understanding':

> by [this] sight I saw that he is in all things, that he does all that is done; . . .
> nothing happens by chance, . . . but rather by the endless forseeing wisdom
> of God. (VIII)

2 *English Lyrics of the XIIIth Century*, ed. Carlton Brown (Oxford, 1932), pp. 61–4, pp.
122–4 (the translations are mine).

And through the sight of the bodily drying of Christ's flesh, in the eighth revelation, Julian understands a spiritual thirst as well:

> This is the ghostly thirst, [God's] love-longing, . . . the incompleteness of his bliss, that he has us not as wholly in him as he shall have [at doomsday] . . . He has mercy and compassion on us, and he longs to have us, but his wisdom and his love do not allow the end to come until the best time. (XV)

The cumulative effect of these corporeal shewings is to reveal to Julian, and to all those who would be Christ's lovers, the meaning of his sacrifice – that we might be comforted, purified, protected through God's omnipotence and love – and that his greatest longing is to be fully united with his loved ones at the end of time.

Thus Julian is a link in the chain of love descending from God; and as she passes on the message of divine love we also come to feel the tender concern she has for us all, the degree to which she wants us all to be drawn in. The process by which this love is transmitted connects directly with Julian's view of herself as disciple, and of her Lord as teacher – an essential feature of their bond. Beyond that, by portraying herself as 'one taught', Julian becomes a figure with whom her readers can identify, thereby allowing us to be included in the dialogue as well.[3]

The tenth revelation – an 'imaginative' shewing which includes 'words formed in her understanding' as well as a bodily sight – again shows her in the act of passing on this love. The vision includes a sight of Christ on the cross, but he is not shown to be in pain, and he speaks directly to Julian.

> Full merrily and gladly our Lord looked into [the wound in] his side, and said these words: 'Lo, how I loved thee.' It was as if he had said, 'My child, if thou canst not look at my godhead, see here how I allowed my side to be pierced, and my heart to be cloven in two, and the blood and moisture therein to flow out. And this is pleasing to me, and so I will that it please thee'. Our Lord showed me this to make us glad and merry. (XIII)[4]

Christ's desire to comfort Julian is the explicit meaning of this vision. He is pleased by his wound, as it is a way of showing his love: 'Lo, how I loved thee'. He recognizes that the greatness of the godhead may be

---

3 See Ritamary Bradley's 'Christ, the Teacher, in Julian's Showings: The Biblical and Patristic Traditions', in *The Medieval Mystical Tradition in England* (Exeter, 1982), pp. 128 ff. She suggests that Julian's disclaimer – 'God forbid that you should say or understand that I am a teacher, for I mean not so . . . For I am a woman, ignorant, weak and frail' (VI) – is not so much an expression of women's insufficiency as a recognition that all of humankind are students, and God the only teacher.

4 The *Nun's Rule* and *The Wooing of our Lord* both include the image of Christ opening his side and showing his heart as a sign of his love.

frightening to her – and as he hangs on the cross and speaks to her, he is of course the ultimate evidence of the process whereby his humanity serves to link mankind with the divine. He then, as she understands, asks Julian to be pleased as well – not afraid, not guilt-stricken, but pleased. And in turn she addresses us and explains that the purpose of the shewing is general, for us all, *'to make us glad and merry'*.

In its simplicity the tenth revelation seems intended to clarify the preceeding one, also imaginative, in which Julian is given an understanding of the Trinity. Its paradoxical triune nature is revealed to her in terms of the happiness of the three Persons: each is happy in a particular way, and so they are distinct; all are happy, and so they are one. Christ asks if she is satisfied by his suffering, and she replies, 'Yea, good Lord, . . . gramercy'; 'If thou art satisfied', he replies,

> '[then] I am satisfied. It is *a joy and a bliss and an endless liking* to me that ever I suffered passion for thee, for if I might suffer more, I would.' (XII)

Julian's understanding is then lifted up to heaven;

> and there I saw three heavens . . . none is greater, none lesser, but all are alike in bliss . . . In these three words [of Jesus] – *a joy, a bliss, and an endless liking* – three heavens were showed to me: for the *joy* I understood the pleasure of the Father; for the *bliss*, the worship of the Son; and for the endless liking, the Holy Ghost. (XII)

Her perception of the Trinity, unified and made equal by mutual bliss, recalls her description of the hazel nut, in which she also saw three parts: 'the first is that God made it, the second is that he loves it, the third is that he keeps it'. So, again, God is triune: the maker, the lover, and the keeper. And we are reminded of Julian's own three wishes, and of the three categories of her visions: as we are made in the divine image, so is the tripartite pattern to be found within us as well. The pervasiveness of Julian's trinitarian thinking is already evident, though it shows itself more extensively in the long text, twenty years later.

IV

It is hardly surprising that anyone with as powerful a vision of God's love, as absolute a conviction of his desire to protect and to be joined to us, should be troubled by the question of evil. Julian's view of the creation is so thoroughly positive that the very presence of sin seems to be a contradiction in terms. In the fifth revelation Julian approaches this problem – a more difficult paradox for her than that of the triune God. In this vision she is allowed to contemplate the bleeding body for a time;

> then, without voice and without opening of lips, were these words formed in my soul: 'Herewith is the fiend overcome'. Our Lord said these words in reference to his passion, as he had showed me before. (VIII)

The equation is straightforward: the power of the devil is negated through the specific agency of the incarnation and passion. The devil's malice remains undiminished, and he obsessively aspires to the fall of mankind; but since the crucifixion, he is powerless. 'Continually he sees that all chosen souls escape him, . . . and that is his great sorrow';

> [the fiend] has as much sorrow when God gives him leave to work as when he works not, for his power is entirely locked in God's hand . . . (VIII)

Now Julian is specific as to how, despite the fact of evil, we can be safe. Sin is only part of the larger whole – the divine design; it is permitted by God and has no independent existence. Not suprisingly this understanding fills Julian with delight:

> On account of this sight I laughed mightily, and this made those who were with me laugh as well; and their laughing was pleasing to me. I wished all my fellow Christians had seen what I saw; then would they all have laughed with me. (VIII)

We can imagine the relief of her friends and family, anxiously gathered about what they thought was her death-bed. It is hardly surprising that they laughed with her, though they can have had no idea as to the cause of her laughter. Her generosity is wonderfully apparent again; even in the midst of her revelation it occurs to her to think of her fellows, and to wish that they too could have seen what she saw: 'then would they all have laughed with me'. Failing that, she faithfully continues to serve as the link, passing on these comforting truths in the record of her revelations: 'I did not see Christ laugh; neverthless it pleases him that we laugh for our own comfort, and rejoice in God: for the fiend is overcome'.

Despite this reassurance as to what she calls the 'unmight' of the devil, Julian continues to worry about sin and the purpose it serves. She wonders, in the thirteenth revelation, why it has to exist at all: 'if there were no sin, we should all have been pure, and like our Lord, as he created us'. But answering her, God replies that sin – 'all that is not good' – actually plays a useful role in the scheme of salvation. For the bodily and spiritual pain caused by sin is comparable to the pain of the passion: as we suffer it we are like Jesus; as we are purged of our own mortal flesh, and of our own misdirected desires, so do we follow him. The struggle against sin, in which we, too, may feel forsaken, is our equivalent of the passion. Nonetheless, it is made clear that sin itself has no substance, no existence of its own; and it can only be known by the pain that it causes.

God's revelation to Julian as to the purpose of sin continues at greater length, but first he pauses, as it seems, to reassure her:

> All this was shown me in a moment, and quickly passed over into comfort; for our good Lord did not wish my soul to be frightened by this ugly sight . . . For the passion of our Lord is a comfort to us against this . . . To all who shall be saved he gives comfort readily and sweetly by his words, when he says, 'But all shall be well, and all manner of thing shall be well'. These words were shown most tenderly, with no manner of blame to me, nor to anyone who shall be saved. (XIII)

She recognizes how incongruous it is for her to blame God for sin when he does not blame her. But still she is troubled. And so she persists, seeking some more explicit clarification 'whereby I might be reassured in this matter'. With great trepidation she asks, 'Ah, good Lord, how is it possible for all to be well, considering all the harm that has been done by sin to thy creatures?'

Her fear, of course, is groundless, and God answers 'meekly',

> and with a loving countenance . . . that the sin of Adam was the greatest sin that ever has been done, or ever shall be, until the end of the world. (XIV)

He instructs her not to contemplate the damage caused by sin, but rather the positive effect of the passion, the glorious reparation:[1]

> for this reparation is more pleasing to the blessed godhead, and more to the furtherance of man's salvation, than the sin of Adam was ever harmful.

It follows that if the greatest sin has been made good, then so shall every lesser one.

God makes clear to Julian that it is not appropriate for her to want to understand everything about the divine purpose: even the 'saints in heaven want to know only what our Lord chooses to show them'.[2] Nonetheless he is willing to provide her with a fuller understanding of sin; his compassion for her distress – and perhaps his respect for her intelligence

---

[1] Julian's word is 'asethe', from the French *asset* (<*assez*), and originally late Latin *ad satis*, ='satisfaction'. Our modern 'reparation' does not express quite so literally the one-to-one nature of the exchange, whereby the loss of the Fall, brought about by the old sin of Adam, is redeemed by the new sacrifice of Christ.

[2] Rolle makes this point as well: 'It is presumption for a man, with his own wit, to pry too deeply into an understanding of ghostly things' (Allen, *op. cit.*, XI, 43).

– seem to be such that he will carry on with these explanations until she is fully comforted: 'and thus our good Lord answered all my questions and doubts'.

Further, the explanations are augmented by words of profound reassurance;

> 'I may make all things well, I can make all things well, I will make all things well, I shall make all things well; and thou shall see thyself that all things shall be well.' (XV)

To share this comfort – recognizing that we, too, may be troubled by the same doubts – Julian immediately provides a gloss, in which we are shown how these words are a reflection of God's tripartite nature :

> Where he says he *may*, I understand the Father; where he says he *can*, I understand the Son; where he says I *will*, I understand the Holy Ghost; where he says I *shall*, I understand the unity of the blessed Trinity, three Persons in one truth; and where he says *thou shall see thyself*, I understand the union with the blessed Trinity of all mankind who shall be saved. (XV)

It is further shown to Julian 'that sin is no shame', and her understanding is again lifted to heaven:

> and then in truth I was reminded of David, Peter and Paul, Thomas of India and the Magdalene, who are known in the earthly church for their sins, which are to their praise. (XVII)

Peter, Paul, Thomas and Mary Magdalene are renowned for being among the most devoted of the Lord's followers, and David was traditionally seen as an Old Testament prefiguration of Christ, the king and saviour. It is striking to say the least to see these figures described as sinners; but so they were – David for his passion for Bathsheba and the killing of Uriah; Peter for the denial of Christ; Paul for assisting at the martyrdom of St Stephen; Thomas for doubting the resurrection; and Mary Magdalene for being a sinner, perhaps a prostitute.[3] Julian is impressed by this dramatic illustration, and as we might expect, seeks to generalize its application for the sake of her fellows:

---

3   The biblical evidence for these sins is as follows: for David, 2 *Samuel* XI; for Peter, *Matthew* XXVI, 69–75; for Paul, *Acts* VII, 58; for Thomas, *John* XX, 25–8; for Mary, *Luke* VII, 37–48. The reference to Thomas being 'of India' arises from an unproven tradition that has him taking the gospel to India after the crucifixion. The bible does not specify the nature of Mary Magdalene's sin, though Jesus says 'Her sins, which are many, are forgiven; for she loved much'.

It is no shame to them that they have sinned; and in the bliss of heaven the token of their sin becomes an honour. Our Lord showed them to me as an example for others, that they shall come thither as well. (XVII)

In the dénouement of this thirteenth shewing, the positive function of sin is revealed to Julian in the most precise detail. It is 'the sharpest scourge with which any chosen soul may be beaten', she tells us – and with the image of the scourging she recalls the link between Christ's passion and our sin; this 'scourge' so lowers us in our own sight that we believe we are only fit 'to sink into hell'.

In this humble, 'noughted' state, the soul becomes susceptible to contrition, which is the first and absolutely fundamental stage to recovery. Simply, the soul recognizes that it has done wrong and becomes ready to make amends: 'when contrition fills [the soul], by the touching of the Holy Ghost, then bitterness turns into hope for God's glory'.

And, as he turns to the life of holy church, [the sinner's] wounds begin to heal, and his soul to come to life again. The Holy Ghost leads him to confession, to willingly, openly and honestly – with great sorrow and shame that he has so defiled the fair image of God – admit his sins. (XVII)

With the image of the quickening soul, Julian again reinforces the parallel with Christ and his resurrection. By the reference to the defiling of the divine image we are reminded that as we commit sin, we separate ourselves further from God; and as we overcome it, we become closer, and more like him. Hell, of course, is the ultimate separation from God's presence – 'those who loved him not suffered pain because of the absence of comfort' (X); 'the pain [of sin] seemed to me the hardest hell, for then [the soul] has not his God' (XVIII).

Penance is dispensed as a result of confession, and its medicinal effect speeds the process of recuperation: 'by this medicine it behooves each sinful soul to be healed . . . Though he be healed, his wounds are still seen by God, not as wounds but as honours'. As we accept punishment here on earth, so shall we be honoured in heaven by the love of our Lord.

The reward that we receive [in heaven] . . . shall be high, glorious and honourable, and so shall all shame turn into honour and more joy. (XVII)

Julian is now evidently satisfied as to the purpose, and the non-existence of sin, for near the end of the *Revelations* she includes this triumphant apostrophe:

Ah, wretched sin, What are you? You are nought. For I saw that God is all things; I saw you not . . . And thus I am sure that you are nought. And

anyone who loves you . . . shall be brought to nought with you, and end-
lessly confounded. (XXIII)[4]

In the course of the revelations, Julian has her own personal struggle with
the forces of evil. During their exchange as to the nature and inevitability
of sin, God has informed her that she, too, will sin; and after the fifteenth
revelation – which has as its message the importance of patience in adver-
sity – she lapses into a state that seems very close to despair:

> As a wretch I was vexed and mourned on account of the physical pain that
> I felt, and it seemed greatly irksome to me that I had to live any longer. And
> I was as barren and dry as if I had never received any comfort. (XXI)

This state of spiritual 'dryness' links Julian with Christ as he thirsts on the
cross; but it also recalls the Dionysian dark night experienced by Mechthild, in which she felt herself to be abandoned by her lover. Julian seems,
however briefly, to have lost contact with her friend and Lord, and to
have forgotten his words of comfort.

A visitor comes to her bedside, and asks how she is feeling; she replies
that she has raved: 'I imagined that the cross that stood at the foot of my
bed bled profusely'. The visitor's response is one of grave amazement; he
recognizes the validity of her revelations, while she has been guilty of
'little faith' and dismissed them as mere delirium. It does not take her
long to realize her error: 'when I saw how seriously and reverently he
took [my words] I was greatly ashamed, and would like to have made
confession'.

> But I could tell it to no priest, for I thought, 'Why should a priest believe
> me, when I believed not our Lord God?' I did believe him during the time
> that I saw him . . . But like a fool I let it pass from my mind. Lo, what a
> wretch I am! It was a great sin and a great unkindness[5] that, on account of
> the folly of my feelings and a little pain, I so unwisely departed from the
> comfort of all his blessed shewing. (XXI)

With the recognition of her lapse, Julian's trust returns, and she falls
asleep. While she is sleeping, and unconfessed, the devil evidently im-
agines her to be at her most vulnerable, and so decides to make his move;

---

4 Julian adds a personal coda to the discussion of sin, in which she points out that just
   because it is part of the divine plan does not mean that it is good to sin, or that a greater
   reward will be given to the sinner: 'when a soul wilfully chooses sin . . . as his god, in
   the end he has nothing'.
5 Julian's word 'unkyndnes' means not only 'unkind' and 'ungrateful', but also 'unnatural', 'against nature' – as it is unnatural to turn away from those who love us.

as she seems on the verge of death, he naturally wants to get possession of her soul if he possibly can.

> In my sleep . . . it seemed to me that the fiend was at my throat and wanted to strangle me, but he could not. Then I awoke from my sleep and was scarcely alive. (XXI)

Those who are by Julian's bed see her distress and wet her temples, in an effort to restore her. 'My heart was comforted', but

> soon a little smoke came in through the door, along with some great heat and a foul stench. I said, 'Blessed be the Lord, is all on fire that is here?' For I imagined it to be a physical fire that was going to burn us all to death. I asked those who were with me if they smelled any stench, and they said No, they smelled nothing . . . Then I realized it was the fiend who had come to tempt me. (XXI)

Her malicious foe, however, has not taken accurate measure of the soul he would so like to corrupt. Julian's moment of doubt has passed, she has repented of her error and wished for confession; she speedily recognizes the devil and knows what he is about; and she has the tools with which to dispatch him:

> straight away I took all that our Lord had shown me that very day, along with all the faith of holy church, for I believe they are one and the same, and I turned to them for my comfort. Immediately [the smoke, stench and heat] all vanished, and I was brought to a state of rest and peace, without bodily sickness or any sense of fear. (XXI)

The devil does not give up quite so easily, and returns after the next vision; this time he seems to have brought reinforcements. The dreadful heat and the vile stench recur, but Julian also hears a sound of chattering and of speech, 'as if there had been two bodies';

> and they jangled at once as if they were busily holding a parliament; all was soft muttering, and I did not understand what they said. (XXIII)

However, she understands their purpose perfectly: 'all this was to stir me to despair'; and again she demonstrates her remarkable courage and steady faith:

> I comforted my soul with actual speech, as I would have done to another who had been similarly travailed . . . I set my bodily eyes on the same cross that I had found so much comfort in before, I occupied my tongue with speaking of Christ's passion and repeating the truths of holy church, and I fastened my heart on God, with all the trust and all the might that was in

me . . . And thus they kept me occupied all night, and into the next morning . . . and then at last they were gone . . . and nothing remained but the stink, which lasted a while longer. (XXIII)

This trial-by-devil turns out to be a reaffirmation of the fifth revelation, in which Julian saw the 'unmight' of the fiend; now it has been her personal experience that the only protection she needs against diabolical temptation is provided by the crucifixion:

I scorned them, and thus I was delivered from them by the virtue of Christ's passion: for therewith is the fiend overcome, as Christ had assured me before. (XXIII)

It is characteristic that the only temptation to which Julian seems to be even remotely susceptible is despair – that most ghostly of sins – which has to do exclusively with the relation of the soul to God. She seems immune to the other sins of the spirit – pride, wrath, envy – which are for the most part directed against a human 'other'. As for the physical sins, such as gluttony or lechery, these hardly need mentioning in the presence of a nature that seems to be as spontaneously spiritual as Julian's. Hildegard's susceptibility to pride; Mechthild's struggles with the flesh; the dangers presented by vanity to the young women addressed in the *Nun's Rule* or the epistles of Rolle – none of these are of the least relevance to Julian: it is appropriate that her brush with sin, however slight, should take the form of doubt.

The grand effort made in the thirteenth revelation to elucidate the purpose of sin is complemented by the subsequent vision in which Julian is led to an understanding of the operation of prayer. This puzzle is not so difficult as that of sin's purpose, and it has not caused her anything like the same distress; yet its explanation helps to reveal another way in which God works to bring the soul closer to him.

Julian notes that when we pray, our trust in God is not always complete, for because of our feelings of unworthiness, we are not sure that he hears us. Sometimes 'we are as barren and as dry after our prayers as we were before . . . and this I have experienced myself'. But this doubt is folly and weakness, for as God explains, 'I am the ground of your beseeching': he makes us want the things we pray for, and then takes pleasure in granting our prayers:

'First it is my will that you have it, then I make you want it, and then I make you pray for it; and if you pray for it, how should it be that you should not have your prayers answered?' (XIX)

In other words, our positive desires – for the spiritual welfare of our fellows, or ourselves – are actually inspired by God, who makes us ask for them.

It is God's will that we pray . . . and that we have our prayers granted, for prayer pleases God. (XIX)

It pleases God partly because, since he loves us, he enjoys giving us what we want; partly because it 'pleases man with himself, making him sober and meek when he had been in strife and travail'. Most important, through the process of prayer, the divine likeness is restored:

> Prayer joins the soul to God, for though the soul is always like God in nature and substance, it is often unlike him in condition, because of sin . . . Prayer makes the soul like God when the soul wills what God wills; and then is it like God in condition as it is in nature . . . Thus prayer brings about an accord between God and the soul, for when man's soul is at home with God, he does not need to beseech. (XIX)

The need for beseeching comes 'when we see God not';

> For when a soul is tempted, and troubled, and left to itself . . . then is it time to pray and make itself humble and obedient to God. (XIX)

Contemplation is thus the highest form of prayer: when our wills are at one with God's, and we are safe in the divine presence, we need ask for nothing, and can rest in reverent beholding.

> Then does God, in the soul's sight, turn to the beholding of the soul, as if it had been in pain or in prison, saying, 'I am glad that you have come to rest, for I have always loved you and now love you as you do me.' (XIX)

V

One of the most extraordinary features of Julian's *Revelations* is her articulation of the doctrine of the motherhood of God, which follows the fourteenth showing. There are hints of this teaching in the short text of her work, but we must look to the longer version for its full expression, which perhaps she only felt the confidence to expand upon after twenty years' meditation. The early Christians had been familiar both with the idea that the divine nature included a feminine aspect, and with the use of the maternal metaphor to express the relation between the feminine aspect of the godhead and the soul.

The early tradition of speaking of Christ as mother was largely suppressed by the fifth century; but the use of the maternal image had recently been revived, notably by Bernard and Anselm, and Julian may have been familiar with their texts.[1] It hardly needs saying, however, that the ecclesiastical establishment continued to insist on viewing the triune God in wholly masculine terms. Julian, as we might expect, seems undeterred by this rejection – measured against the power of her own revelation, she is left with no choice: this is what she has been shown, and this is what she must pass on. According to her revelation, the maternal aspect of the godhead is not figurative but literal; Christ is not like a mother, he is our Mother: in her words, 'God is as really our Mother as he is our Father'.[2]

The fact that Julian was herself a woman has perhaps given her the particular sensitivity to experience and articulate the maternal aspect of the godhead so fully, even as we have seen Hildegard and Mechthild's individual understanding of their Creator to be enhanced by their womanhood. However, it is also important to recall that some of the earliest recorded Christian references to God as mother were articulated by those pillars of the esablishment, the Church Fathers: Clement of Alexandria, in the late second century, maintained that

> God himself is love; and out of love to us became feminine. In His ineffable essence He is Father; in his compassion to us He became Mother. The Father by loving became feminine . . . The body of Christ . . . nourishes by the word the young offspring, which the Lord Himself brought forth in throes of flesh . . . The nutriment is the milk of the Father . . . The Father's breasts of love supply milk.

Then, in the fourth century, Ambrose remarked that 'Christ is the virgin who entered into marriage, carried us in her womb, gave birth to us, and fed us with her own milk'; and soon after, Augustine is seen to employ the maternal image, though unlike the others he stipulated that its use was metaphorical:

> Just as a mother, suckling her infant, transfers from her flesh the very same food which would otherwise be unsuitable to the babe, . . . so the Lord, in order to convert His wisdom into milk for our benefit, came to us clothed in flesh.[3]

---

1 See 'The Motherhood Theme in Julian of Norwich', Ritamary Bradley, *14th Century English Mystics Newsletter*, II, 4 (December, 1976), pp. 25 ff.; also Colledge and Walsh (*op. cit.*), pp. 149 ff. and Molinari (*op. cit.*), pp. 169 ff. For a discussion of the systematic suppression of early Gnostic texts that referred to the feminine aspect of the godhead see Elaine Pagels, *The Gnostic Gospels* (New York, 1979).

2 Wolters (*op. cit.*), p. 167. Subsequent quotations from Julian on the doctrine of the motherhood of God are from this translation, chs 58–61 (the numbers in brackets refer to Wolter's chapter divisions).

3 Quoted in Bradley ('The Motherhood Theme,' *op. cit.*), pp. 26–7. Bradley also points to

Nonetheless, until the mid-1970s, Julian's translators and editors tended to dismiss her treatment of the motherhood of God as 'a mere metaphor', with a scriptural basis 'far too flimsy for any doctrine to be built upon it';[4] since then it has fortunately begun to receive the attention it deserves. (What we witness here, then, are two distinct waves of misogynist censorship: one in the fifth century, which sought to suppress the doctrine of God-as-mother; and the second in the twentieth, which until the past few years has tended to treat this aspect of Julian's work with dismissive condescension.)

What then is the substance of Julian's teaching on the motherhood of God? It will come as no surprise by now that her explication is complex and difficult; in itself it could be, and indeed has been, the subject for prolonged and detailed inquiry.[5] But if we are to approach a full understanding of Julian and her work, some effort must be made to grasp the major aspects of this doctrine. Her introduction of the motherhood theme occurs after the fourteenth revelation, on the operation of prayer. Technically, it could be said to be based on meditations arising from this revelation; as the shewing on prayer focusses on God's tender love for the soul – his pleasure in pleasing us by granting what we pray for – it is an appropriate 'springboard' for Julian's understanding of his maternal nature.[6]

However, her teaching on this subject goes far beyond the particular question of prayer, to elucidate such fundamental Christian mysteries as the triune God, creation, and salvation. When God made us, she explains, 'he joined and united us to himself'; by such a union 'we are kept as pure and noble as when we were first made'. This bond is essential to our redemption, and the three Persons of the Trinity are equally but differently involved in its creation.

when he made us God almighty was our kindly Father, and God all-wise

thirteenth-century texts by Albert the Great and Bonaventure in which the motherhood of God is discussed, and through which this similitude entered the Dominican and Franciscan traditions; the use of the similitude would have been introduced to the Benedictines through Anselm (see André Cabassut, 'Une dévotion médiévale peu connue. "La dévotion à Jesu notre Mère" ', *Revue d'Ascetique et de Mystique* 25, 1949). See also Molinari (*op. cit.*), p. 171; and Caroline Walker Bynum, 'Jesus as Mother and Abbot as Mother: Some Themes in Twelfth Century Cistercian Writing', *Harvard Theological Review* 70 (1977).
4 Walsh (*op. cit.*), p. 10; Wolters (*op. cit.*), p. 34.
5 See, for example, Caroline Walker Bynum, *Jesus as Mother: Studies in the Spirituality of the High Middle Ages* (Berkeley, 1982).
6 In referring to God-the-mother as 'he', I follow Julian, who is unperturbed by using the 3rd person masculine pronoun even as she is referring to Jesus as female, a mother who gives birth and suck.

was our kindly Mother, and the Holy Spirit their love and goodness; all one God, one Lord. (58)

Here, the second Person of the Trinity is explicitly 'our kindly Mother' – though he never ceases also to be the Son of God – whose wisdom is necessary for the formation of this bond with God. We are enabled, by such a union – which is kinetic rather than static – to sustain our loving relationship with God: pleasing, praising, thanking, rejoicing forever; it is a 'plan continually at work in every soul to be saved'.

Thus Julian is shown not only the characteristics of the Trinity, but also its operation:

> I saw the blessed Trinity working. I saw that there were these three attributes: fatherhood, motherhood, and lordship – all in one God.

The Father has sustained and blessed us from before the beginning of time; this function has to do with our 'created natural being'. The Holy Spirit looks after us when our physical lives are over. The essential attribute of the second Person at the point of creation was wisdom, but the Mother's ongoing role is to tend us during our time here on earth:

> By [his] skill and wisdom . . . we are sustained, restored, and saved with regard to our sensual nature, for he is our Mother, Brother, and Saviour.

Julian has seen that as we are in God's image, and as the godhead consists of three parts, so also does our nature. Further, as she says, 'our life too is threefold'; there are three 'stages' to our lives: (1) natural being (which was first created by the Father before time), (2) growth (which occurs in the course of our physical/sensual lifetimes), (3) perfection (which through grace is brought about by the Holy Spirit).

It is in the second Person that we are able to move towards redemption. As he is our Mother 'with regard to our essential nature', so has

> that same dear Person become our Mother in the matter of our sensual nature. We are God's creation twice: essential being and sensual nature. Our being is that higher part which we have in our Father . . . and the Second Person of the Trinity is Mother of this basic nature . . . But he is our Mother also in mercy, since he has taken our sensual nature upon himself.

The higher, essential aspect of our nature maintains its divine likeness, but during the sensual 'stage' of our lives, when we are vulnerable and susceptible to error, we are most in need, and it is then that our Mother cares for us, even to the point of joining us in our flesh and in our mortality.

154

In our Mother, Christ, we grow and develop; in his mercy he reforms and restores us; through his passion, death, and resurrection he has united us to our being . . . In our merciful Mother we have reformation and renewal.

Although our essential nature is 'entire in each person of the Trinity', only the Mother is directly linked to our sensual being, which 'is in the Second Person alone, Jesus Christ' – the Mother who looks after our rescue:

In and by [Jesus Christ] we have been taken out of hell with a strong arm and . . . wonderfully raised to heaven.

As we see the cooperation of the Persons of the Trinity, its mystery begins to unfold. There are three aspects within one godhead, each with its own nature, each caring for a different stage of our existence; each plays a part in the process that begins with creation and has its consummation in our ultimate redemption; each is distinct, yet part of one whole. So we thank and praise our Father for creating us, beseech 'our Mother for mercy and pity, and . . . the [Holy] Spirit for help and grace'. (59)

Julian has much more to say about the special attributes of the second Person;

He is our Mother . . . by grace, because he took our created nature upon himself. All the lovely deeds and tender services that motherhood implies are appropriate to the Second Person. (60)

The ongoing process of 'reformation and renewal' is carried out by our Mother, who

laid the foundation of his work in the Virgin's womb . . . It was in this lowly place that God most high . . . adorned and arrayed himself with our poor flesh, ready to function and serve as Mother in all things.

For Julian, the mother's role is 'the most intimate, willing, and dependable of all services, . . . the truest of all'. Yet, as she contrasts Jesus with earthly mothers, she shows us how wholly superior he is: they bear us to pain and death, he bears us to joy and eternal life; his labour involves the most terrible pain imaginable, and ends in his death. While the human mother suckles her child with milk,

our Mother Jesus feeds us with himself . . . by means of the Blessed Sacrament, the precious food of all true life . . . The human mother may put her child tenderly to her breast, but our tender Mother Jesus simply leads us into his blessed breast through his open side.

Julian is not suggesting that our own mothers are insufficient; rather she uses the human ideal to show that Jesus is better even than they: in essence, she explains, 'motherhood means love and kindness, wisdom, knowledge, goodness'.

> A kind, loving mother who understands and knows the needs of her child will look after it tenderly just because it is the nature of a mother to do so. As the child grows older she changes her methods – but not her love,

eventually allowing it to be punished so that faults may be corrected and virtues developed.

> This way of doing things . . . is our Lord at work in those who are doing them. Thus he is our Mother in nature, working by his grace in our lower part, for the sake of the higher.

The relationship between mother and child is the closest we come on earth to that between Jesus and the soul, and it is his will that we understand his maternal nature by comparing it with its earthly counterpart.

> Often when we are shown the extent of our fall and wretchedness we are so scared and dreadfully ashamed that we scarcely know where to look. But our patient Mother does not want us to run away . . . His desire is that we should do what a child does: . . . [run] to mother for help as fast as it can . . . And he wants us to copy the child who always and naturally trusts mother's love though thick and thin. (61)

> Beautiful and sweet is our heavenly Mother in the sight of our souls; and in the sight of our heavenly Mother, dear and lovely are all the gracious children . . . The natural child does not despair of mother's love; . . . the natural child loves mother, and the other children. These are beautiful qualities, . . . and with them all our heavenly Mother is served and pleased . . . And I understood that there is no higher state in this life than that of childhood . . . (63)

The final, sixteenth, 'ghostly' vision is the exalted climax of the *Revelations*, weaving together Julian's perception of God's almighty triune nature, the divine image within the human soul, God's tender concern for that soul, and his assurance that it shall not be overcome.

> Our Lord opened my ghostly eyes and showed me my soul in the midst of my heart. I saw my soul . . . as a glorious city. In the midst of this city sits our Lord Jesus, very God and very man, a fair person, and of large stature, the worshipful, highest Lord: and I saw him clad in honour. He sits in the soul in peace and rest, and he rules and governs heaven and earth and all that is. The manhood sits in peace with the godhead . . .

And my soul is joyously dwelling with the godhead that is sovereign might, sovereign wisdom, sovereign goodness. Jesus shall never depart from the place that he occupies in our soul, for in us is his most comfortable home, the most pleasing for him to dwell in.

Julian understands that the beholding of this 'delectable and restful sight' brings the soul to a likeness of that image, and fills it with peace. His tender love for each soul is reaffirmed by the fact that it is there that he is happiest to dwell; with all his infinite potential for magnificence, he would still prefer his 'homeliest home', with and within our dear souls. As with the other visions, the meaning of this shewing is general, for the comfort of all Christians; but God reveals his affection for Julian as an individual in the last words he speaks to her. These words are formed meekly, 'without voice and without opening of lips', as before; but this time they are meant for her alone:

'Know this to be true, it was no raving that thou saw today. Take it, and believe it, and keep it, and thou shall not be overcome'. (XXII)

Despite Julian's protestations as to her unworthiness, and her insistence that her revelations were not a sign of personal distinction, God seems determined to give her a special sign of his favour with these final words. He is aware of her momentary doubt, of her dismissal of the visions as delirium. But he is also aware of her earnest contrition, and particularly wants her to know that she is quite forgiven for her lapse. Julian's courage and honesty and devotion have made her the perfect conduit for God's message; but she also emerges as its consummate embodiment. If we have any doubt that we 'shall not be overcome', we need only look as far as Julian for reassurance. In her ordeal she has indeed become Christ-like, the intercessor between God and humanity even as Jesus was on the cross.

Epilogue

Hildegard, Mechthild and Julian would have been considered extraordinary in any time or place; it is my hope that this introduction will encourage readers to seek a further acquaintance with all of them.

Each of these women has emerged as strikingly individualistic. Hildegard, we have seen, was a figure of major prominence in her own time, seizing power for herself, so as to be able to carry out the divine precepts received in the course of her illuminations. For her, the assumption of power ranged from becoming abbess at the Disibodenberg, to moving – despite the strenuous objections of her abbot – to Rupertsberg, where she founded a new convent for her sisters; it included the adminstration of this new establishment, lengthy speaking tours to various monastic communities in Germany and France, and a vigorous and often vociferously critical correspondence with many of the most influential male leaders, in both the religious and secular spheres, of her time; it concluded in old age with a principled defiance of ecclesiastical authority that resulted in the excommunication of her entire community at Rupertsberg.

In keeping with her assertive, active nature, Hildegard's image of herself in relation to her Lord was cast in the Germanic, military mold; she saw herself as the faithful vassal, and God as her omnipotent and utterly trustworthy commander. With this divine authority she eagerly cooperated, and it superseded that of any earthly power, even pope or king. She understood the history of the world to be dominated by the struggle between good and evil; constant vigilance was required to guard against the assaults of Lucifer and his forces, and in this sense her role as lieutenant of the Creator was vital to the process of salvation. A range of powerful female figures – Sapientia, Ecclesia, Zion, Synagogue – dominated her writing, and it is difficult to avoid the conclusion that in some fundamental way she identified with these grand, larger-than-life women; adherence to God's will seems to have been an empowering experience for her, one which liberated her from conventional views of women's duty to be submissive and silent.

Mechthild early expressed her rejection of social privilege by deciding to join a beguinage rather than the upper class convent that her family's station would have suggested. This act reflected a thoroughgoing, life-

158

long repudiation of a value system based on status or wealth, and a corresponding commitment to the idea of hierarchy based solely on virtue and the love of God. Like Hildegard, she was outspoken in her condemnation of corruption and hypocrisy, even if it meant incurring the displeasure of powerful church authorities. The egalitarian beguinage, essentially independent from the male-dominated ecclesiastical power structure, included women from many levels of society and required no formal vows for admission. Mechthild never allowed her personal spritual life, crucial as it was, to divert her from the 'mixed life' of the Beguines, which combined private contemplation with acts of charity towards the poor or sick; this was also the ideal embodied by two of her favourite saints, Francis and Dominic, whose example she sought to follow. And ultimately, of course, it was the model set by the life of Christ; Mechthild's zealous imitation of him included not only the need for charitable responsibility, but also a welcoming of the world's scorn – as its values were false, so was its favour to be shunned. In this state of being 'despised', as well as in her experiences of physical and emotional suffering, Mechthild felt herself growing closer to Christ.

Ardent by nature, Mechthild seems to have been drawn to the erotic metaphor, and her descriptions of ecstatic union are glowingly described in terms of passionate, sexual love. She has adapted many of the courtly conventions from the *minnesingers*, although her repudiation of the human activity they advocated was unequivocal. God is the soul's beloved; she waits in fervent longing for their encounters to be repeated; the rest of her earthbound life is drab misery. Contemporary heterosexual models tended to be unequal: in marriage, the husband was dominant; in the courtly relationship the knight became the vassal, bowing down before his often aloof lady. But the lovers in Mechthild's experience are equal because they are of the same nature, and their longing for one another is fully mutual. With this affirmation of her essential participation, by nature, in the divine, Mechthild transcended the medieval misogynist view of women as 'naturally' corrupt, and found the confidence to speak out – insisting on the legitimacy of her own voice and experience.

Julian's profound modesty has meant that it is very difficult to find out anything about her personally. Fortunately, her revelations, which she was bound to record, took place during the course of a severe illness, about which she was thus forced to provide some details. The illness came to her as the answer to a longing to be closer to Christ through a more intense experience of the crucifixion; as she was meditating on the crucifix by her bedside, apparently at the point of death, the cross 'came to life', as it were, before her eyes. The sixteen ensuing revelations included a sort of re-enactment of the passion and the pains endured by Christ, but also an expression of happiness on his part in being able to express his infinite love for humanity through this ultimate sacrifice. In some of the shewings Christ spoke to Julian directly – words were 'formed' in her understanding – and in some, the revelations were purely spiritual. In every case, God's tender love was affirmed, and conversely, the power of the devil negated. Julian's optimism managed to find a function even for sin within the order of the creation, and inspired an evidently egalitarian understanding of heaven in which all souls who have loved God will be equally rewarded. Unlike Hildegard and Mechthild, Julian appears to have been what might be called naturally spiritual, having no interest in matters beyond her direct relationship with God; her function, as she saw it, was to pass on these 'comforting words' to all of Christ's lovers, acting as a kind of link in the chain of love between heaven and earth. To her Christ was as a kindly teacher, and she his student; in imitation of him she reiterated this relationship and herself became a teacher for us all.

When Julian, at thirty, had her revelations, she was probably still living at home with her mother. Subsequently she became an anchoress, making the decision to withdraw from the world and devote herself to a life of meditation. For the next twenty years she was committed to the contemplation of her sixteen revelations, and at the end of this time produced a second, longer account. Although Julian apparently had none of the outspoken, defiant qualities of Hildegard or Mechthild, and indeed seems to be incapable of indignation or bitterness, she nonetheless felt it imperative to be heard; puzzled as she may have been by her Lord's choice of her, she recognized the transmission of these revelations as an incontrovertible obligation. Quiet she was, and understated; but not silent. We can surmise that being blessed with the responsibility of passing on the assurance of God's love was, simply, as great a joy to her as having herself first received it; in combination the two became the great central fact of her existence in this life.

Different as these three women were, there are some important features that they shared. Doubtless they were, in their respective ways, inclined by nature to independence. Although they lived during a period that sought the silence and submission of women, Hildegard, Mechthild and Julian all were able to resist this pressure. In each case the quality of their bond with the divine, in conjuction with their own personal strength, enabled them to transcend their societies' misogynist beliefs. While all reflected to some degree the influence of their contemporary cultures, they also possessed superior powers of selection: Hildegard and Mechthild could adapt the fashionable heroic and courtly literary conventions to their needs without being subsumed by them; Julian could embrace the popular eremitic ideal and yet reject its dualistic emphasis on fear and guilt.

This ability to be at once grounded in temporal reality and able to transcend it has made their work the more accessible – the fact of being able to glimpse these women as real people means that their inspiration and strength can be more effectively shared. It is also the mark of what might be called the sure-footedness of their liberation, their clarity of mind. Despite their assertions of inadequacy, their voices exude authority. Difficult as it may be for the sceptical twentieth-century reader to believe as they did, these three never give the impression of instability, nor do their experiences seem to have been pathological. Although they all experienced pain or illness at some point, their physical symptoms could easily have resulted from pent-up emotion, and evidently faded as the women were able to set down what had happened to them; it is perhaps worth noting that they all lived to a remarkably ripe old age: Hildegard to 81, Mechthild perhaps to 87, and Julian at least to 73.

The power of faith surely had much to do with this sense of balance, with keeping them so apparently sane in the wake of these dramatic and unsettling experiences. Beyond this, as visionaries, they shared with the greatest artists a power of the creative spirit that could not be refused. Although their illuminations separated them from their conventional peer groups – and would have done even if they had been kept secret – they also provided them with a new and higher reality. Along with the profound joy that they found in their connection with the infinite, they were able to bring their spiritualized femaleness to fruition in various ways. Hildegard and Mechthild created new families of daughters and sisters for themselves at Rupertsberg, in the beguinage and at Helfta; being women, they brought a special understanding to the role of the feminine in the process of salvation, which in Hildegard's case manifested itself in the presence of such powerful figures as Sapientia and Ecclesia, in Mechthild's in the elevation of the Virgin to the level of the divine, at the left hand of God. Although Julian was wholly at peace as a solitary, it seems possible that she drew upon a close relationship with her mother in achieving her remarkable serenity, and in being able so fully to articulate her doctrine of the motherhood of God. For them, in their lifetimes, it was not possible to be 'normal'; instead they transcended the man-made restrictions of their societies, found magnificent emotional fulfilment in the love of God, rejoiced in the creation in all its potential glory as the image of its loving Creator – and compromised their womanhood not one whit.

APPENDIX

Julian's Revelations as listed in the Long Text

I. The first revelation tells of Christ's precious crowning with thorns. It included and demonstrated the Trinity, the incarnation, and the unity between God and the soul of man. There were many splendid revelations of eternal wisdom, and many lovely lessons about love, and all the subsequent revelations are based on these.

II. The second concerns the discolouring of his fair face, the sign of his most dear passion.

III. The third shows that our Lord God, almighty, all-wisdom, and all-love, has made everything, and also works in and through everything.

IV. The fourth speaks of the flogging of that tender body, and of the blood shed copiously.

V. The fifth reveals that the Fiend is conquered through Christ's pitiful passion.

VI. The sixth describes the great honour of God's gratitude and the heavenly reward for his blessed servants.

VII. The seventh depicts the recurring experience of delight and depression. The former is God's touch of grace and radiance, and brings real assurance of external joy; the latter is a temptation caused by the dullness and frustration of our life in the body. There is the spiritual knowledge that we are kept secure in love, through delight and depression, by God's goodness.

VIII. The eighth speaks of Christ's final sufferings and his cruel death.

IX. The ninth relates the pleasure that the Blessed Trinity has in the grievous passion of Christ, and his pitiful death. In this joy and pleasure God wants us to be comforted and cheered along with him until we come to our fulfilment in heaven.

X. The tenth shows our Lord Jesus rejoicing to display, in his love, his blessed heart, riven in two.

XI. The eleventh is a high and spiritual revelation of his beloved Mother.

XII. The twelfth shows our Lord to be the being of all that is, and most worthy.

XIII. The thirteenth declares the will of God to be that we should greatly value all his works: the noble nature of all creation, the excellency of man's creation, the supremest of his works, and the precious atonement he has made for man's sin, turning our blame into eternal splendour. He says, 'Look. By my same mighty wisdom and goodness I shall make what is not right to be all right. And you shall see it'. In all this it is his will that we hold on to the faith and truth of Holy Church, and not be anxious to know his secrets now, but only in so far as we are able in this life.

XIV. The fourteenth declares that our Lord is the foundation of our prayers. There are two considerations here: right praying, and sure trust. He wants both alike to be generous. So our prayer will delight him, and through his goodness he will answer it.

XV. The fifteenth says that we shall be taken suddenly from all our pain and distress and by the goodness of God attain heaven, where the Lord Jesus will be our reward, and we shall be filled with joy and bliss.

XVI. The sixteenth affirms that the Blessed Trinity, our Creator in Christ Jesus our Saviour, lives eternally in our soul. There he rules in honour and governs all things; by his might and wisdom he saves and keeps us for love's sake; we will not be overcome by our enemy.

(This listing is taken from Wolter's translation of the *Revelations of Divine Love*, *op. cit.*, pp. 60–3.)

WORKS CITED

Aldhelm: The Prose Works, ed. Michael Lapidge and Michael Herren (Ipswich, 1979).

Alighieri, Dante. *The Divine Comedy*, trans. H.R. House (New York, 1954).

The Ancrene Riwle, trans. M. B. Salu. (London, 1955).

Andreas Capellanus. *The Art of Courtly Love*, trans. J.J. Parry (New York, 1969).

d'Ardenne, S.T.R.O., ed. *The Liflade ant te Passiun of Seinte Iuliene*, EETS OS 248 (London, 1960).

d'Ardenne, S.R.T.O. and E.J. Dobson, eds. *Seinte Katerine*, EETS SS 7 (Oxford, 1981).

Aristotle. *On the Generation of Animals*, trans. A.L. Peck (Cambridge, Mass., 1953).

Attwater, Donald, ed. *The Penguin Dictionary of Saints* (Harmondsworth, 1956).

Bernard of Clairvaux. *On the Song of Songs*, trans. a Religious of C.S.M.V. (London, 1952).

———. *Life and Works of St. Bernard*, ed. Dom John Mabillon (London, 1889).

The Book of Margery Kempe, ed. S.B. Meech and H.E. Allen, EETS OS 212 (London, 1961).

Bostock, J. Knight, ed. *A Handbook on Old High German Literature*, 2nd. ed. rev. K.C. King and D.R. McLintock (Oxford, 1976).

Bradley, Ritamary. 'The Motherhood Theme in Julian of Norwich', *14th Century English Mystics Newsletter*, II, 4 (December, 1976).

Brown, Carlton, ed. *English Lyrics of the XIIIth Century* (Oxford, 1932).

Bugge, John. *Virginitas: An Essay in the History of a Medieval Idea* (The Hague, 1975).

Bynum, Caroline Walker. 'Jesus as Mother and Abbott as Mother: Some Themes in Twelfth Century Cistercian Writing', *Harvard Theological Review* 70 (1977).

———. *Jesus as Mother: Studies in the Spirituality of the High Middle Ages* (Berkeley, 1982).

Cabassut, André. 'Une dévotion médiévale peu connue. "La dévotion à Jesu notre Mère" ', *Revue d'Ascetique et de Mystique* 25 (1949).

Chambers, R.W. 'On the Continuity of English Prose from Alfred to More and his School' (Oxford, 1933).

Chance, Jane. *Woman as Hero in Old English Literature* (Syracuse, New York, 1986).

Chaucer, Geoffrey. *The Legend of Good Women*, trans. and intro. by Ann McMillan (Houston, Texas, 1987).

———. *The Riverside Chaucer*, ed. L. Benson (Boston, 1987).

Clay, Rotha Mary. *The Hermits and Anchorites of England* (London, 1914).

Comper, Frances. *Life of Richard Rolle* (London and Toronto, 1928).

Crump, G.C. and E.F. Jacob, eds. *The Legacy of the Middle Ages* (Oxford, 1926).

Cynewulf. *Juliana*, ed. Rosemary Woolf. Methuen Old English Library (New York, 1966).

Daly, Lowrie J. *Benedictine Monasticism. Its Formation and Development Through the 12th Century* (New York, 1965).

D'Aygalliers, A. Waulter. *Ruysbroeck the Admirable*, trans. F. Rothwell (Paris, 1923).

Dictionnaire d'Histoire et de géographie ecclésiastiques (Paris, 1937).

Dictionnaire de Spiritualité (Paris, 1937 ff.).

Dronke, Peter. *Fabula: Explorations into the Uses of Myth in Medieval Platonism* (Leiden and Cologne, 1974).

———. *Poetic Individuality in the Middle Ages* (Oxford, 1970).

———. *Women Writers of the Middle Ages* (Cambridge, 1984).

Eckenstein, Lena. *Woman Under Monasticism* (Cambridge, 1896).

Encyclopedia Britannica, eleventh edition (Cambridge, 1910).

Flores, Angel, ed. *An Anthology of Medieval Lyrics* (New York, 1962).

Gordon, R.K., trans. *Anglo-Saxon Poetry* (Cambridge, 1954).

The Holy Bible: A Translation from the Latin Vulgate in Light of the Hebrew and Greek Originals (London, 1956).

Fiero, Gloria K., Wendy Peffer, Mathe Allain, trans. and eds. *Three Medieval Views of Women* (New Haven, 1989).

Fleckenstein, Josef. *Early Medieval Germany*, trans. Bernard K. Smith (New York, 1978).

Gardner, Edmund. *Dante and the Mystics* (London, 1913).

Gillingham, J.B. *The Kingdom of Germany in the High Middle Ages (900–1200)* (London, 1971).

Greenfield, Stanley B. *A Critical History of Old English Literature* (New York, 1965).

Haverkamp, Alfred. *Medieval Germany (1056–1273)*, trans. H. Braun and R. Mortimer (London, 1990).

Hildegard of Bingen. *Scivias*, trans. Mother Columba Hart and Jane Bishop (New York and Mahwah, 1990).

———. *Scivias*, trans. Bruce Hozeski (Santa Fe, New Mexico, 1986).

———. *Symphonia armonie celesium revelationum*, ed. Barbara Newman (Ithaca, New York, 1988).

Hildegardis Scivias, ed. Adelgundis Führkötter and Angela Carlevaris, *Corpus Christianorum: Continuatio Medieualis* XLIII and XLIIIa (Turnhout, 1978).

Home, G. *Evolution of an English Town: Pickering* (London, 1905).

Horstmann, C. *Yorkshire Writers* I (London, 1895).

Hozeski, Bruce. 'Hildegard of Bingen's Ordo virtutum: The Earliest Discovered Liturgical Morality Play', *American Benedictine Review* 26 (1975).

Jeremy, Sister Mary O.P. *Scholars and Mystics* (Chicago, 1962).

Jones, Rufus. *The Flowering of Mysticism: The Friends of God in the Fourteenth Century* (New York, 1931) repr. 1971.

Julian of Norwich. *Revelations of Divine Love*, trans. Grace Warrack (London, 1901).

————. *Comfortable Words for Christ's Lovers*, trans. Dundas Harford (London, 1911).

————. *Revelations of Divine Love Shewed to a Devout Ankress by Name Julian of Norwich*, trans. Roger Hudleston (London, 1927).

————. *Sixteen Revelations of Divine Love*, Sister Anna Maria Reynolds, Doctoral Thesis, Leeds University, 1956.

————. *A Shewing of God's Love: The Shorter Version of Sixteen Revelations by Julian of Norwich*, trans. F. Reynolds (London, 1958).

————. *Revelations of Divine Love*, trans. James Walsh (London, 1961).

————. *Revelations of Divine Love*, trans. Clifton Wolters (Harmondsworth, 1966).

————. *Julian of Norwich: A Revelation of Divine Love*, ed. Marion Glasscoe (Exeter, 1976).

————. *Revelations of Divine Love*, trans. M.L. delMaestro (New York, 1977).

————. *Julian of Norwich's Revelations of Divine Love*, ed. Frances Beer (Heidelberg, 1978).

————. *A Book of Showings to the Anchoress Julian of Norwich*, ed. E. Colledge and J. Walsh (Toronto, 1978).

Jung, Carl G., ed. *Man and his Symbols* (New York, 1964).

Lambert, Malcolm. *Medieval Heresy: Popular Movements from Bogomil to Huss* (New York, 1976).

deLubac, H. *Exégèse Médiévale* (Paris, 1964).

Mack, Frances, ed. *Seinte Marherete*, EETS OS 193 (London, 1958).

Mechthild of Magdeburg. *The Flowing Light of the Godhead*, trans. Lucy Menzies London, 1953).

————. *Flowing Light of the Divinity*, trans. Christiane Mesch Galvani, ed. and intro. Susan Clark (New York and London, 1991).

————. *Revelationes Gertrudianae et Mechthildianae*, vol II (Poitiers and Paris, 1877).

————. *Offenbarungen der Schwester Mechthild von Magdeburg, oder das fleissende Licht der Gottheit, aus der einzigen Hanschrift des Stifes Einsiedeln*, ed. Gall Morel (Ratisbonne, 1869, repr. Darmstadt, 1963, 1967).

The Medieval Mystical Tradition in England (Exeter, 1982).

Menzies, Lucy. *Mirrors of the Holy: Ten Studies in Sanctity* (London, 1928).

Migne, J.-P., ed. *Patrologiae cursus completus, Ser. Graeca* (Paris, 1855).

———. *Patrologiae cursus completus. Ser. Latina* (Paris, 1882).

Millett, Bella, ed. *Hali Meiðhad, EETS OS* 284 (London, 1982).

Millett, Bella and Jocelyn Wogan-Browne, eds. *Medieval English Prose for Women: The Katherine Group and Ancrene Wisse* (London, 1990).

Molinari, Paul. *Julian of Norwich: The Teaching of a 14th Century Mystic* (London, 1958).

Morris, R. *Old English Homilies (1220–30), EETS OS* 29 (London, 1867).

McDonnell, Ernest W. *The Beguines and Beghards in Medieval Culture* (New Brunswick, New Jersey, 1954).

McNeill, John T. and Helena M. Gamer, eds. *Medieval Handbooks of Penance* (New York, 1938).

Newman, Barbara. 'Jesus as Mother and Abbot as Mother: Some Themes in Twelfth Century Cistercian Writing', *Harvard Theological Review* 70 (1977).

———. *Jesus as Mother: Studies in the Spirituality of the High Middle Ages* (Berkeley, 1982).

———. *Sister of Wisdom: St. Hildegard's Theology of the Feminine* (Berkeley and Los Angeles, 1987).

Nichols, J.A. and L.T. Shank, eds. *Distant Echoes* (Kalamazoo, Michigan, 1984).

O'Faolain, Julia and Lauro Martines, eds. *Not in God's Image* (New York, 1973).

Pagels, Elaine. *Adam, Eve and the Serpent* (New York, 1988).

———. *The Gnostic Gospels* (New York, 1979).

Pantin, W.A. *The English Church in the Fourteenth Century* (Notre Dame, Indiana, 1963).

The Pearl, trans. Sara de Ford (Northbrook, Illinois, 1967).

Pomerius, Henricus. *De origine monasterii Viridis Vallis, Analecta bollandiana*, vol. IV (Brussels, 1885).

Power, Eileen. *Medieval English Nunneries* (Cambridge, 1922).

Price, Jocelyn. 'The Liflade of Seinte Iuliene and Hagiographic Convention', *Medievalia et Humanistica* (New Series, 14), 1986.

Quinn, E. A., trans., *The Fathers of the Church* (New York, 1959).

Reeves, Marjorie. *The Influence of Prophecy in the Later Middle Ages* (Oxford, 1969).

Reynolds, F. 'Some Literary Influences in the Revelations of Julian of Norwich', *Leeds Studies in English and Kindred Languages* 7 (1952).

Rickert, Margaret. *Painting in Britain in the Middle Ages* (London, 1954).

Riehle, Wolfgang. *The Middle English Mystics* (London, 1981).

Rolle, Richard. *The Fire of Love* (Harmondsworth, 1972).

———. *Writings Ascribed to Richard Rolle, Hermit of Hampole*, ed. Hope Emily Allen (London and New York, 1927).

———. *English Writings of Richard Rolle*, ed. Hope Emily Allen (Oxford, 1931).

———. *Richard Rolle: The English Writings*, trans. and ed. Rosamund S. Allen (Mahwah, New Jersey, 1988).

The Rule of St. Benedict, ed. Timothy Fry, O.S.B. (Collegeville, Minnesota, 1980).

The Rule of St. Benedict, trans. and intro. by Cardinal Gasquet (New York, 1966).

Sacks, O. *Migraine: Understanding a Common Disorder* (Berkeley, 1985).

Schmitz, Dom Philibert. *Histoire de l'Ordre de Saint Benoît* (Maredsous, 1956).

Shepherd, Geoffrey, ed. *Ancrene Wisse,* (London and Edinburgh, 1959).

Singer, C. *From Magic to Science* (New York, 1958).

Southern, R.W. *The Making of the Middle Ages* (New Haven and London, 1961).

———. *St. Anselm and his Biographer* (Cambridge, 1963).

Stiller, Nikki. *Eve's Orphans: Mothers and Daughters in Medieval Literature* (Westport, Connecticut and London, 1980).

von Strassburg, Gottfried. *Tristan*, trans. A.T. Hatto (Harmondsworth, 1960).

Strayer, Joseph R. *Western Europe in the Middle Ages* (New York, 1955).

Tacitus, Cornelius. *De Origine et Situ Germanorum*, ed. J.G.C. Anderson (Oxford, 1938).

Thompson, W. Meredith, ed. *The Wohunge of Ure Lauerd. EETS OS* 241 (London, 1958).

Tolkien, J.R.R. 'Ancrene Wisse and Hali Meiðhad', *Essays and Studies* 14 (1929).

deVinck, José. *Revelations of Women Mystics: From Middle Ages to Modern Times* (New York, 1985).

Wilson, Katharina, ed. *Medieval Women Writers* (Athens, Georgia, 1984).

Woolf, Rosemary. *Art and Doctrine: Essays on Medieval Literature*, ed. Heather O'Donoghue (London, 1986).

The Works of Dionysius the Areopagite, trans. Rev. J. Parker, 2 vols. (Oxford, 1897).

INDEX

Italic page numbers refer to illustrations.

Paul, 2
Pythagoras, 3
Tertullian, 3, 22
'Vices of Women', 4
Nuptial imagery, sources of, 23, 91–92
Nun's Rule, 3, 4, 10, 11, 67, 72–75, 115, 118, 121, 130, 150
Pearl, and heavenly company, 23
Porete, Marguerite, 13
Proverbs, 27, 31, 33
Revelation of St John, 23, 27
Richard of St Victor, commentary on the Apocalypse, 33n.
Rolle, Richard:
    as spiritual advisor, 10, 113, 114–118 *passim*, 122–129
    calor, canor, dulcor, characteristics of mystical experience, 111, 117, 128
    Commandment, 113, 122, 124–125
    corruption of clergy, 112
    Daltons, 111–112
    devil, 111, 112, 126
    Ego Dormio, 113, 114–118 *passim*, 121, 124–125, 127n.
    Emendatio Vitae, 124

English Psalter, 122
eremitic ideal, 110–111
Fire of Love, 111, 123
Form of Living, 113, 122, 123, 125–129 *passim*
Hampole, 119, 122, 123
love language, 115–129 *passim*
lukewarmness, 112, 126, 128
misogyny, 10, 11, 112, 129
Margaret Kirkby, 119, 122–129 *passim*
Office, 109–112 *passim*, 122, 123
stages of love, 115–129 *passim*
Song of Songs, 91, 114
St Juliana, 67, 68–69, 70
St Katherine, 67, 70–71
St Margaret, 67, 69–70
Tacitus' *Germania*, 56
Tristan, 4
Twelfth-century renaissance, 20
Virgin Mary, 1, 7, 39, 41, 42, 66, 137, 161
Virginity, ideals of, 59–65 *passim*, 68, 72
Wooing of Our Lord, 67, 75–77, 117, 140
Yorkshire nunneries, 113–114, 119